Stephen Najda
in
New York City

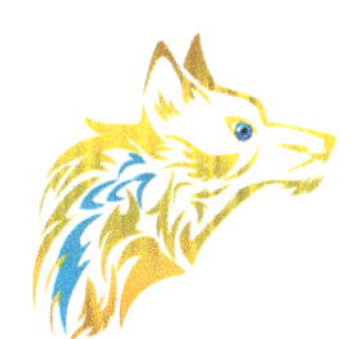

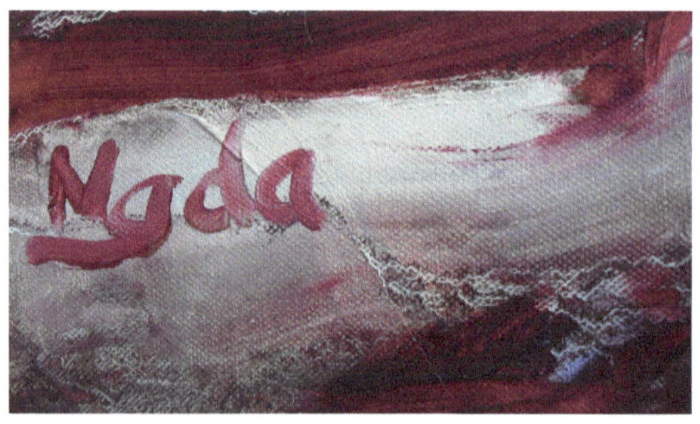

On the cover:
"Three views of Stob Coire Sgreamhach, Glencoe, Scotland"

Painting technique: Acrylic painting on Canvas
Size: 180 cm x 150 cm
Year: 2018

*** * ***

Layout Cover and Internal by: Wolf Graham

ISBN 978 1-911424-69-7

Publishing Company:
Black Wolf Edition & Publishing Ltd.
Scotland (UK)
www.blackwolfedition.com

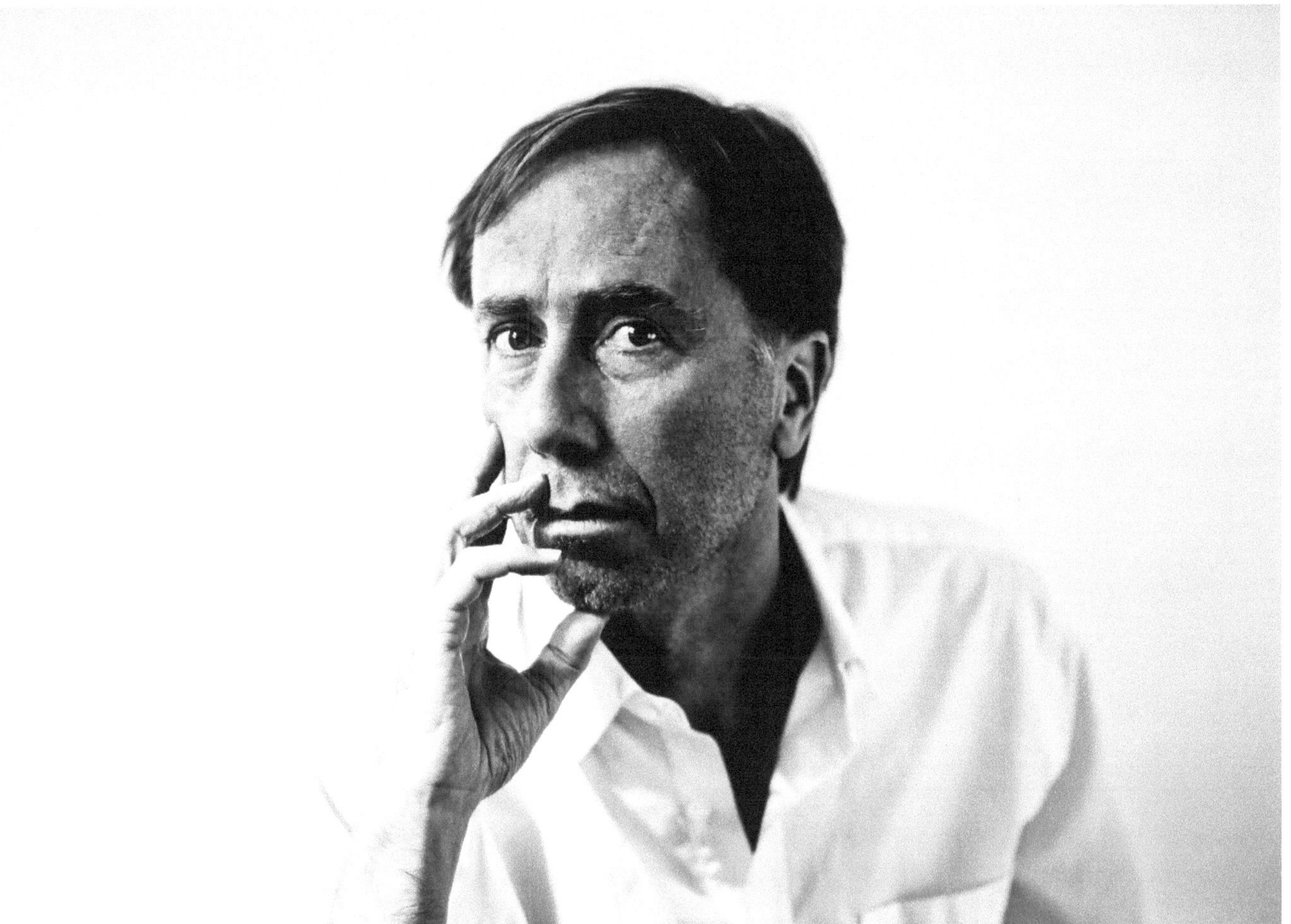

Was born in a Glasgow tenement of Scottish-Polish parentage. The Scottish mountains were an early lure. Since then, Stephen has climbed extensively in the wilderness mountain areas of Europe, the Middle-East, Africa, Asia and the Americas.

Stephen graduated with a PhD in physics from St. Andrews University. Followed by research posts in physics at Tokyo University, CNRS Grenoble and Oxford. Stephen returned to Glasgow to work with a photonics high-tech company and has been 're-born' in Poland with another high-tech venture.

Stephen discovered art by chance and good fortune, pre-empting a 'new path' of discovery and self-expression. Najda's art spans the complete spectrum of human emotion from simple beauty of sensual curvaceous women; through captured moments from the artist's travels; through a wide range of scientific, social, political, philosophical and intellectual questions and debates; to the provocative and challenging brutal reality of war, disease and human tragedy. These theoretical concepts are brought into focus through the medium of oil on canvas to create a unique visual experience. The art is both, wonderful and enlightening, pleasurable and challenging, beautiful and harrowing, complex and terrifying, producing powerfully evocative images that are entirely relevant to the modern world and questioning our path into the future.

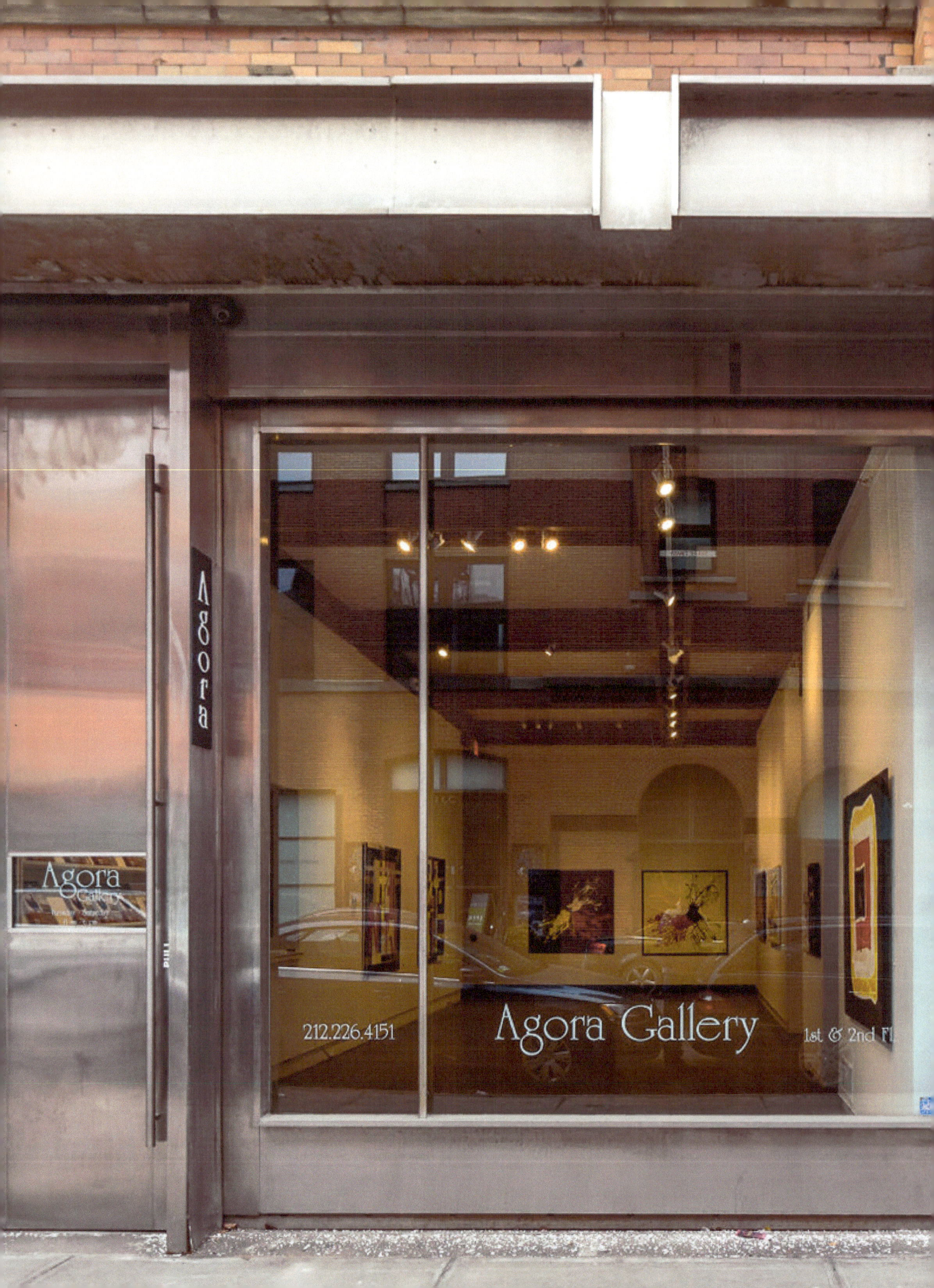

Agora
Agora Gallery
212.226.4151
Agora Gallery
1st & 2nd Fl

Stephen Najda's landscape paintings

The art of Stephen Najda crosses many boundaries, over a wide spectrum of subjects, and using a multitude of techniques. A common thread runs through all his artwork – a bold vision of vivid colour, delineating line and fluid paint to produce a powerful narrative. Many of his works bear a certain qualitative aspect of impenetrability – an ambiguity, allowing the imagination of the viewer to enter into the narrative and explore the abstraction.

Stephen Najda's powerful and expressive landscape paintings are as enigmatic and individualistic as the artist himself. Born and bred in Scotland, Najda has had a lifetime experience of being 'in' the Scottish landscape with an intimate knowledge of the land, the mountains, the sea, the rivers – hiking, sailing, canoeing, climbing...in all seasons and all weathers.

Stephen Najda's paintings captures what he terms the 'primitive-self', exploring the space between imagination and dream, to produce an 'abstraction of thought'. Najda is better known as a figurative painter, in the style of Picasso-Matisse-De Kooning, but brings an unique vision of spontaneity and emotion to painting.

The artwork is embedded in the wild and dramatic landscape of the Scottish Highlands and Islands. This is a land of stunning unspoilt nature of rugged mountains, deep lochs, and majestic coastlines – a geology almost as old as planet earth. Ever-changing weather gives a magical touch of unique space and light, one moment you can see the hills, the next moment they are gone. This land is special – a land intermingled with a sad and bloody history, with dark tales of eerie ghosts, myths and legends. Games are played in the mind like a mystical charmed instrument. A gleam of sun light through dark cloud, shadows move over the hills, faces appear on rocks, a drama unfolds, a sudden curtain of heavy rain and blustering wind, and the scene is gone forever.

Najda paints immersed 'in' the landscape 'en plein air' in all weathers, often high in the winter mountains or exposed to full Atlantic gales, capturing the savage beauty of the land and sea. Creating the art is risky and radical, and breathtakingly courageous in challenging conditions in the wilderness areas of Scotland. Hiking into the mountains by himself for days on end with a large canvas, dealing with freezing and stormy weather, and improvising with what's available, stones, branches, moss...to create a piece of art. And there's always a risk in the middle of a storm, the canvas will be blown away, never to be seen again.

The work is a juxtaposition of vivid colour, delineating line, intriguing form and fluid paint to create a powerful image. A 'rock-on-rock' technique is often used that creates a brusque, almost nonchalant, mottled and scored effect that enhances the emotion of the moment.
With a large canvas, painted on an uneven surface, nothing is pinned down or complete. This is not formula painting but creating an intense image of simple complexity from a large element of chance.

The artwork is an emotional response to everything 'in' the landscape, angry clouds, a glimpse of a mountain, fast ice-melt water, a screech of a raven overhead...transforming the transient beauty of the landscape into spontaneous pure visual poetry distilled onto canvas. This is a voyage of discovery, an exploration of the primitive-self, exploring the boundary between human and nature, imagination and dream to produce an 'abstraction of the experience' of being 'in' the landscape.
The artwork is feral, ethereal, rugged and dramatic like the Scottish landscape.

Angela Di Bello,
Executive Director
Agora Gallery 530 W 25th St, New York, NY 10001, USA
and Editor-in-Chief of ARTisSpectrum Magazine.

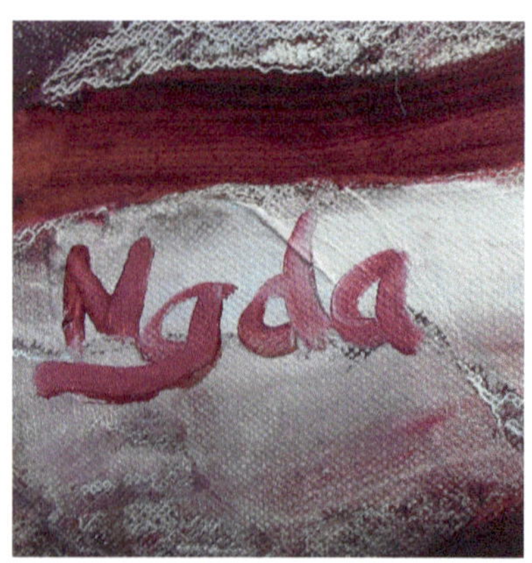

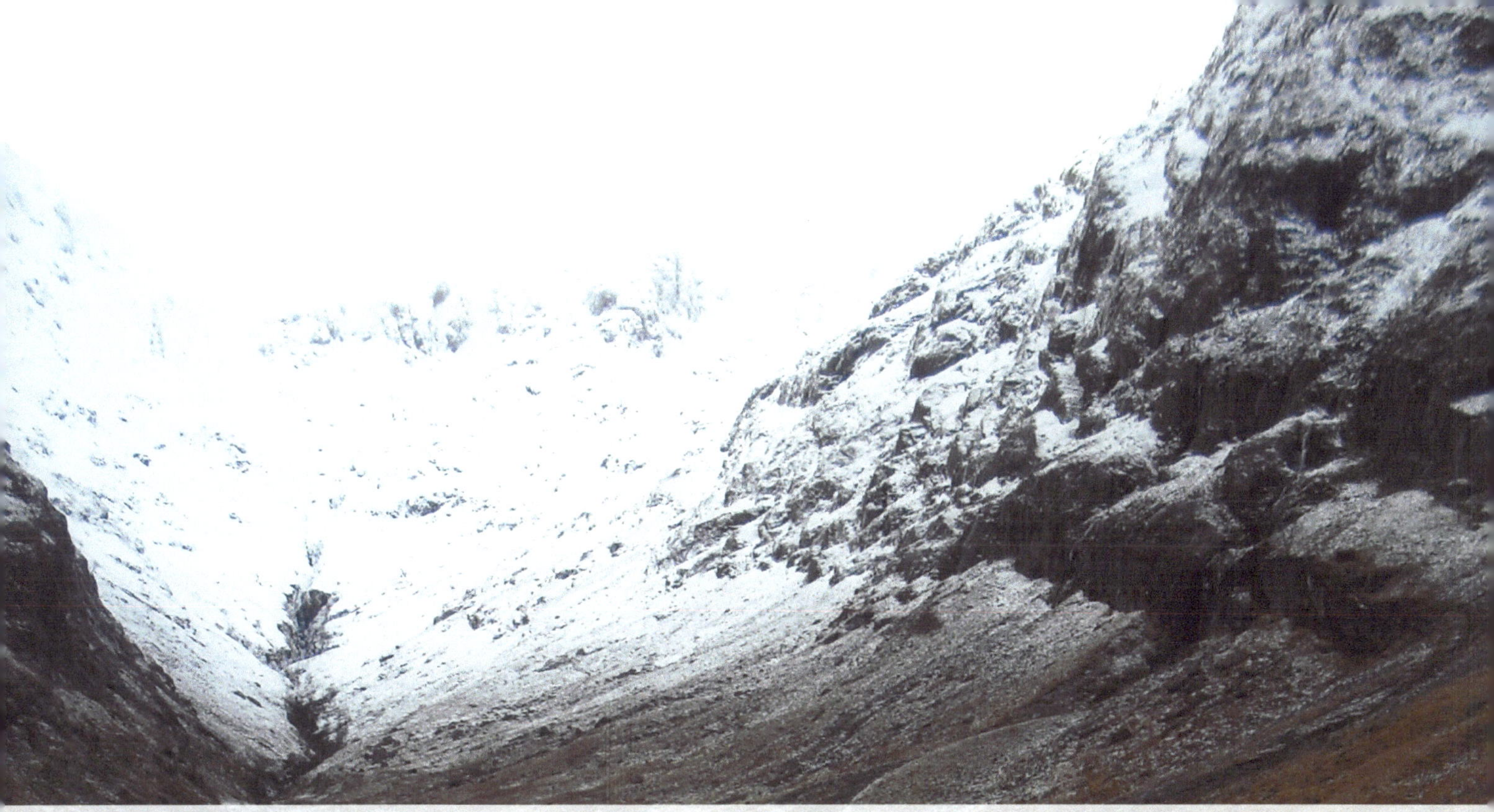

The Scottish Landscape in New York City

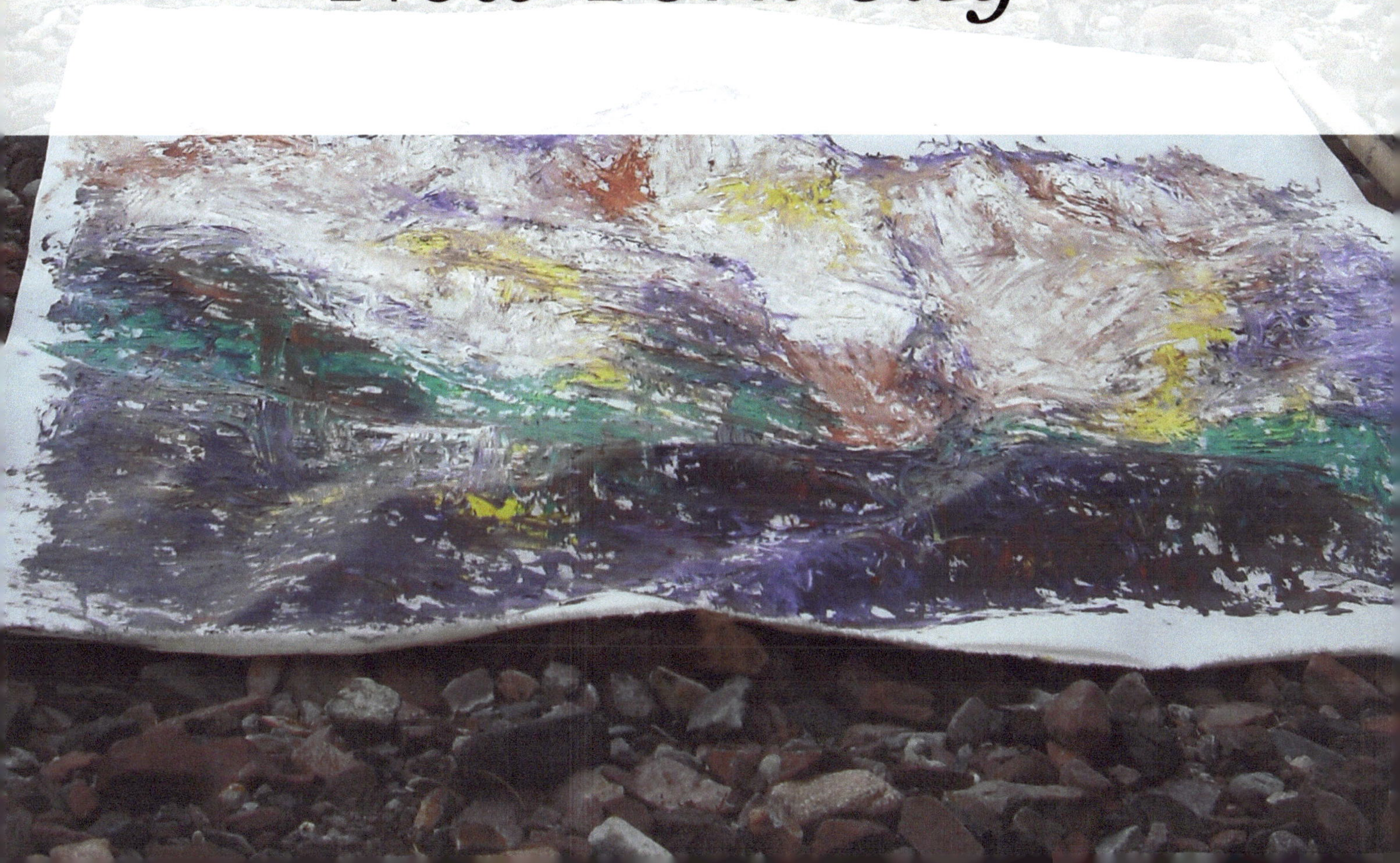

Agora
Gallery

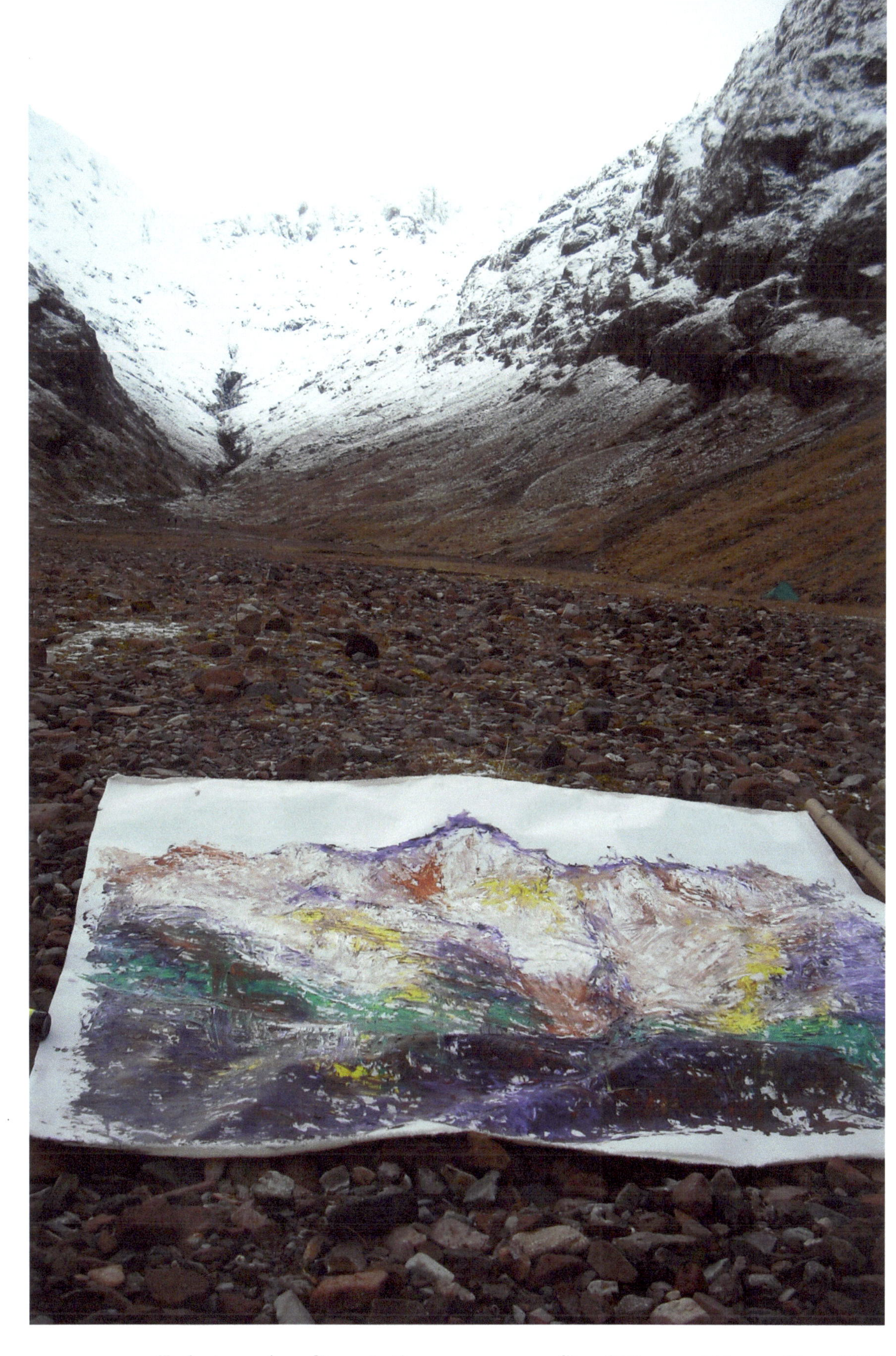

Technique: **Acrylic painting on canvas** - Size: **180 cm x 150 cm** - Year: **2018**

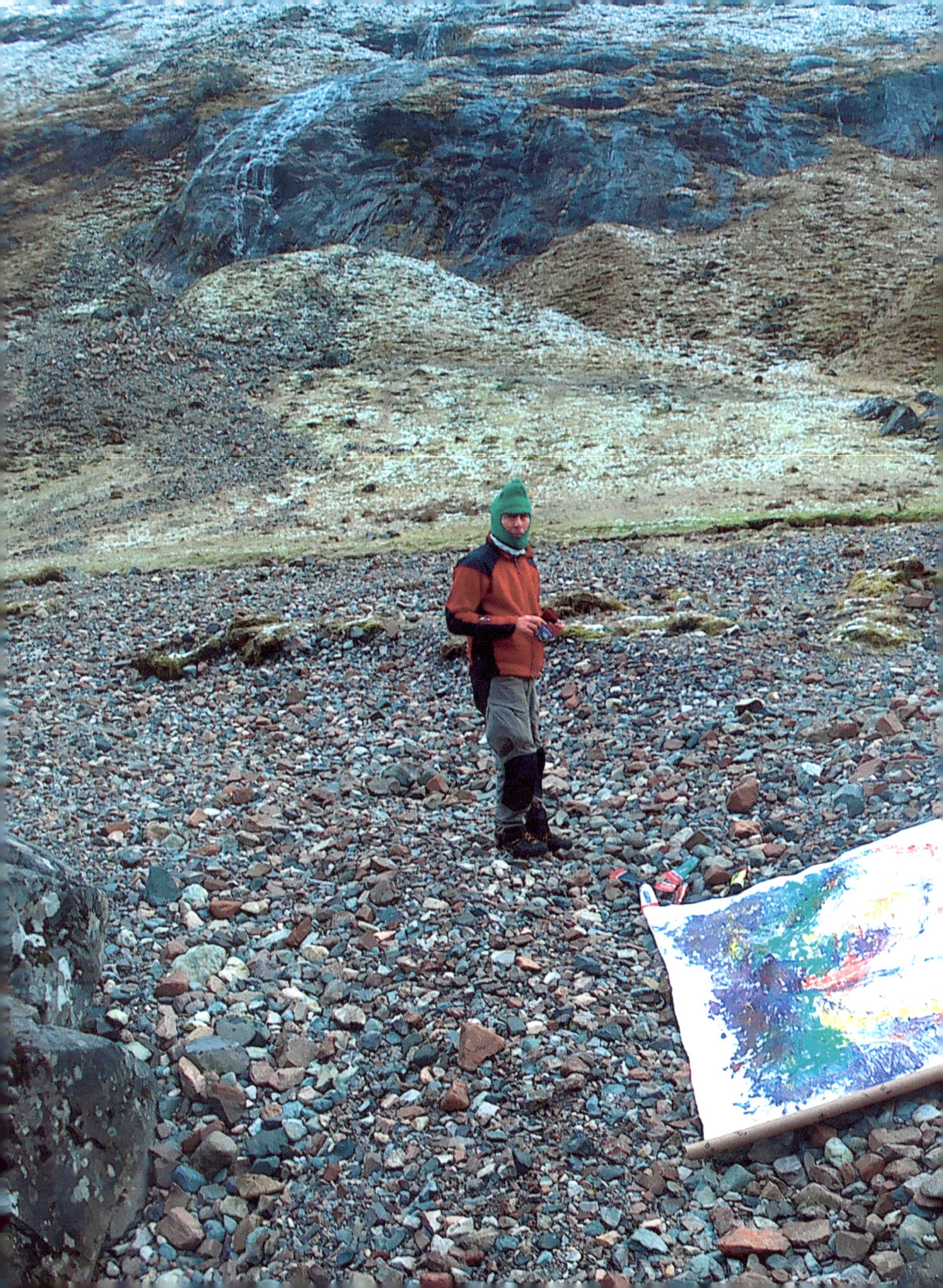

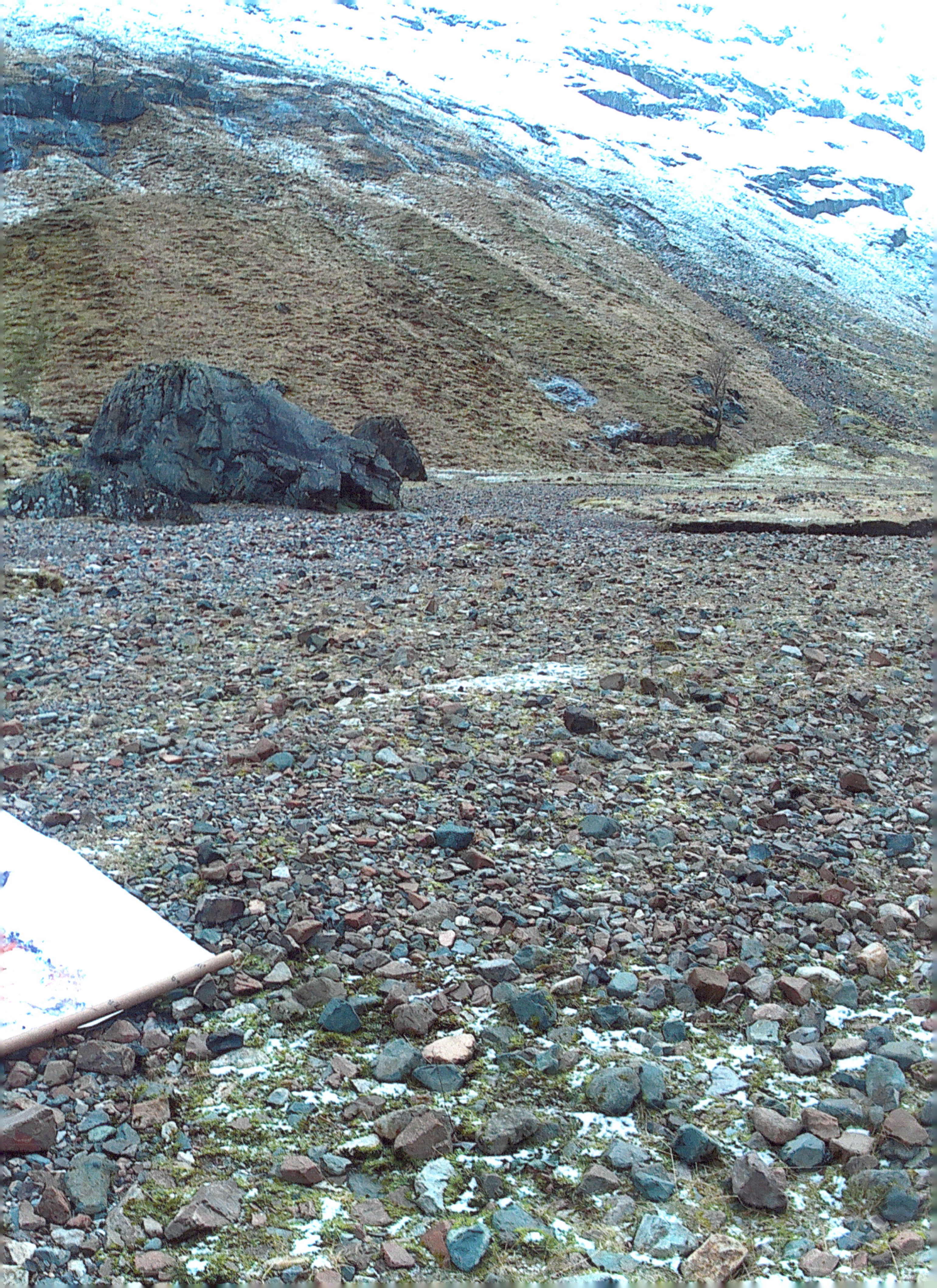

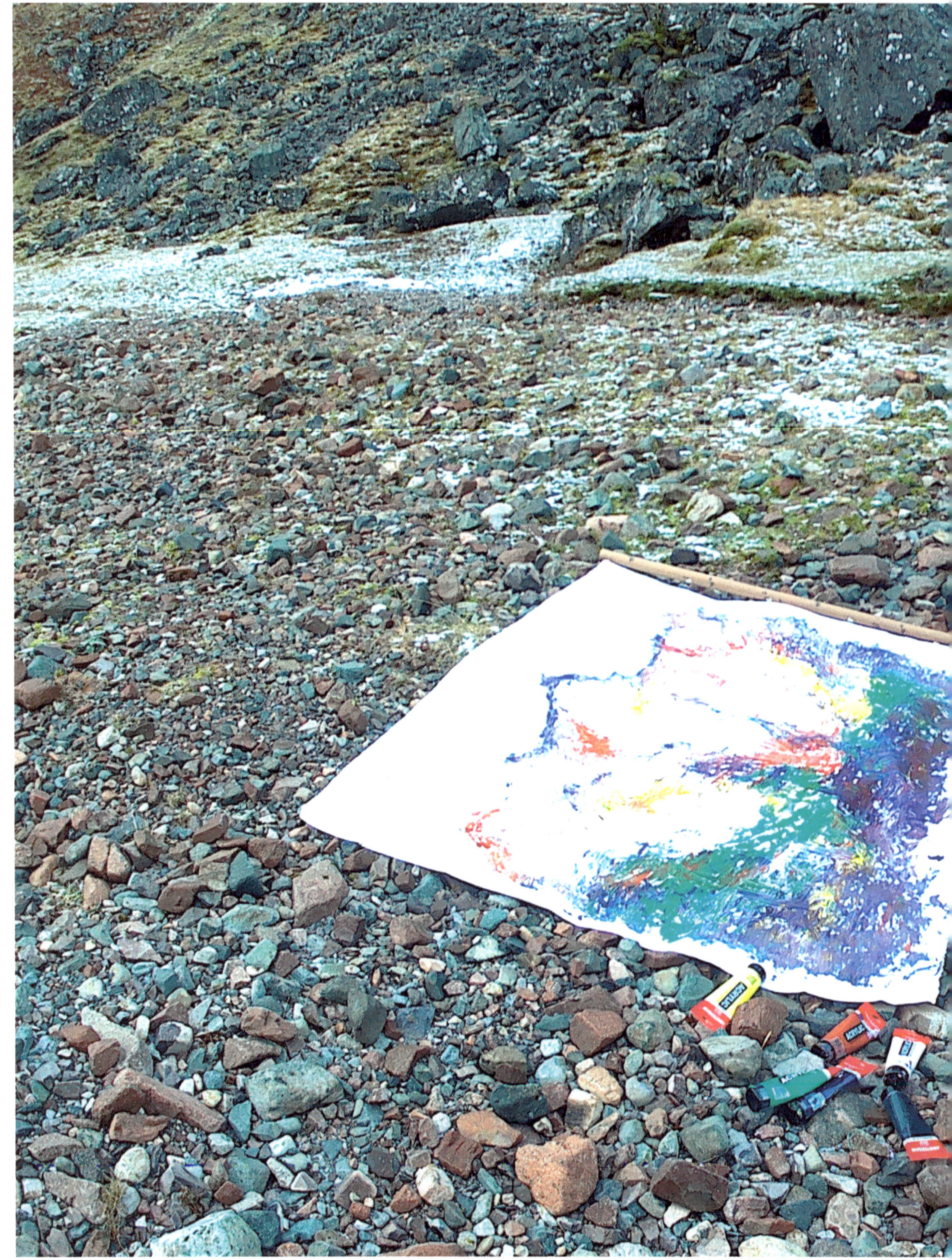

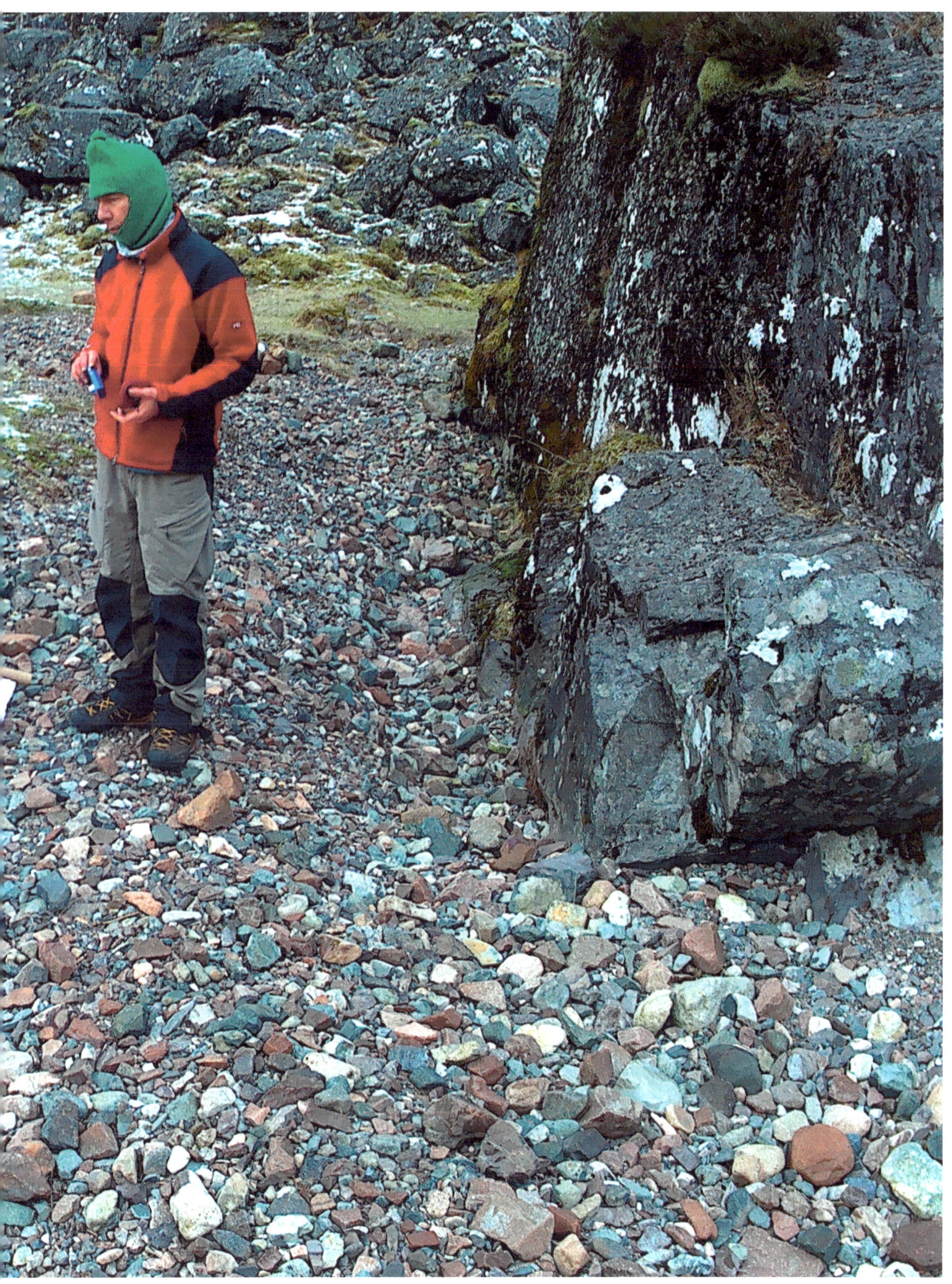

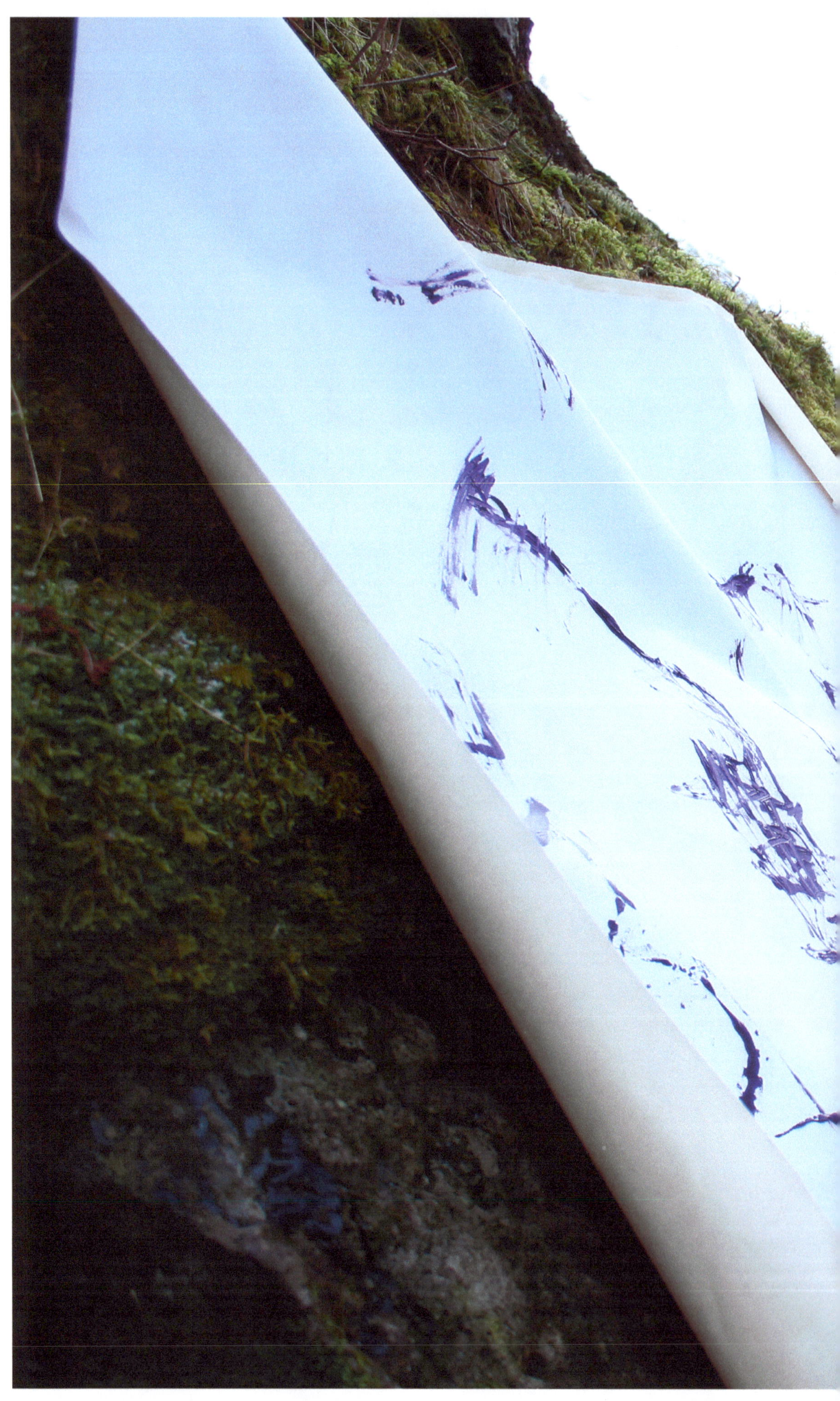

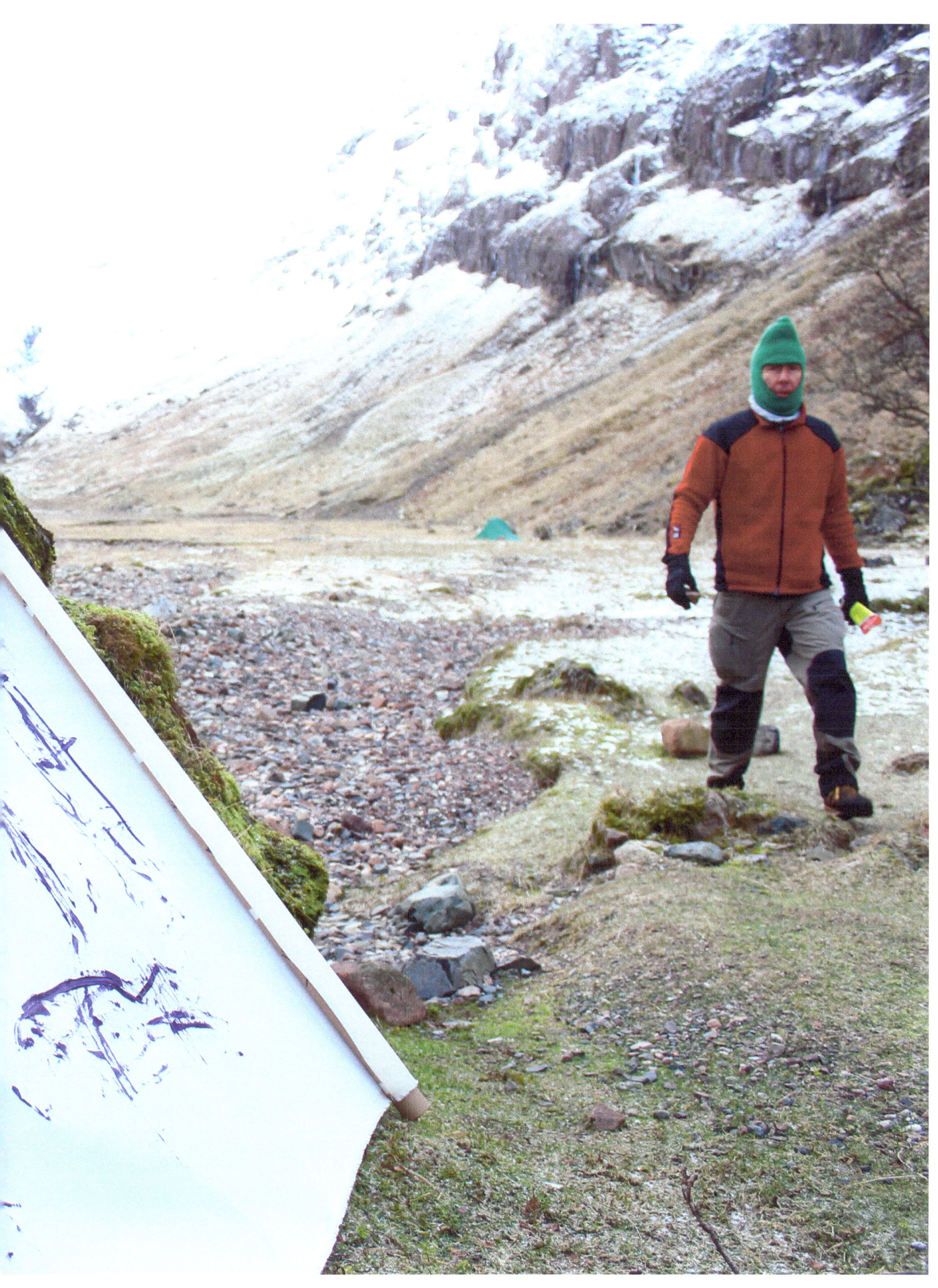

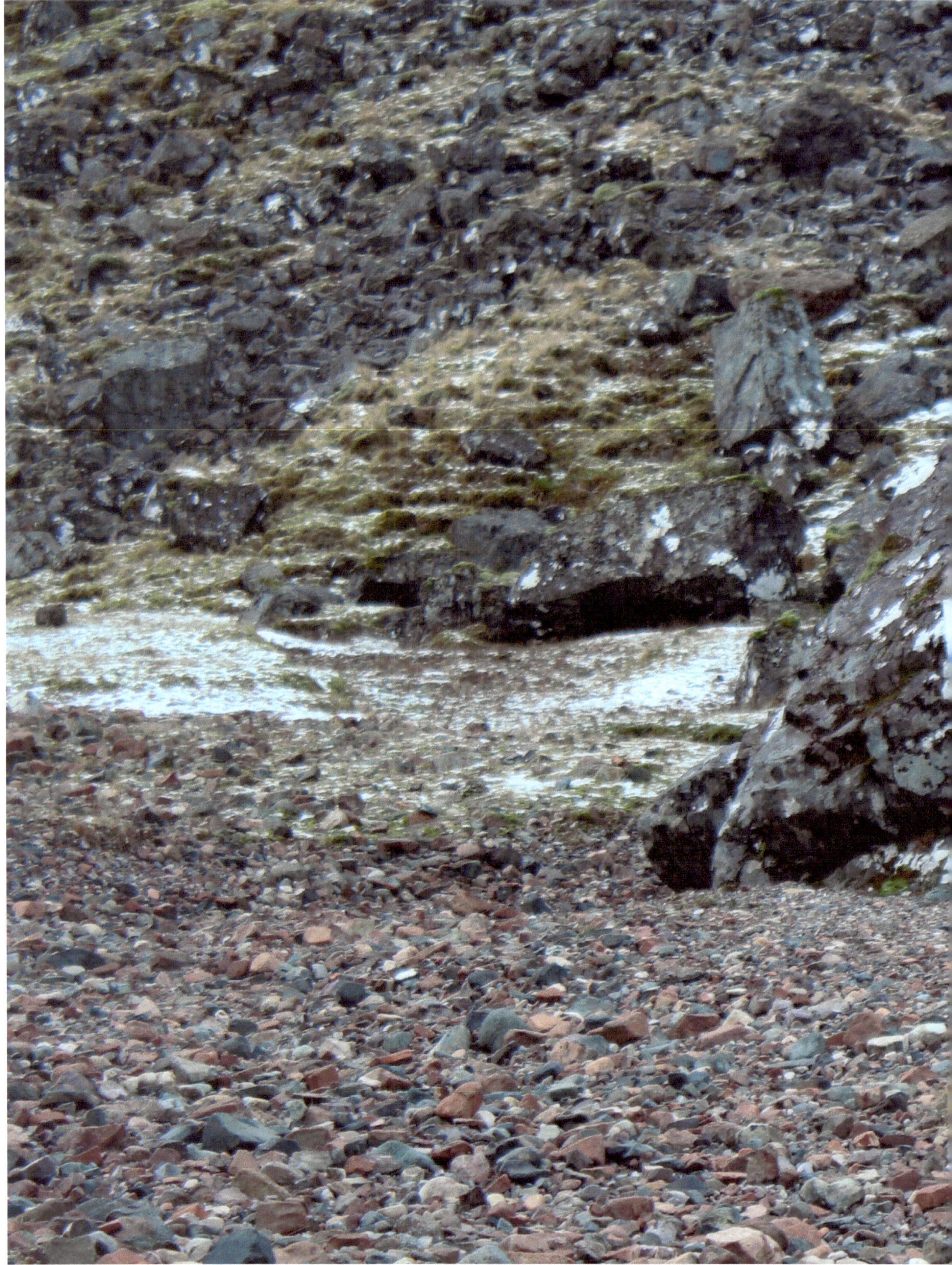

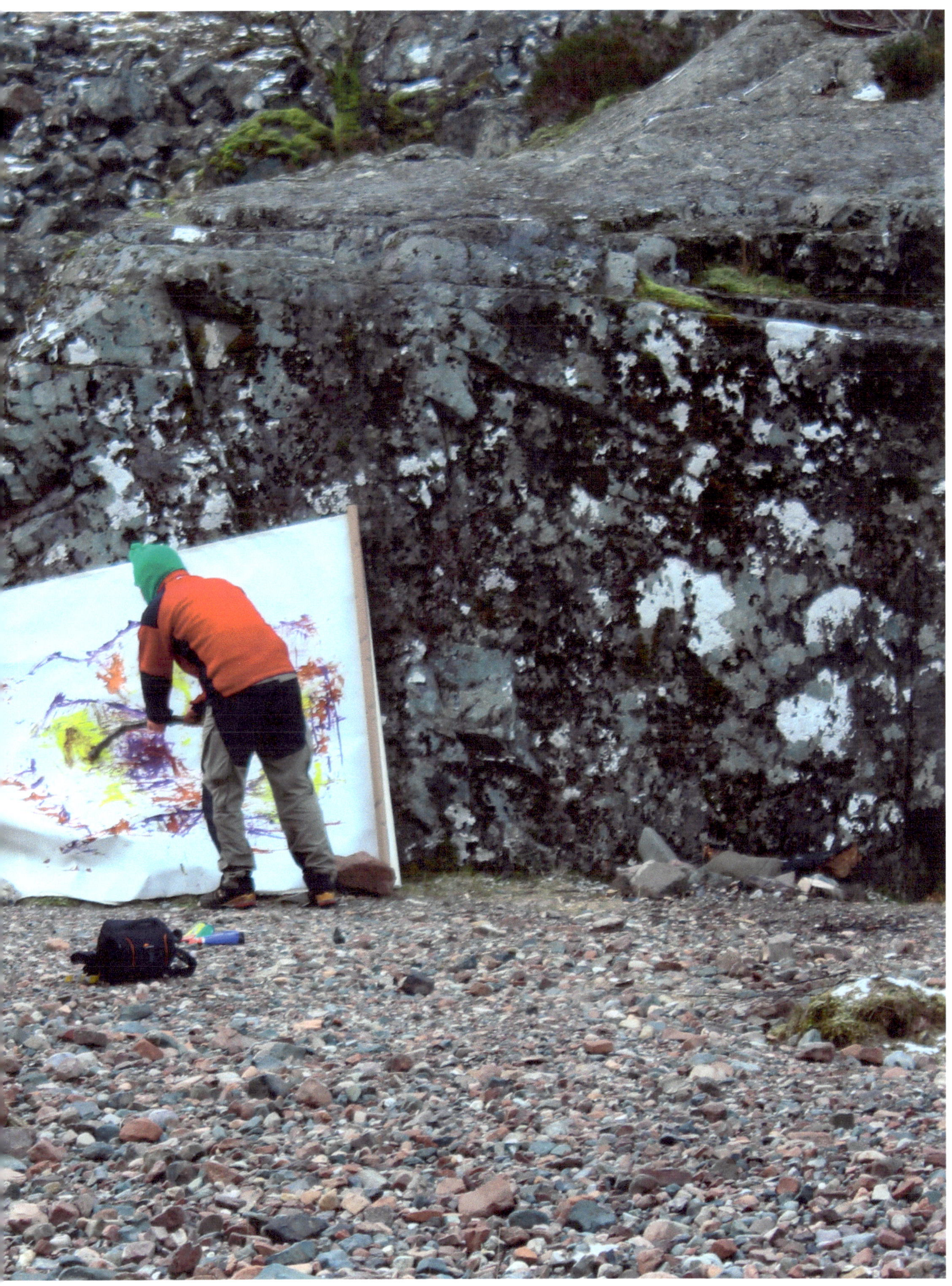

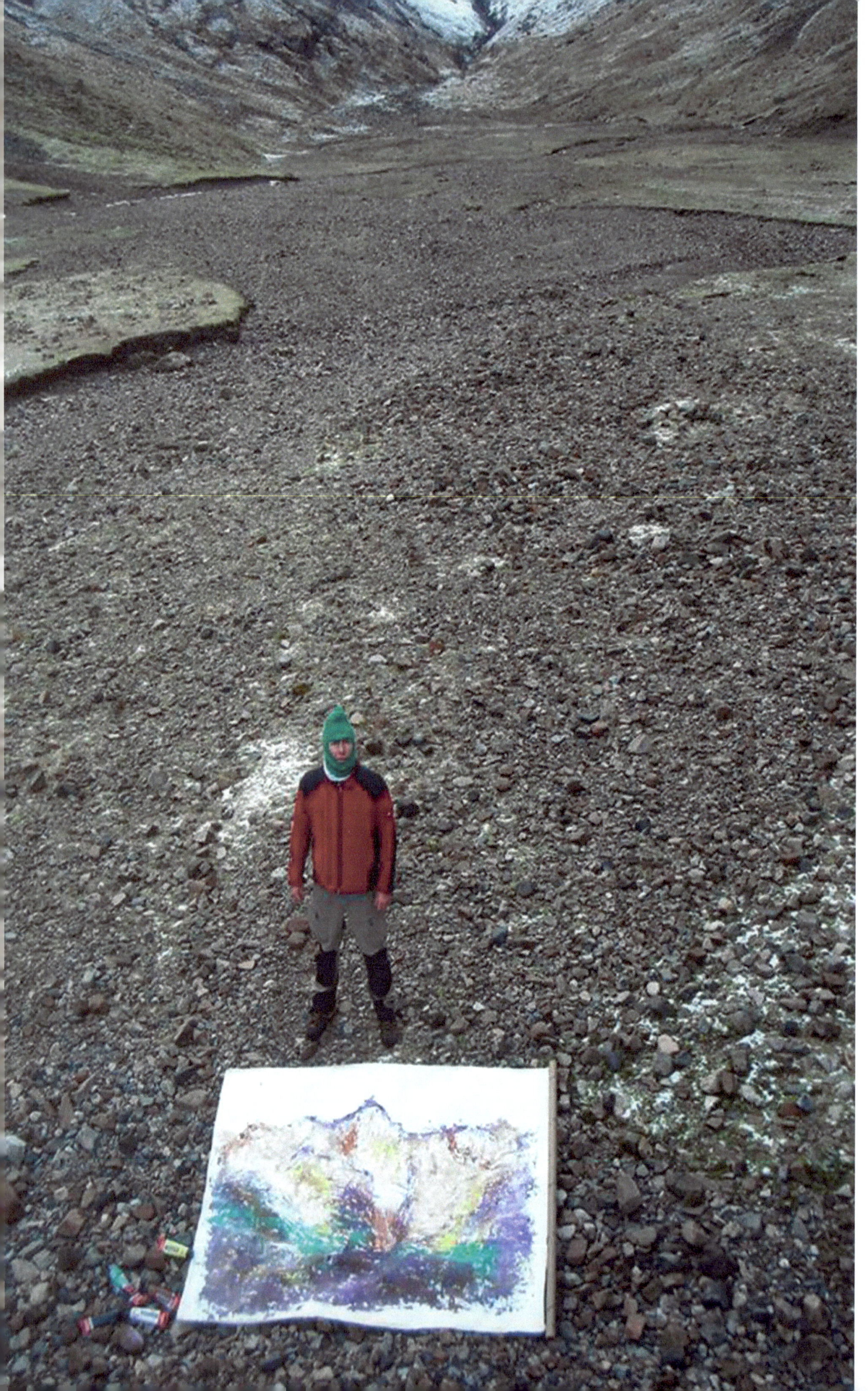

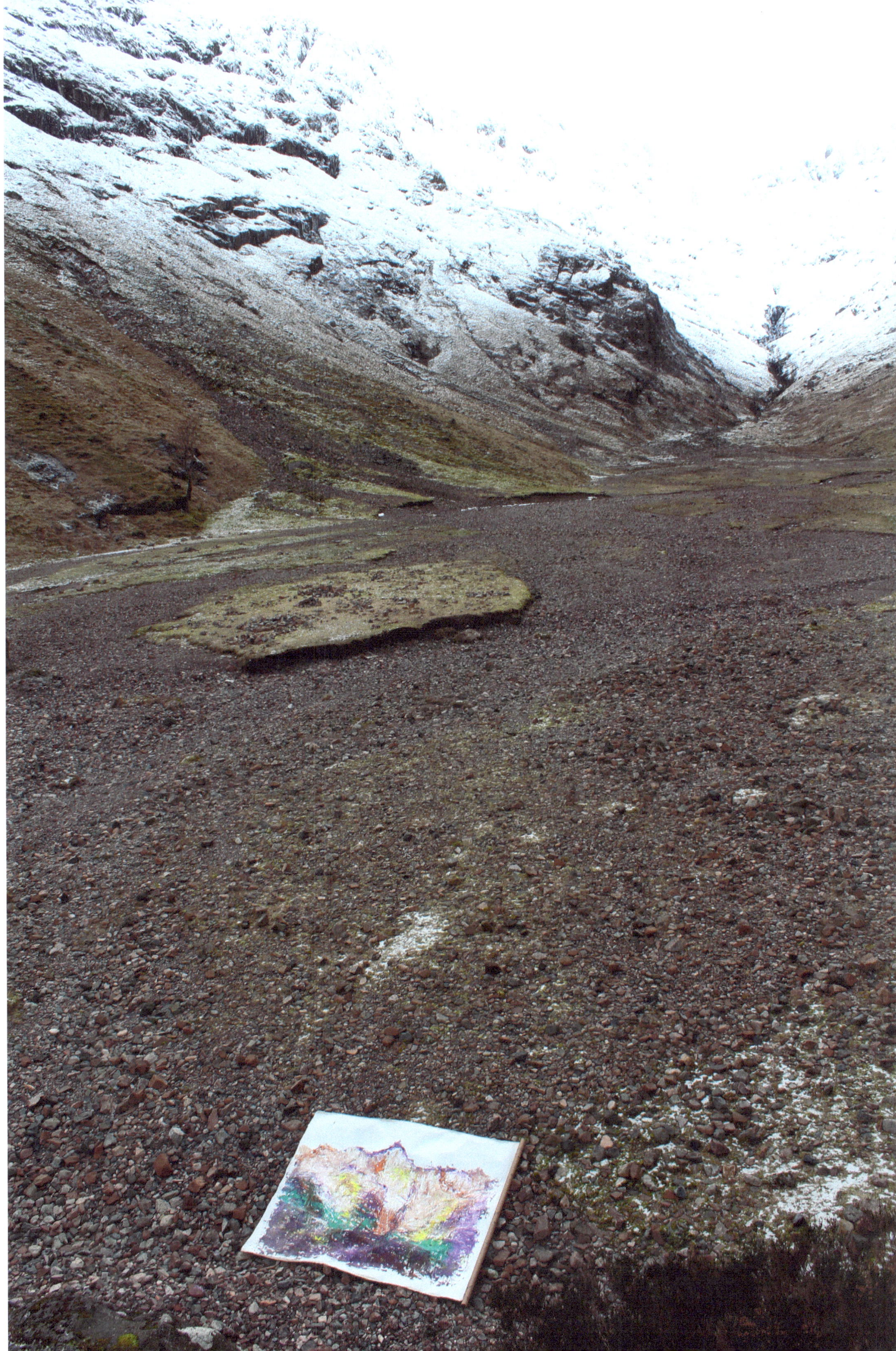

THREE VIEWS OF STOB COIRE SGREAMHACH, GLENCOE, SCOTLAND

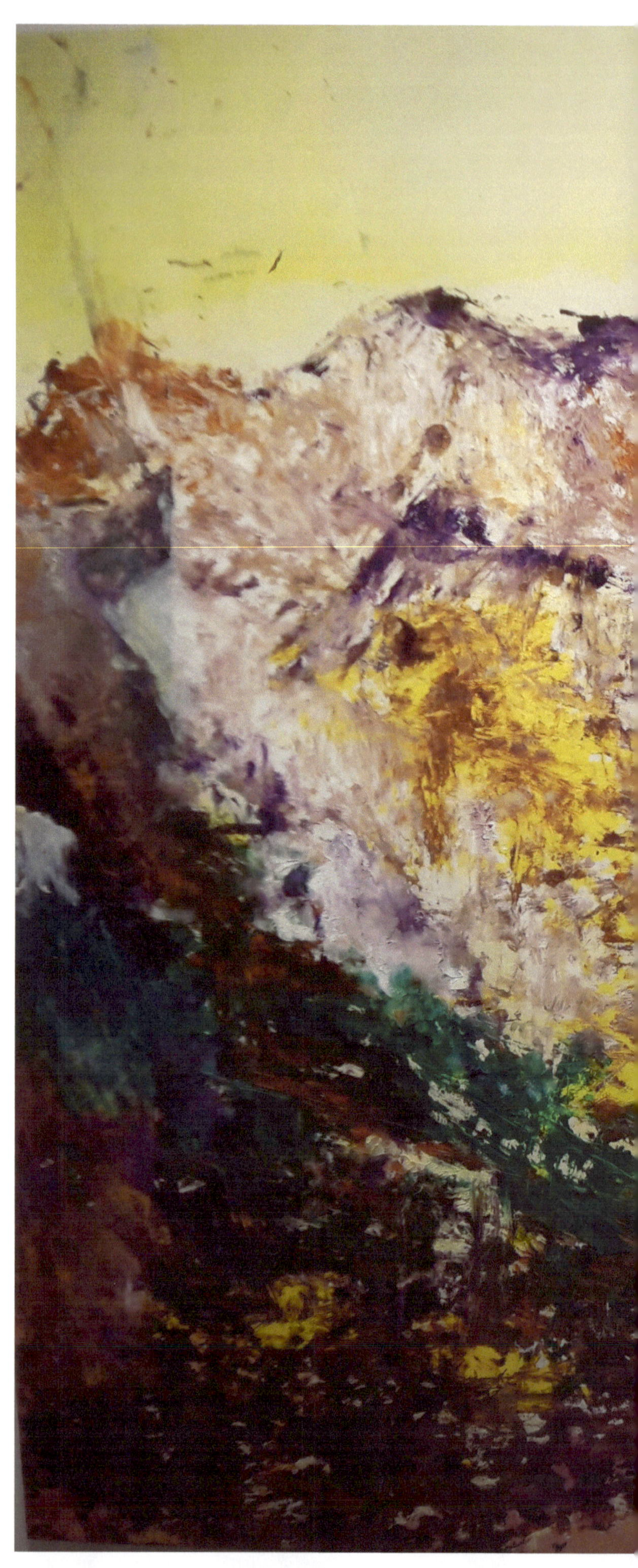

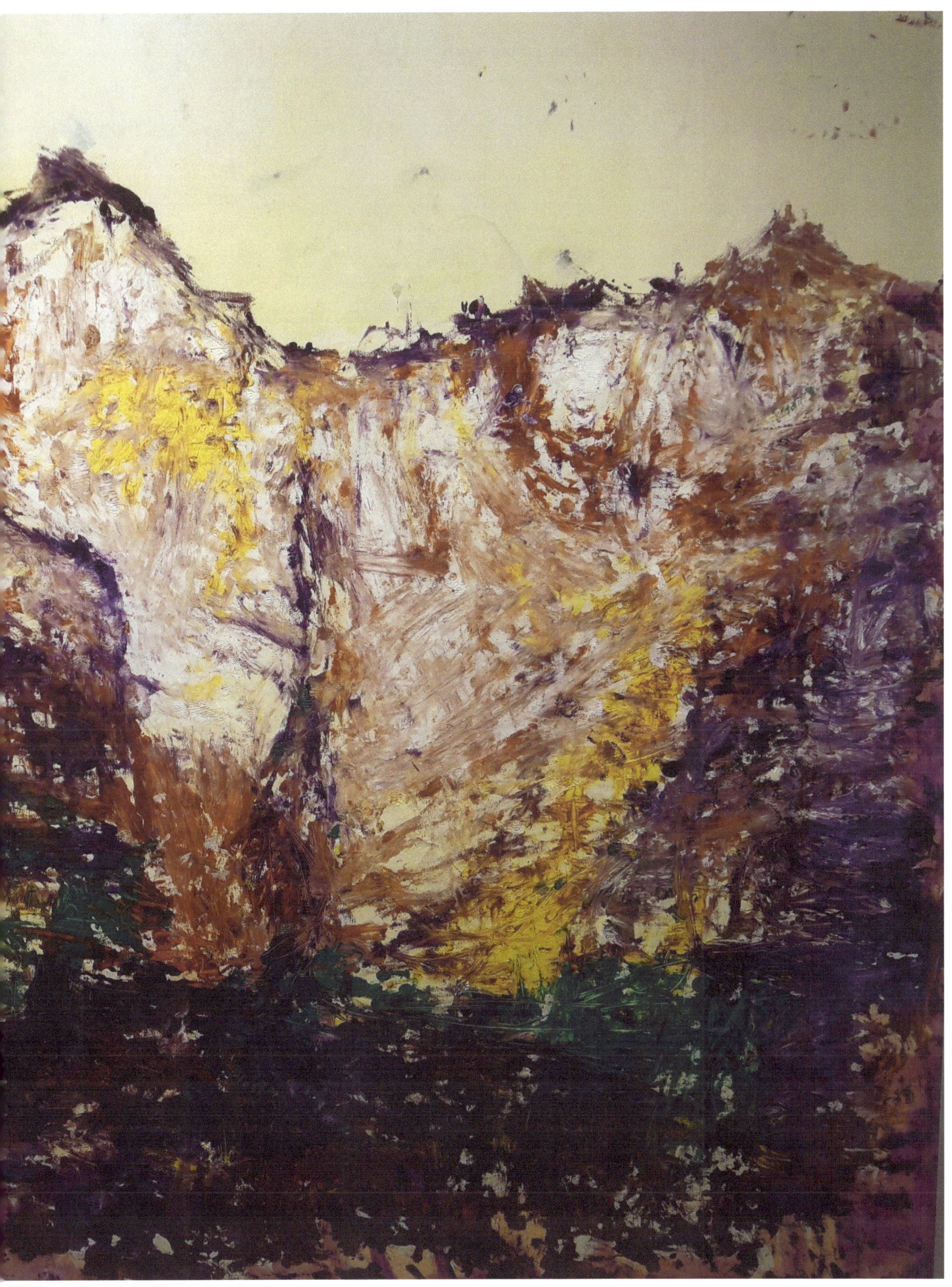

Detail 1

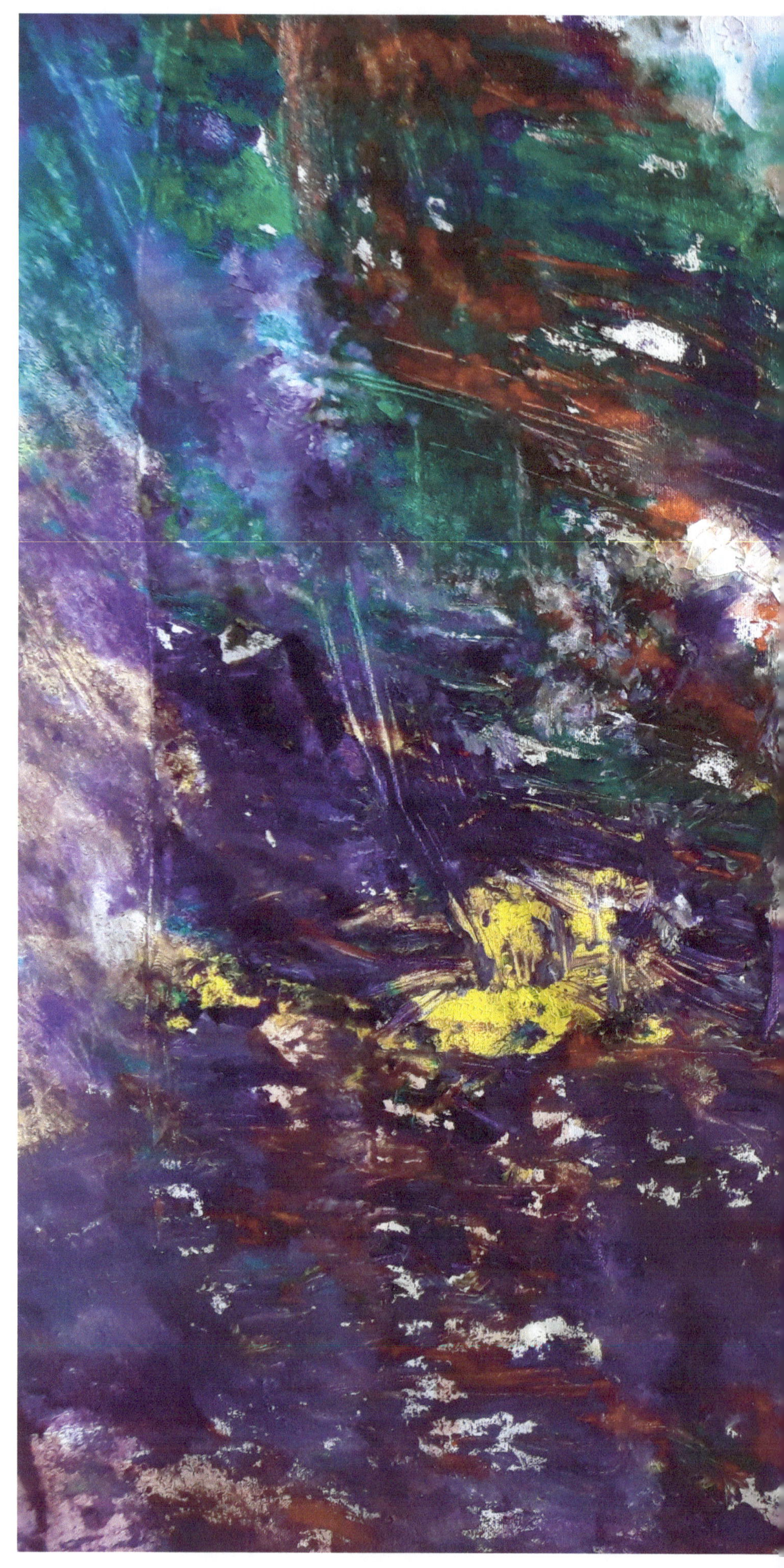

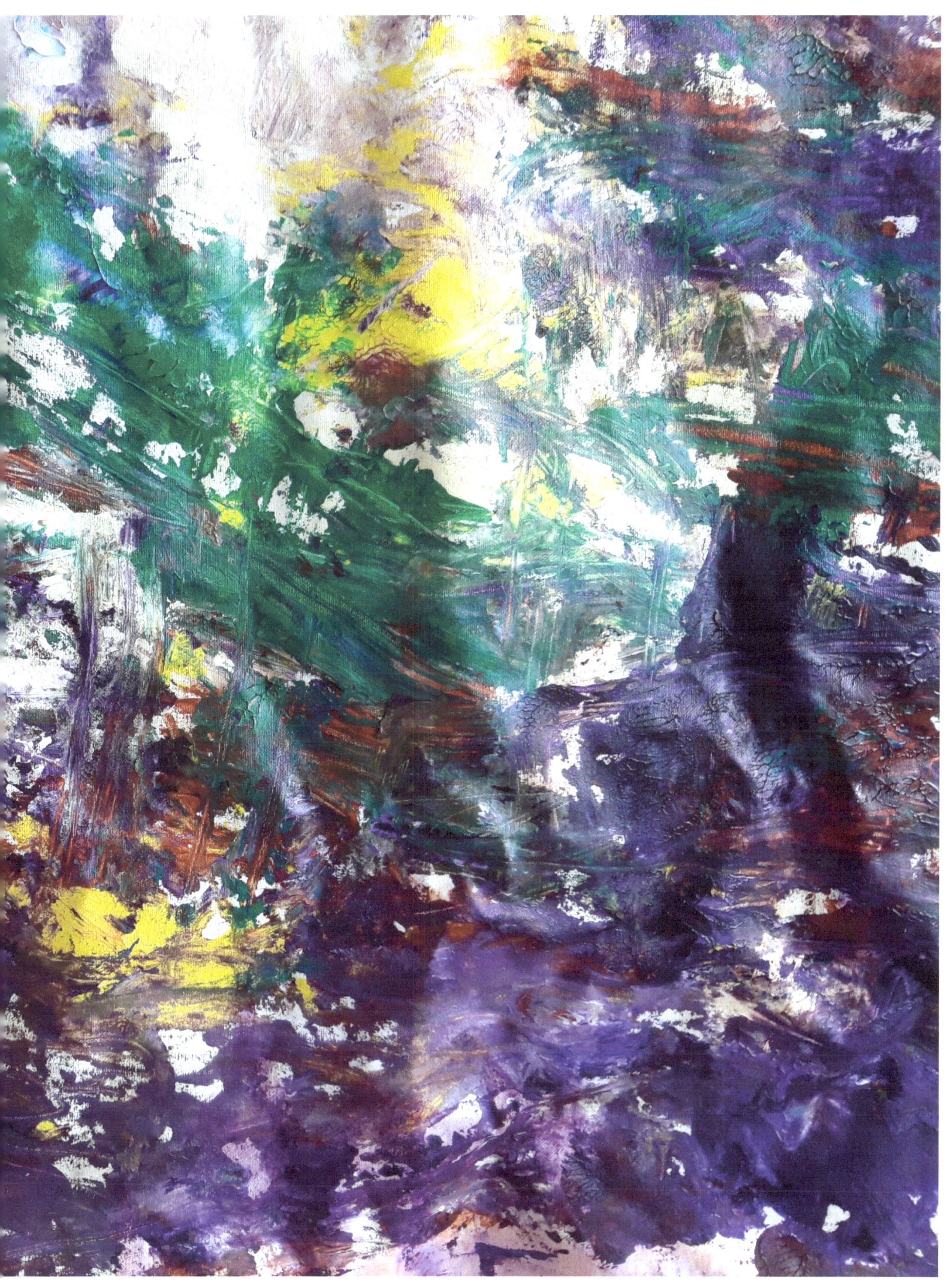

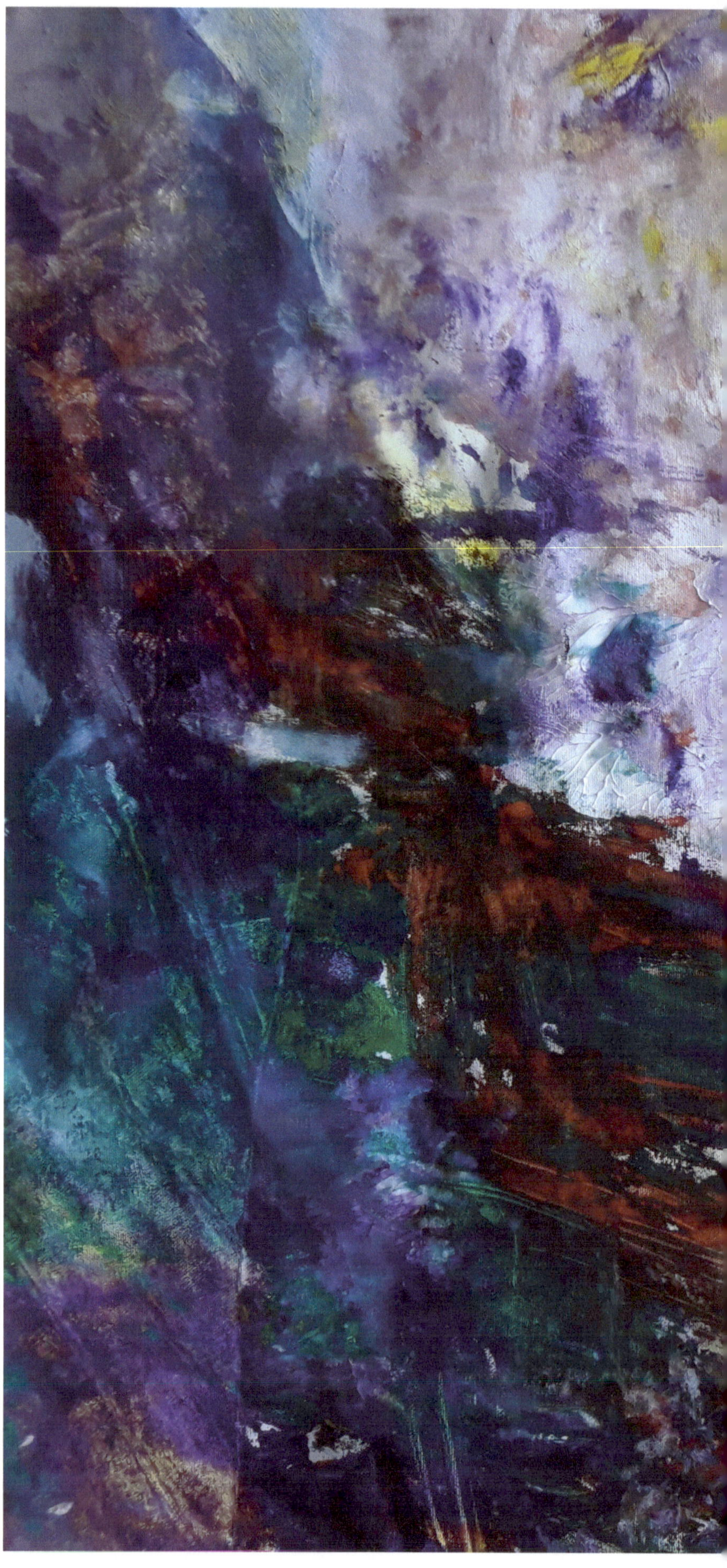

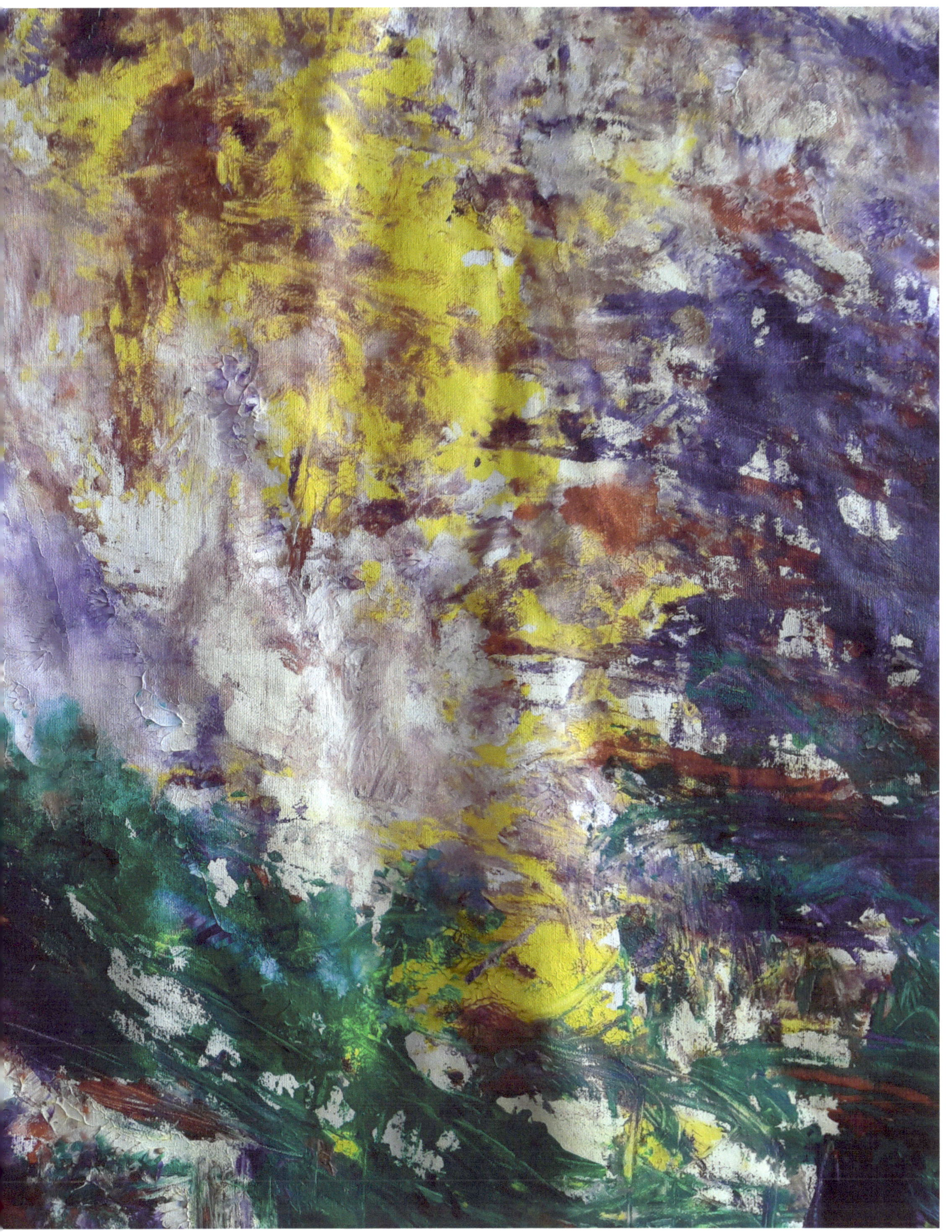

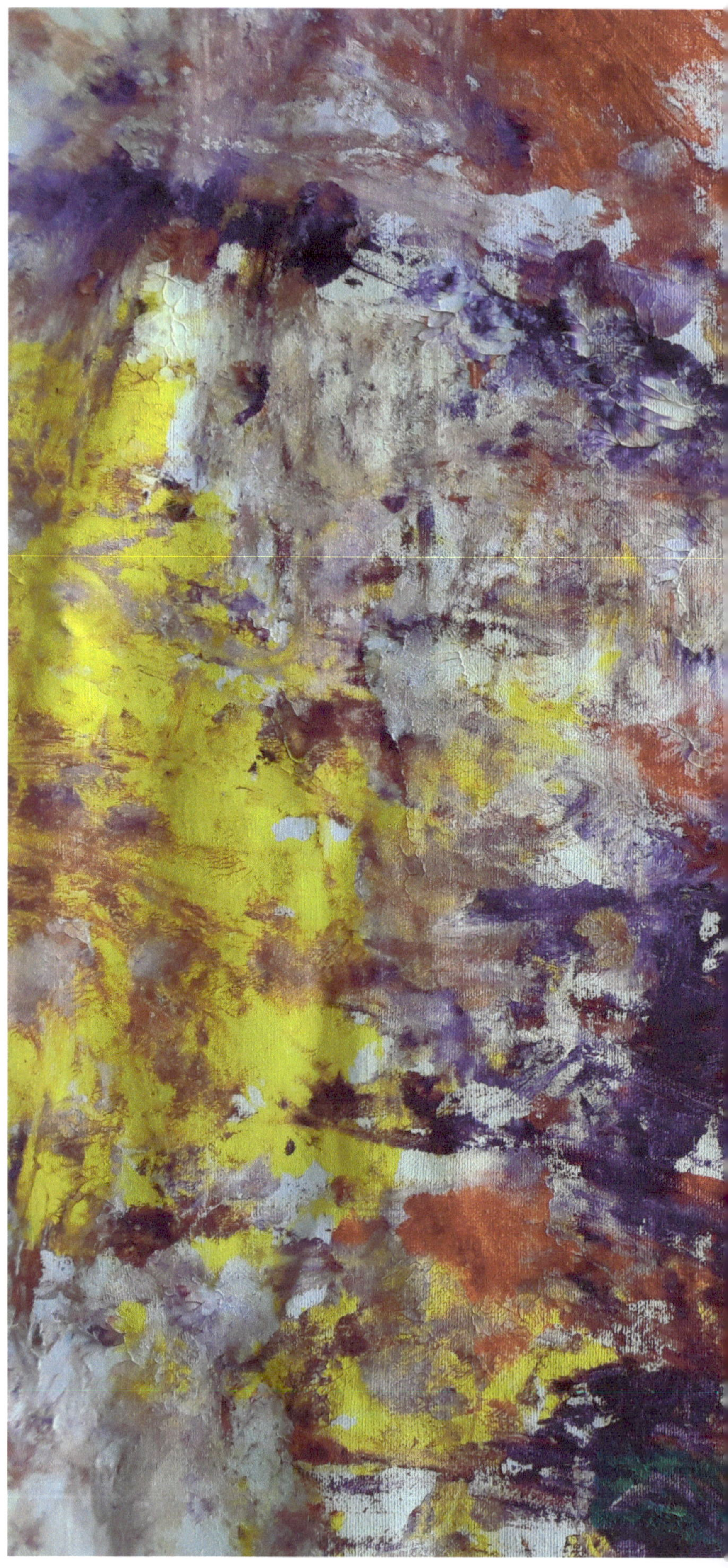

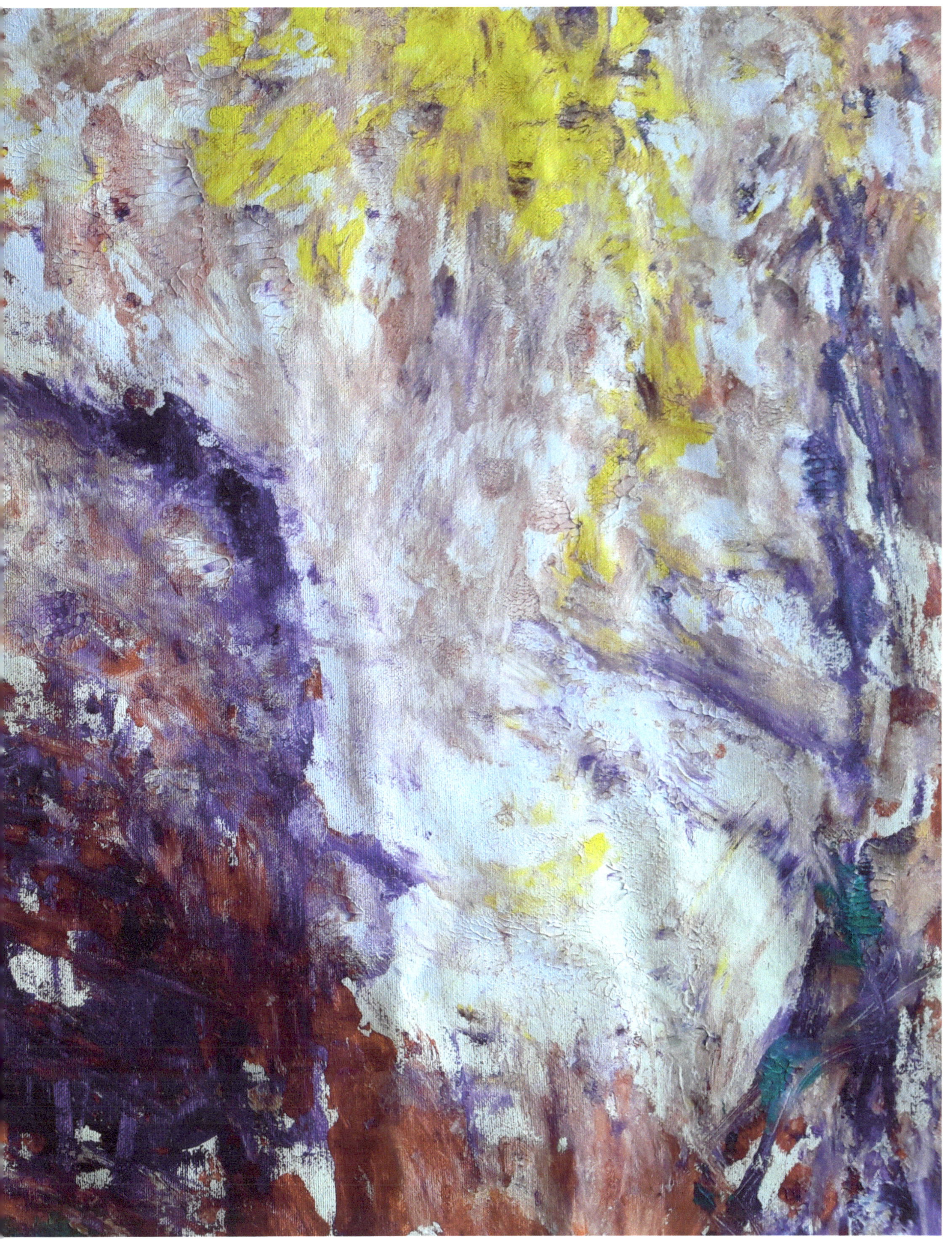

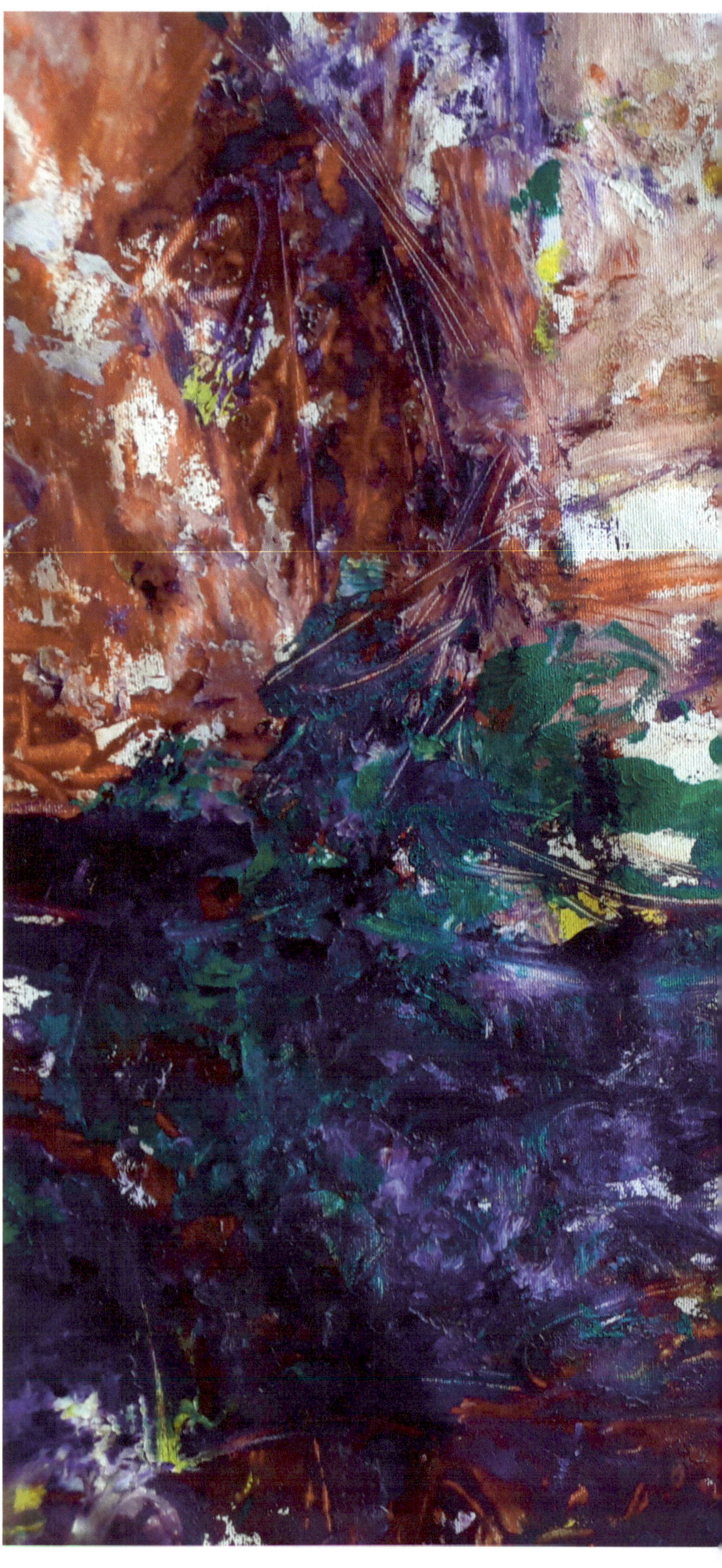

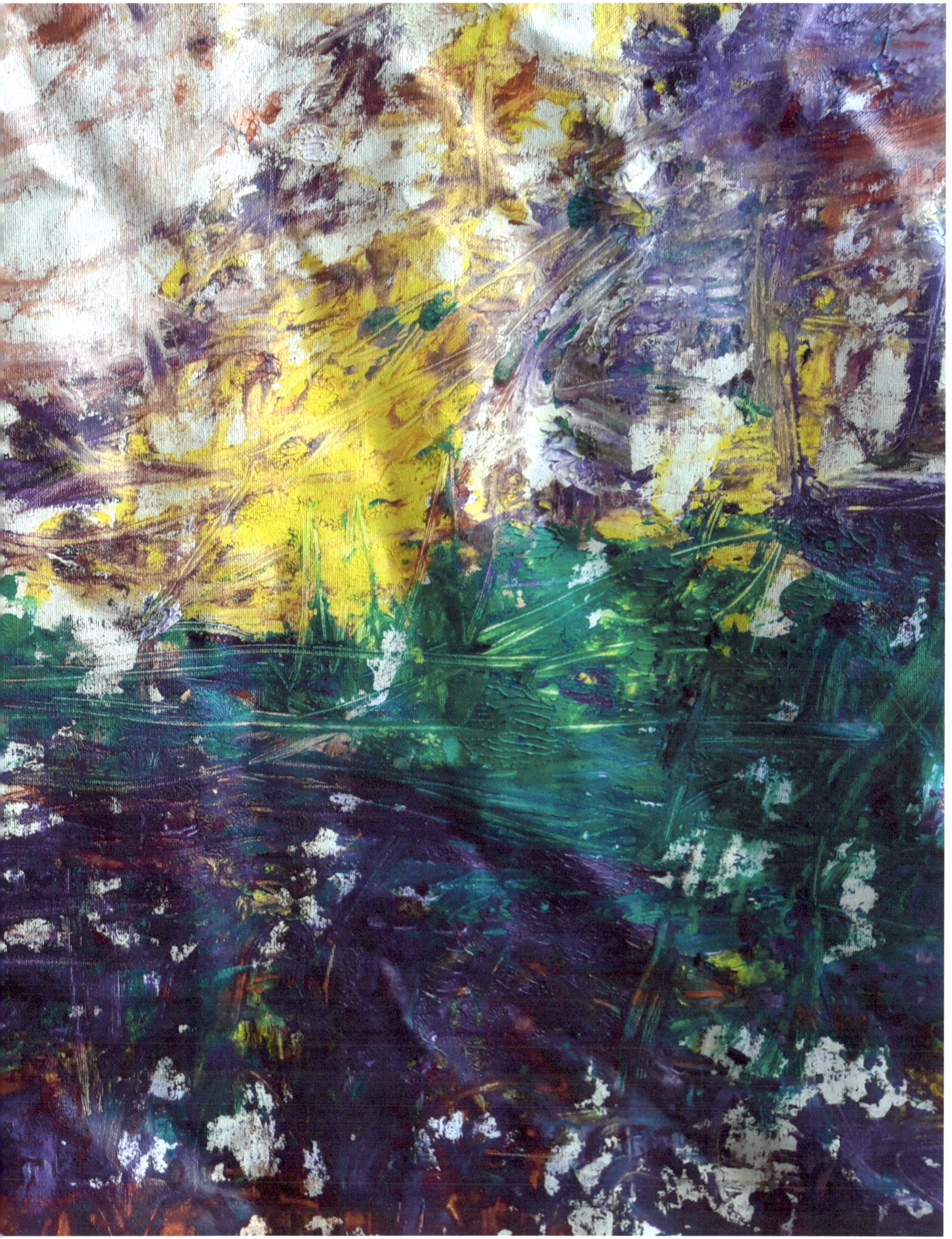

Detail 5

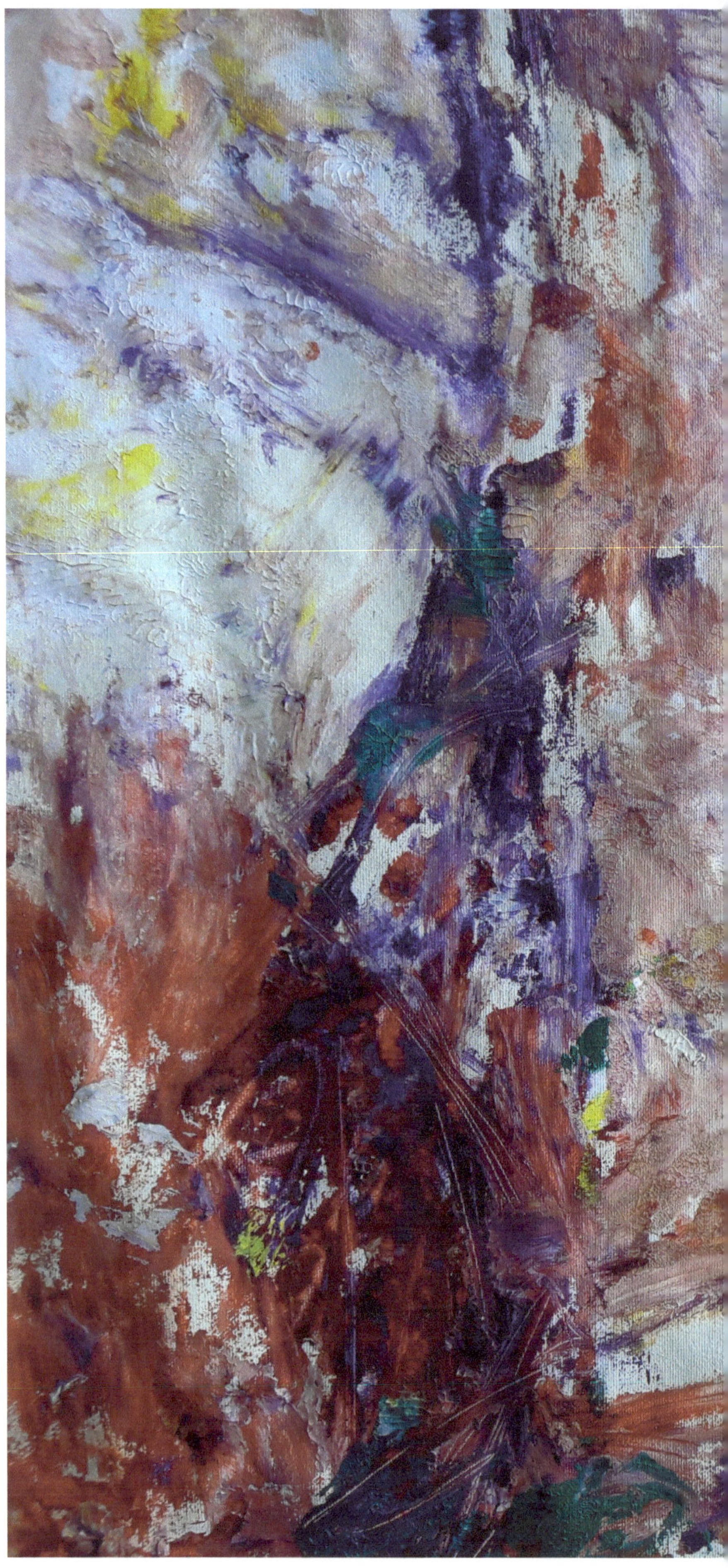

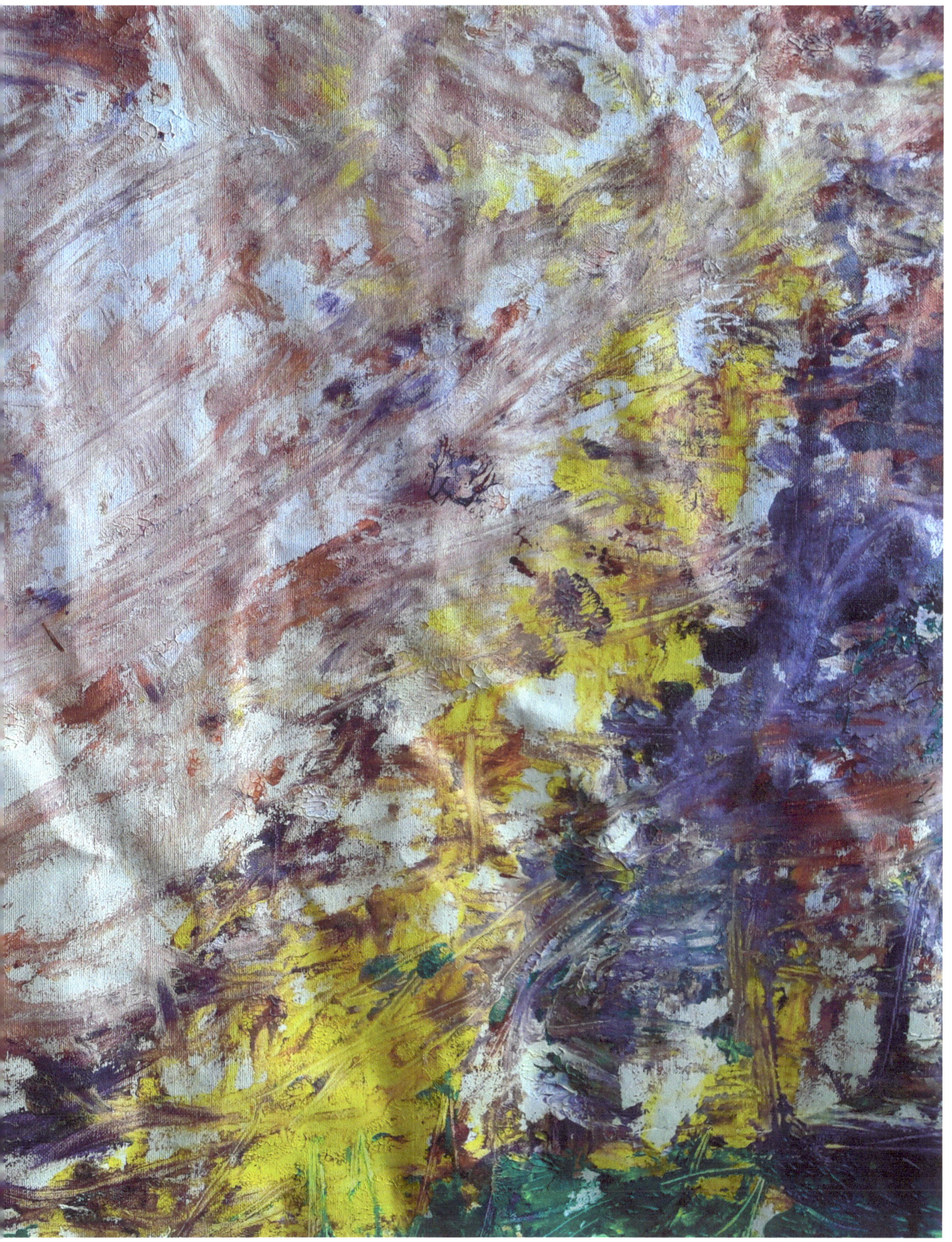

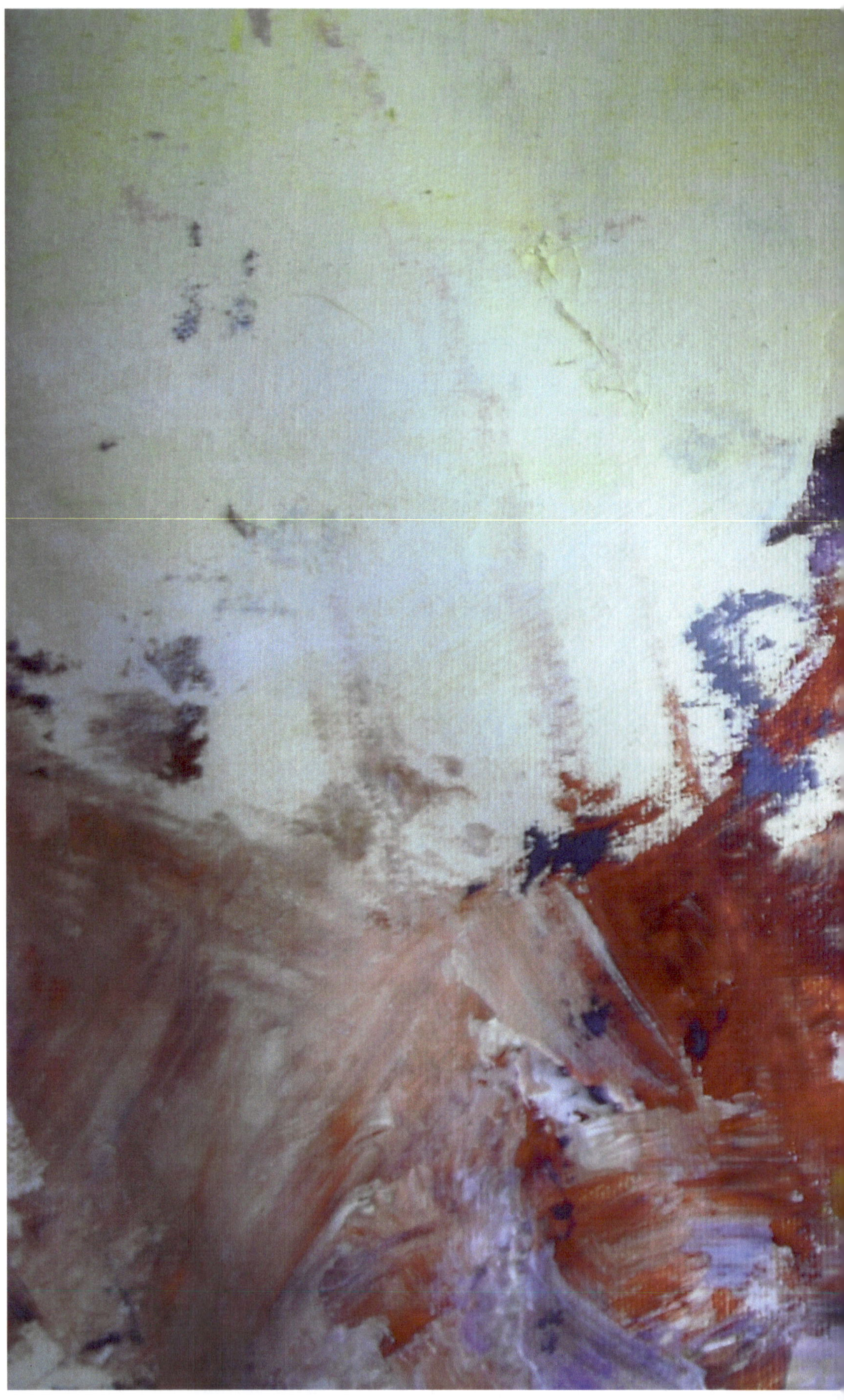

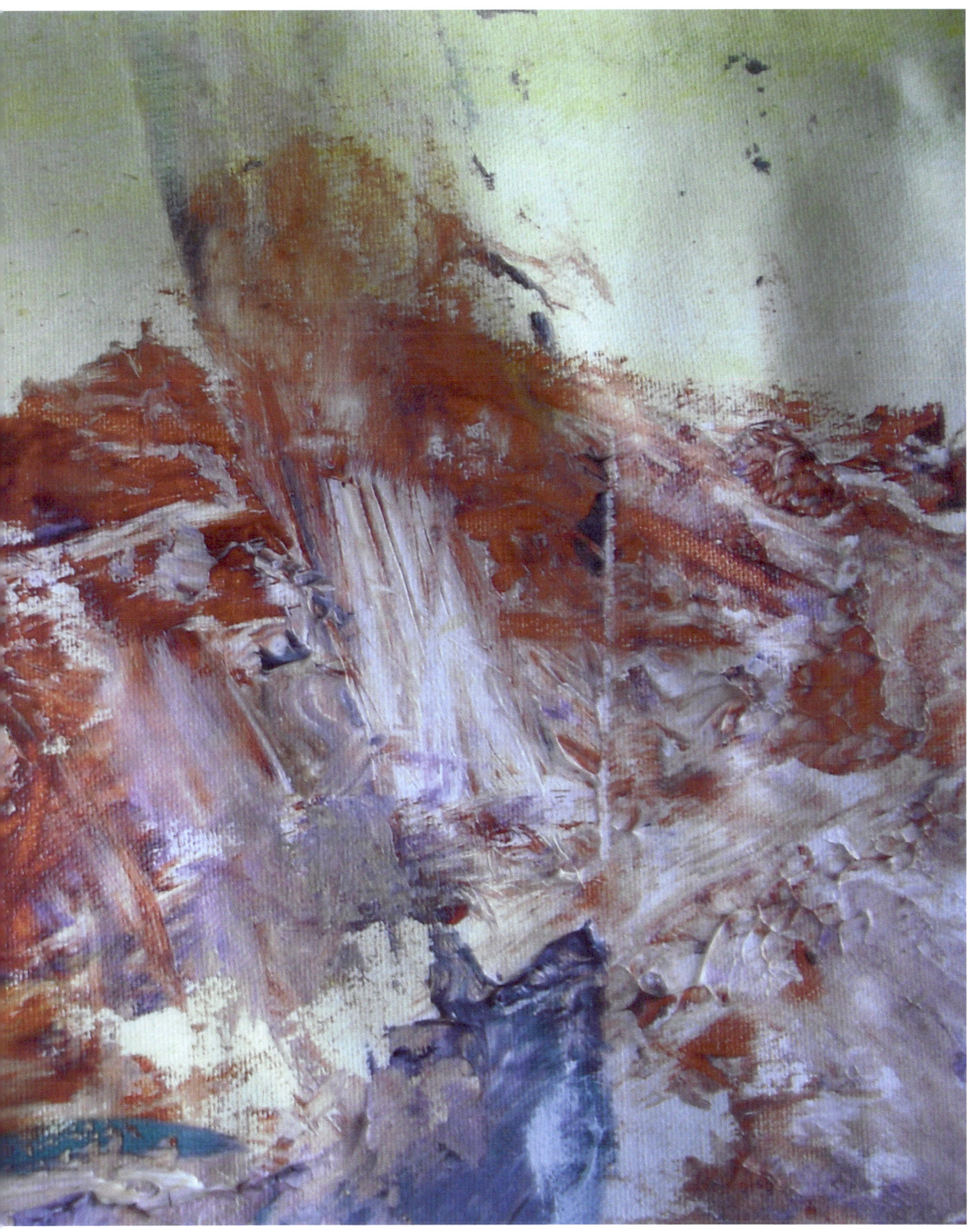

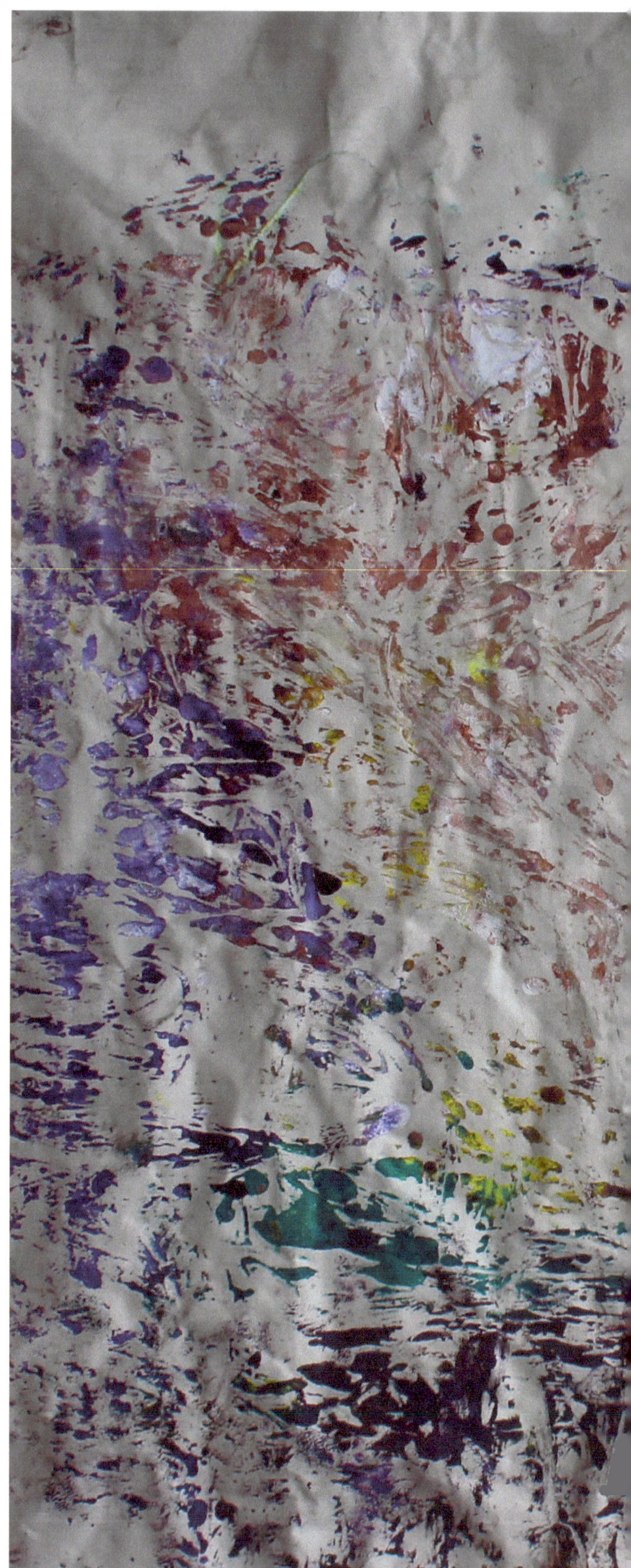

THREE VIEWS OF STOB COIRE SGREAMHACH

(FULL IMAGE OF BACKSIDE CANVAS)

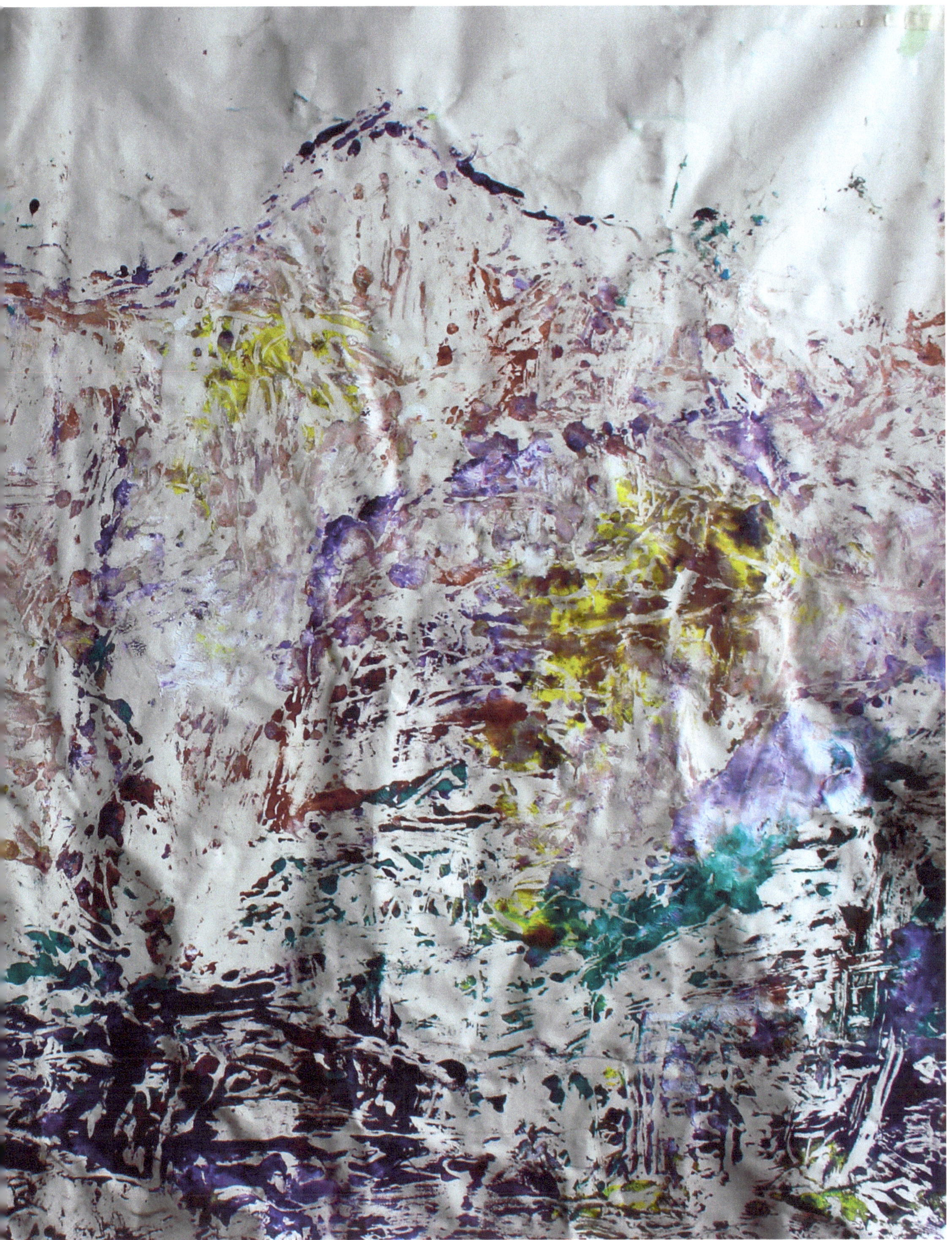

Detail 1

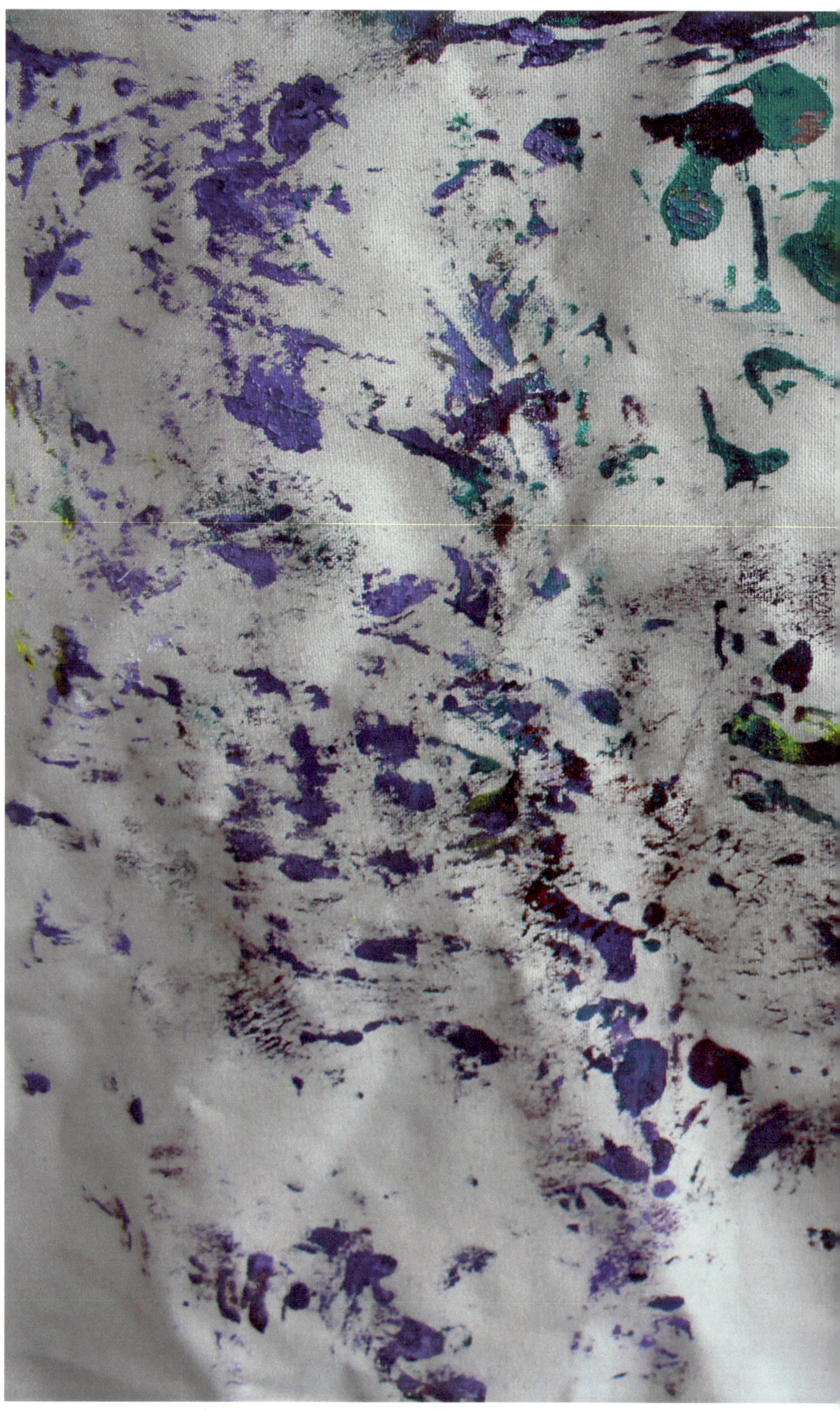

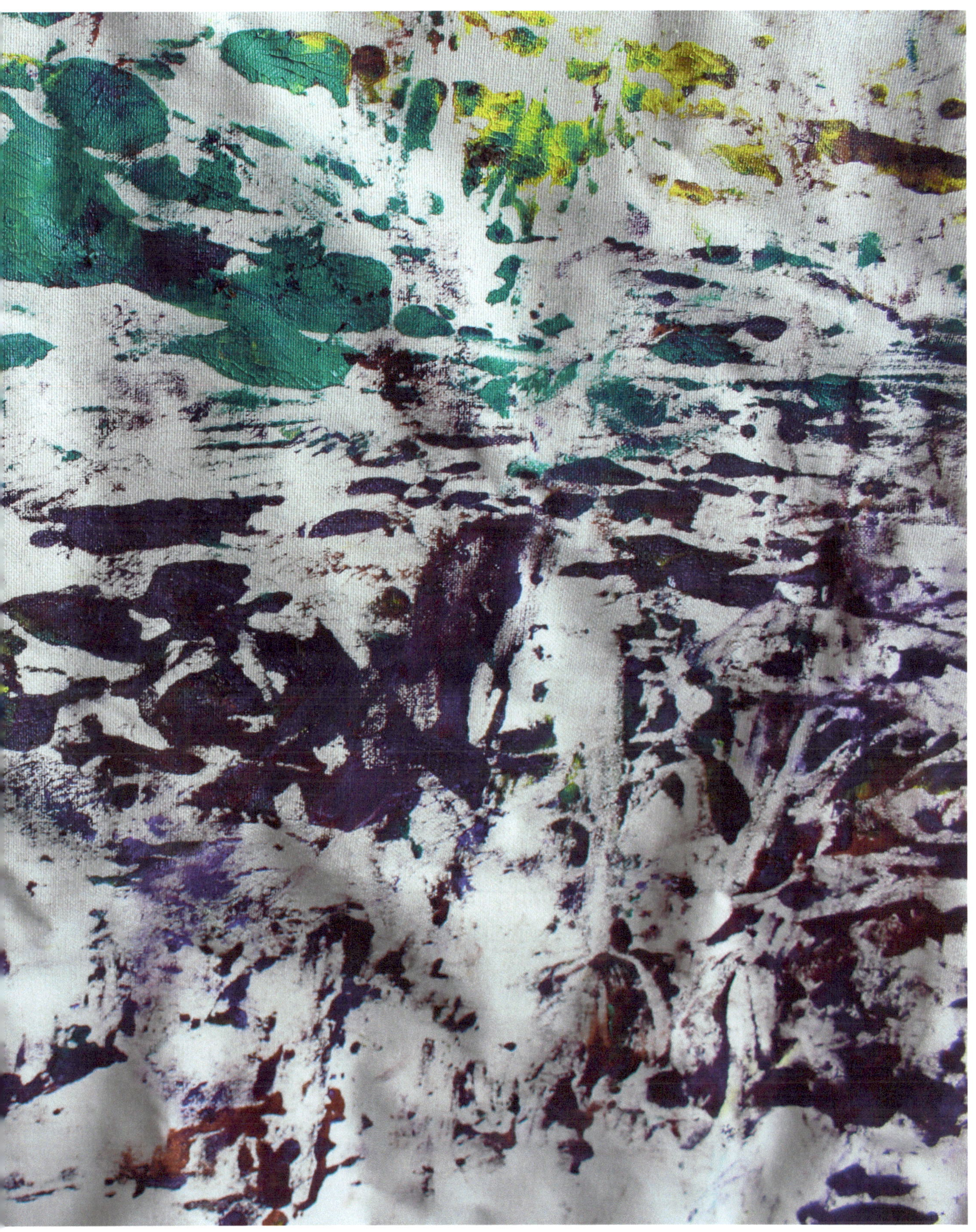

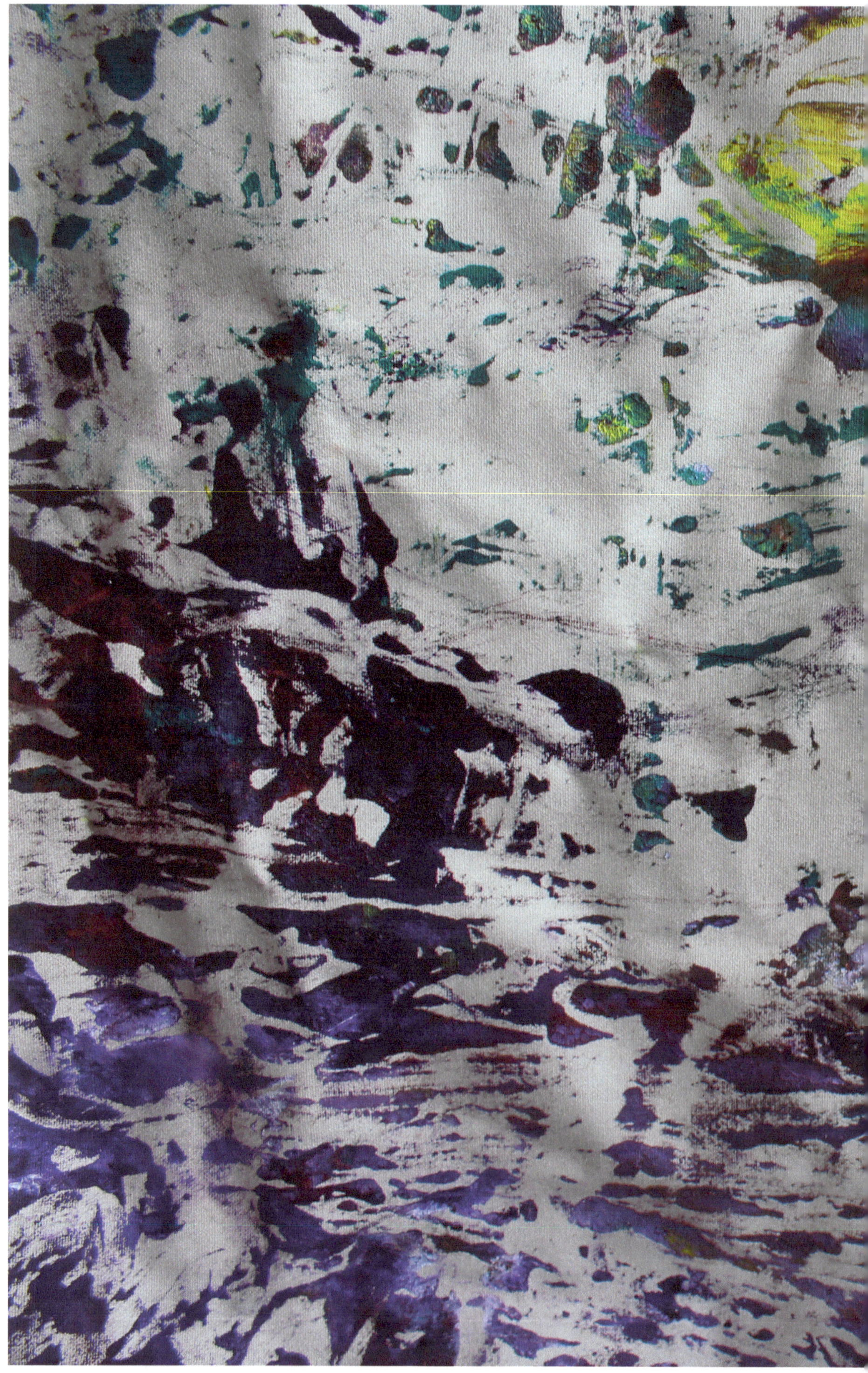

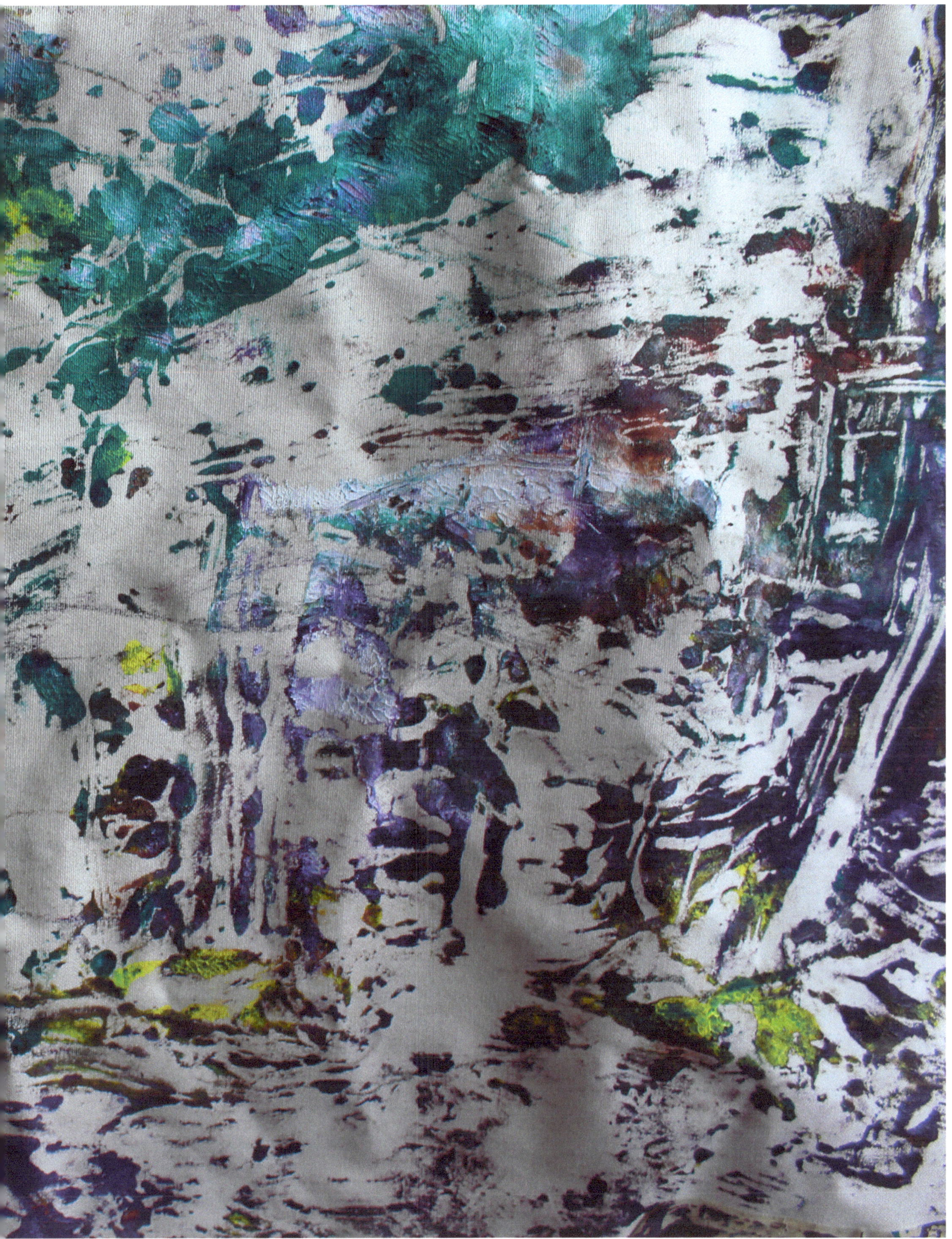

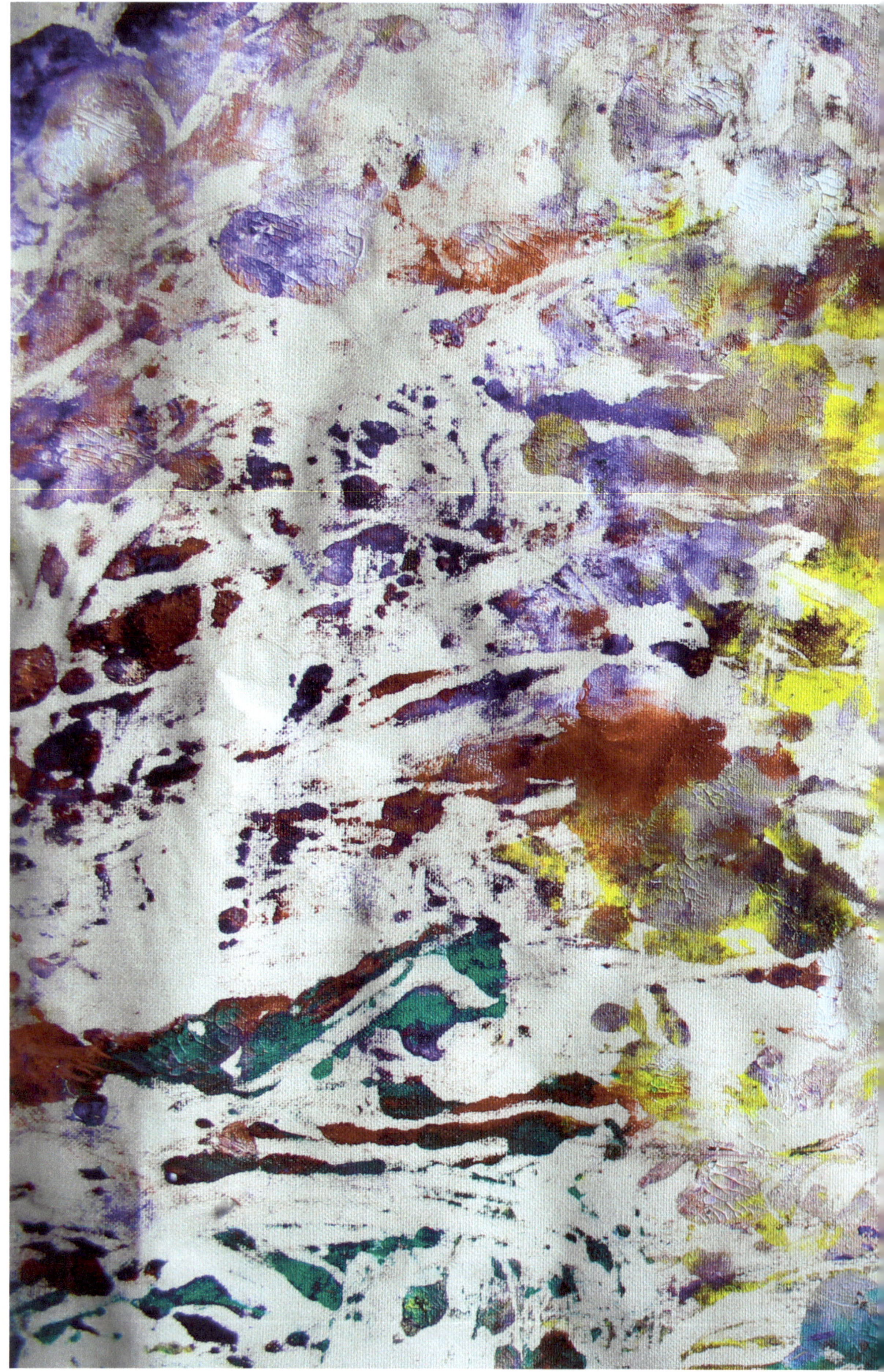

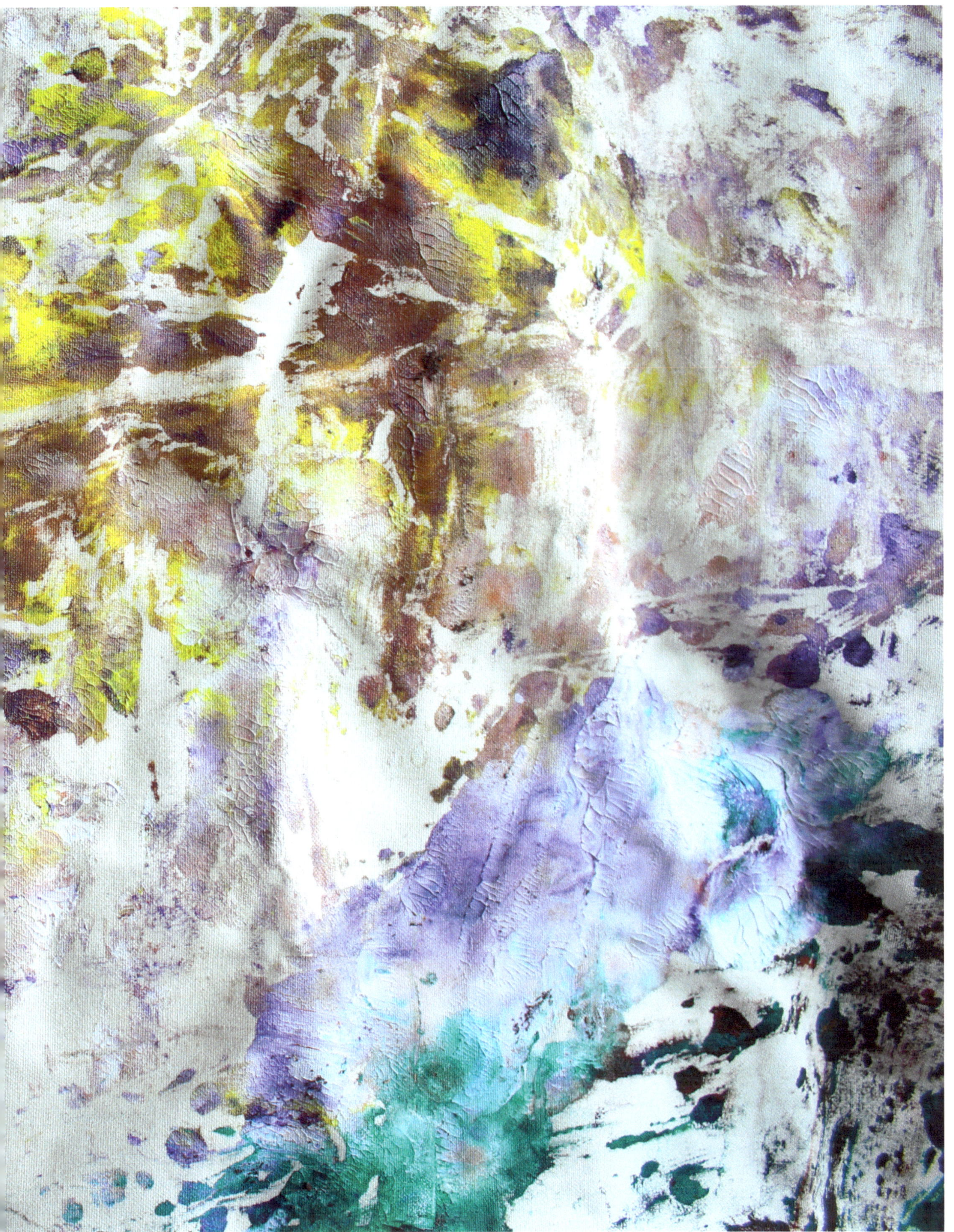

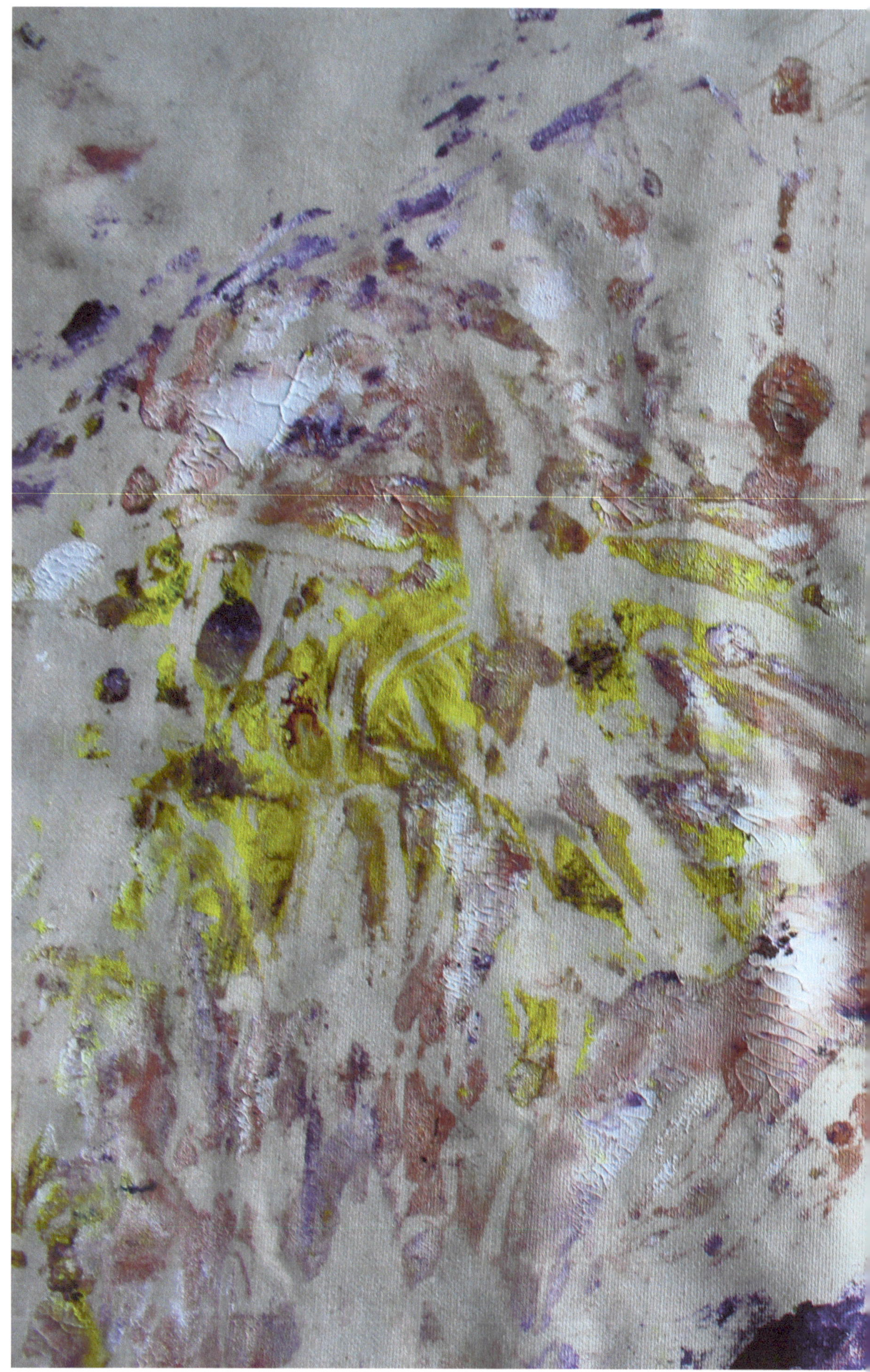

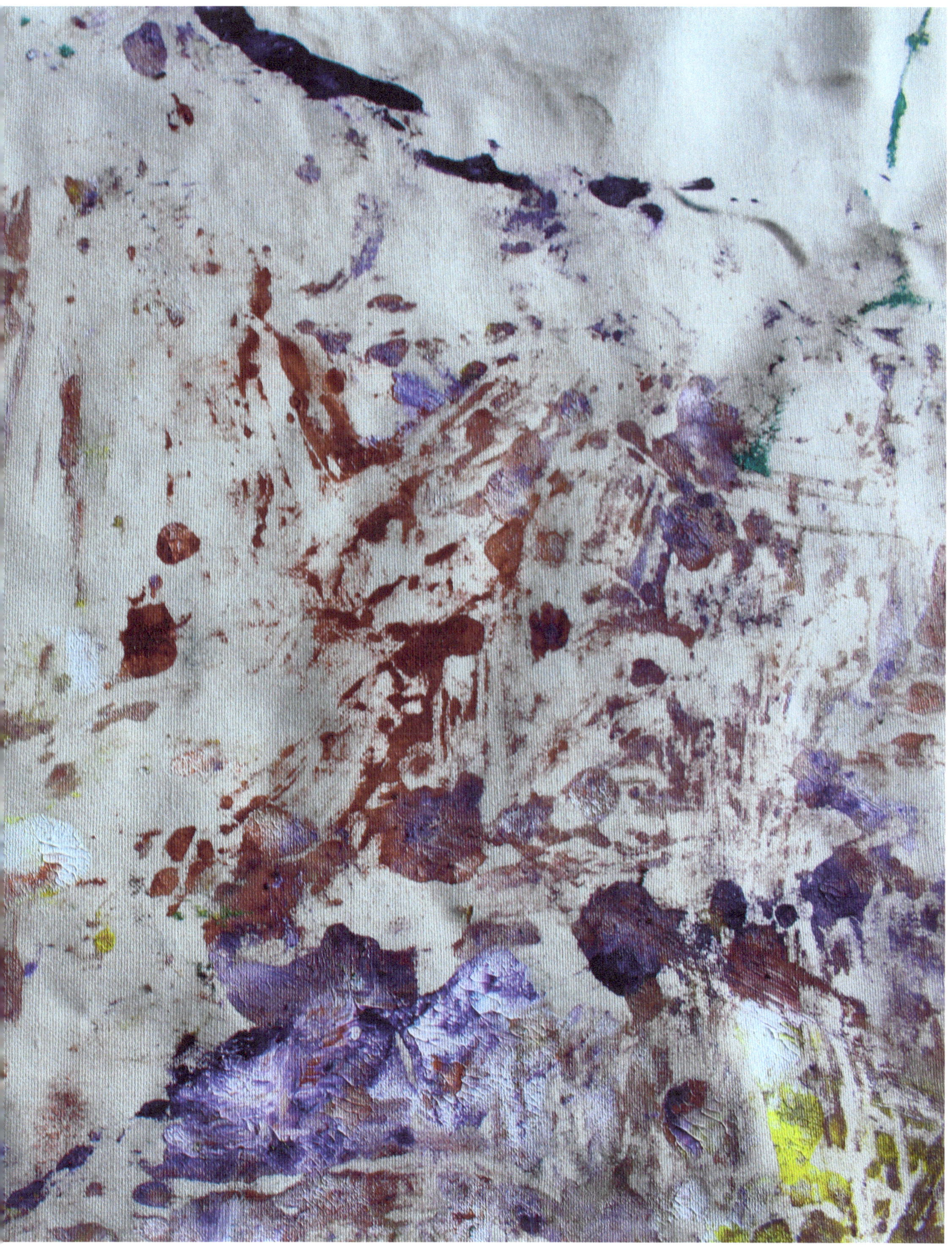

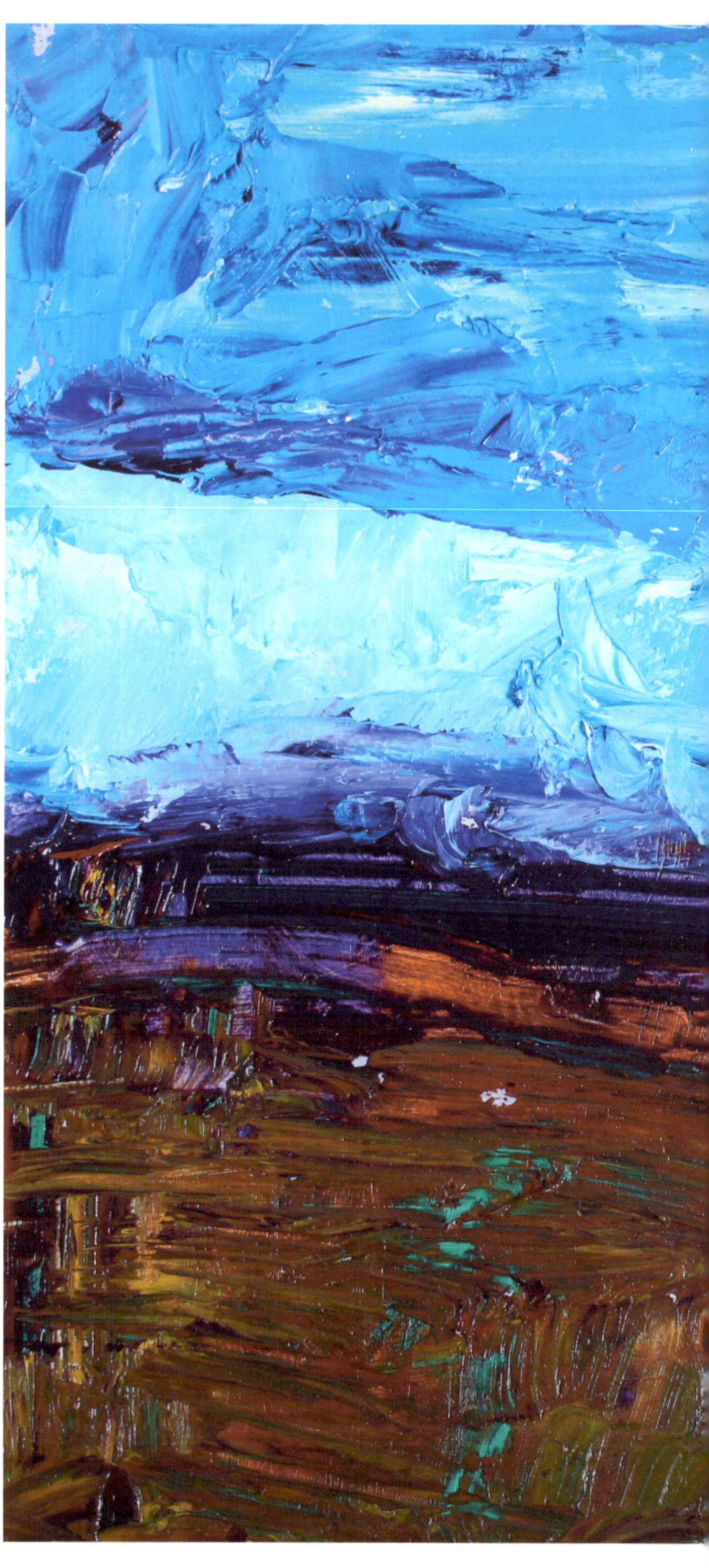

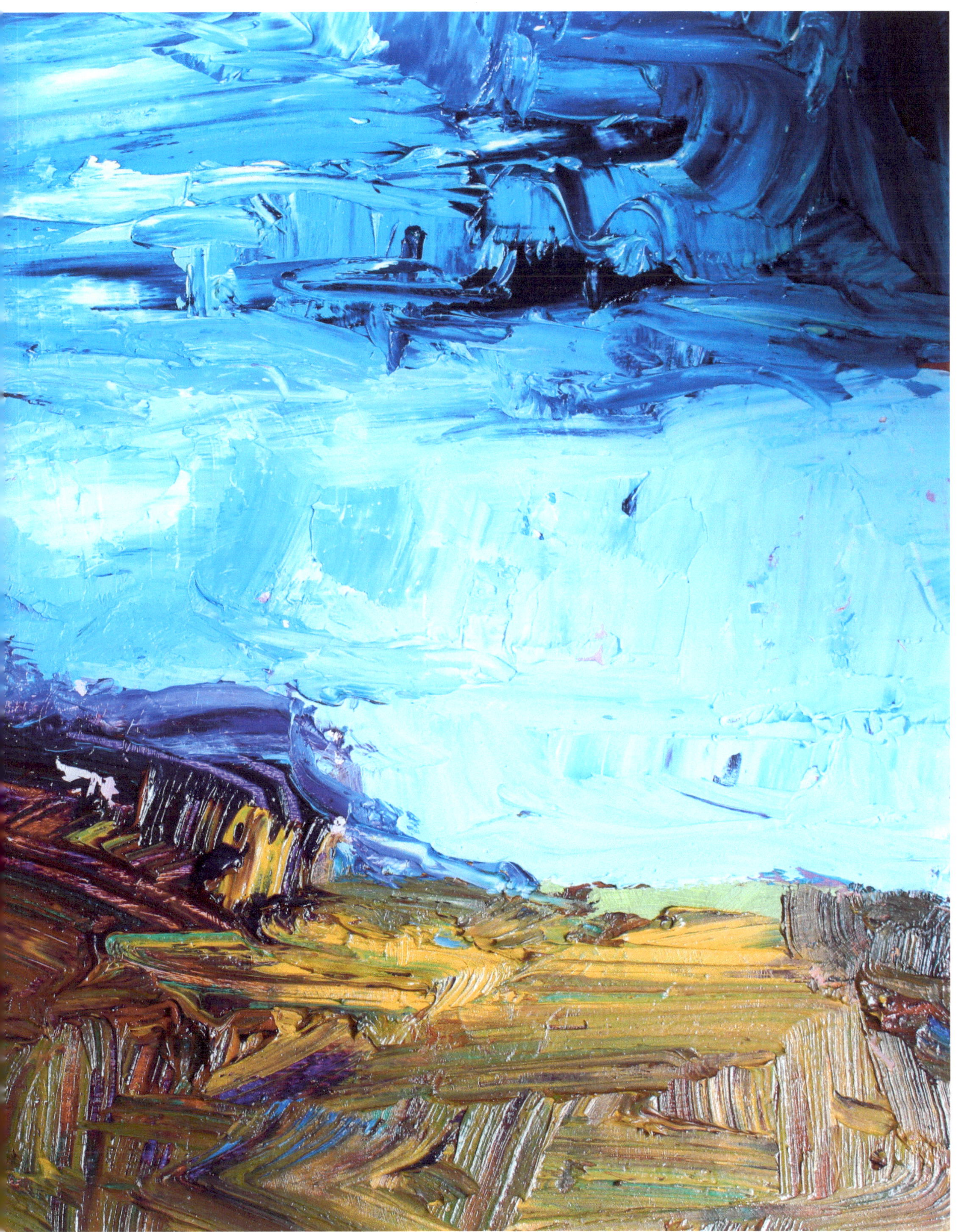

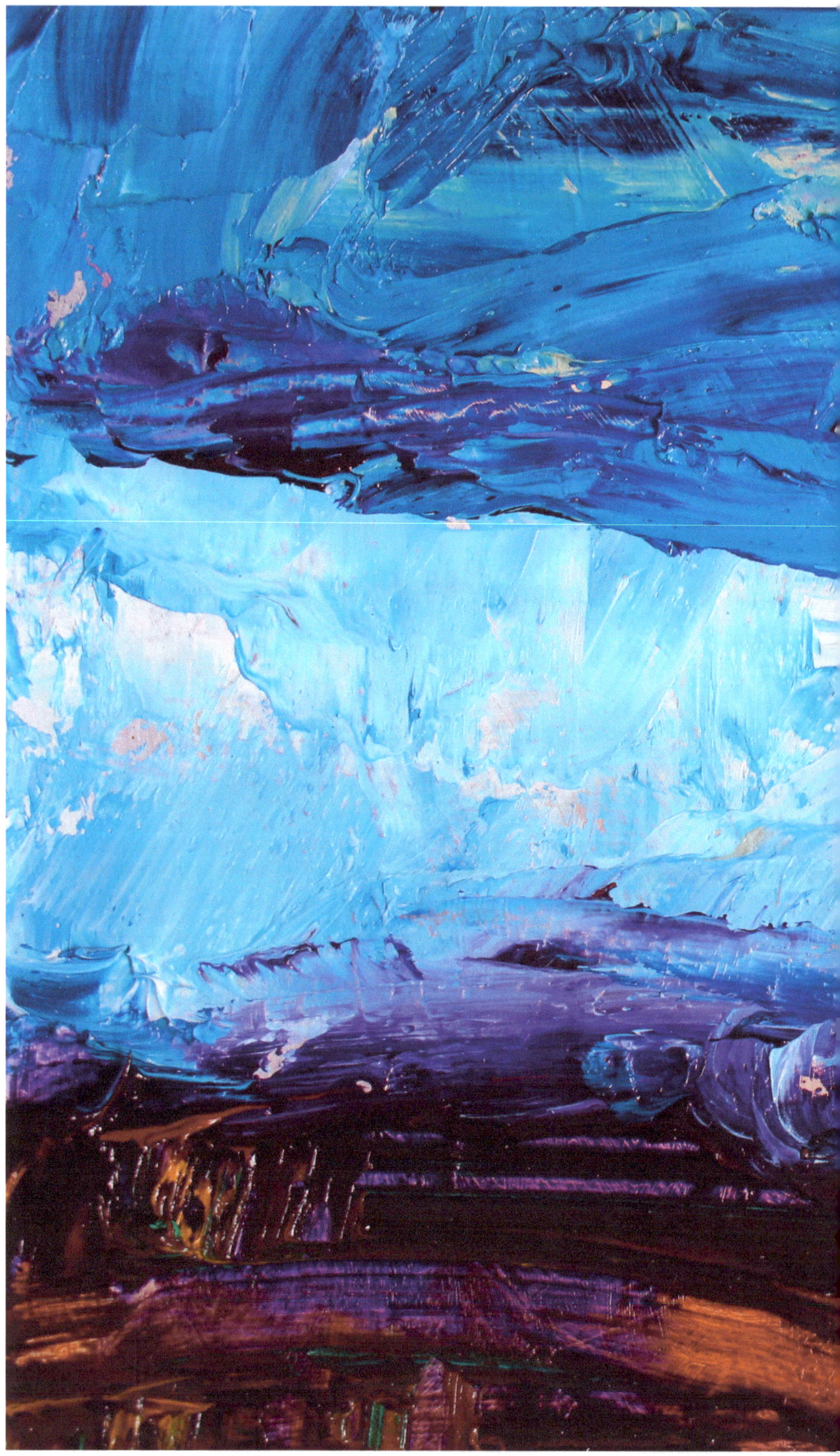

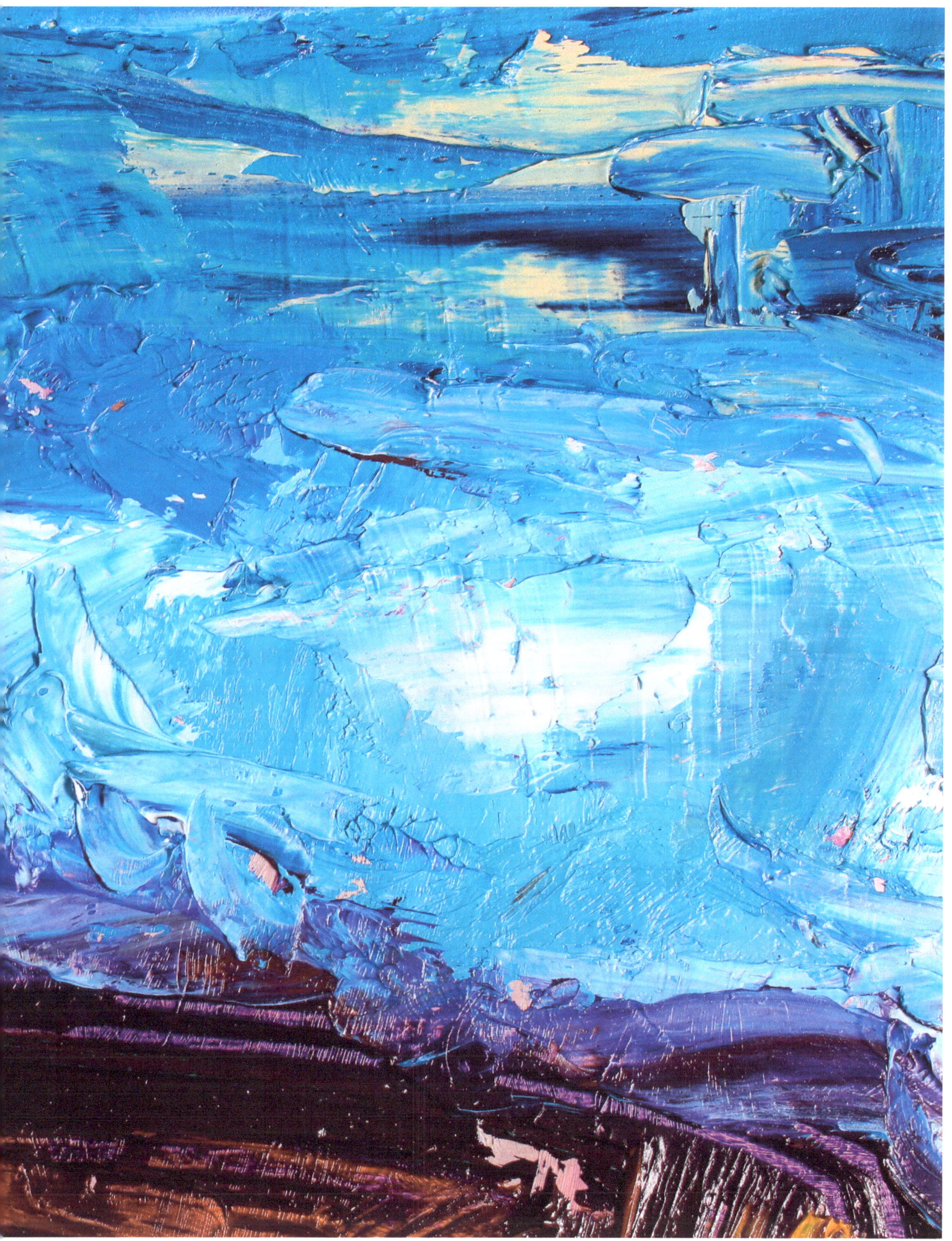

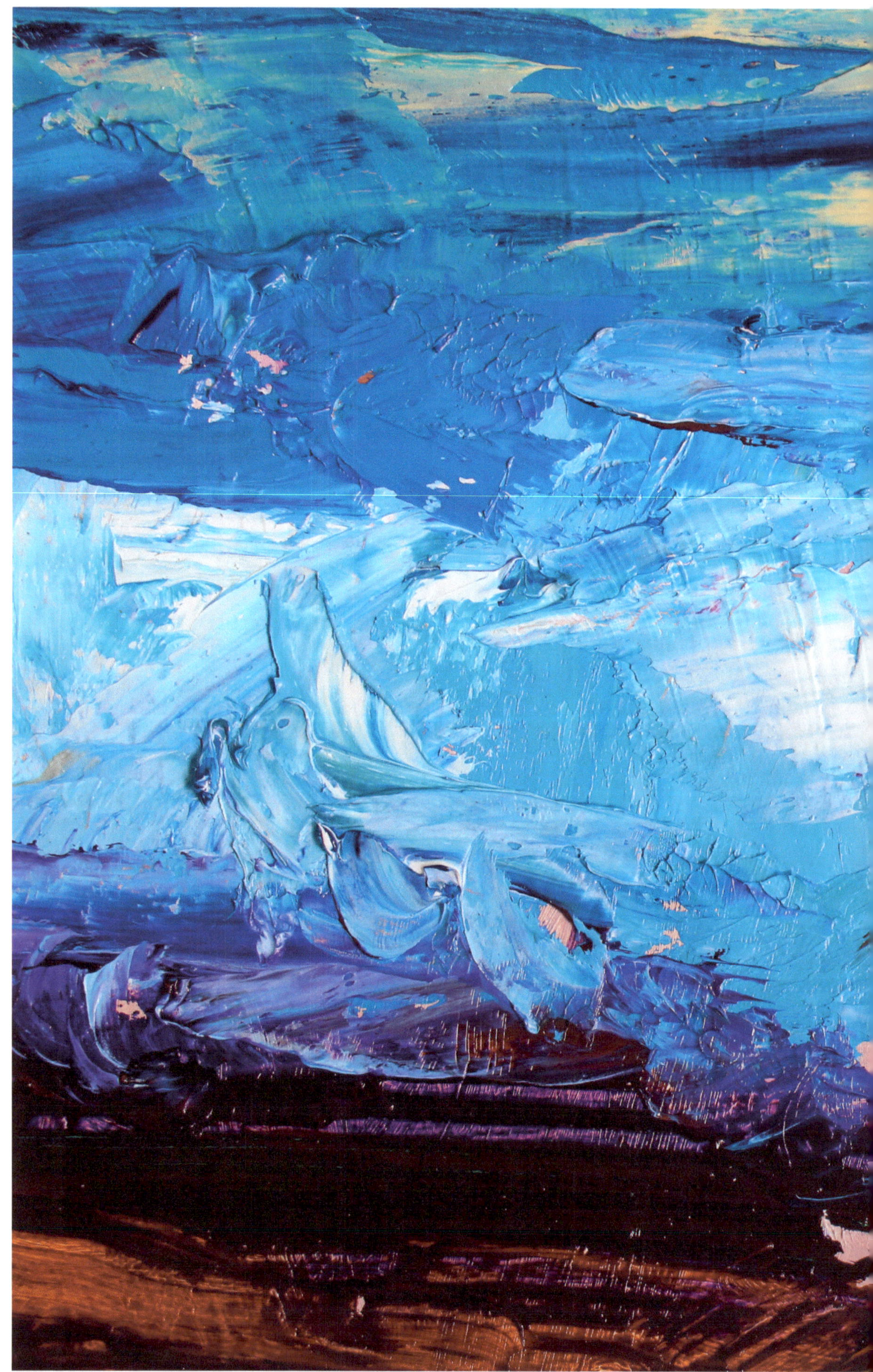

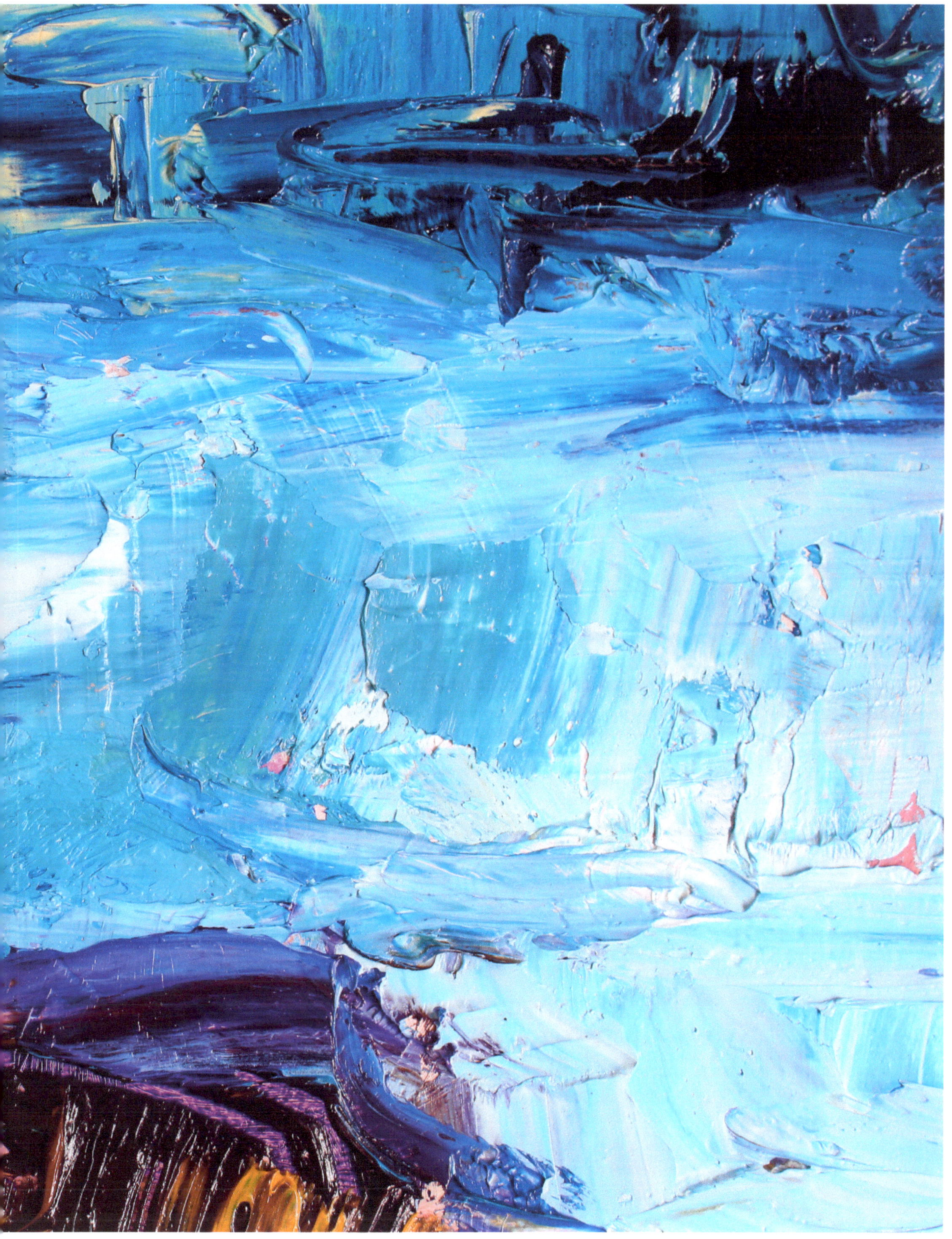

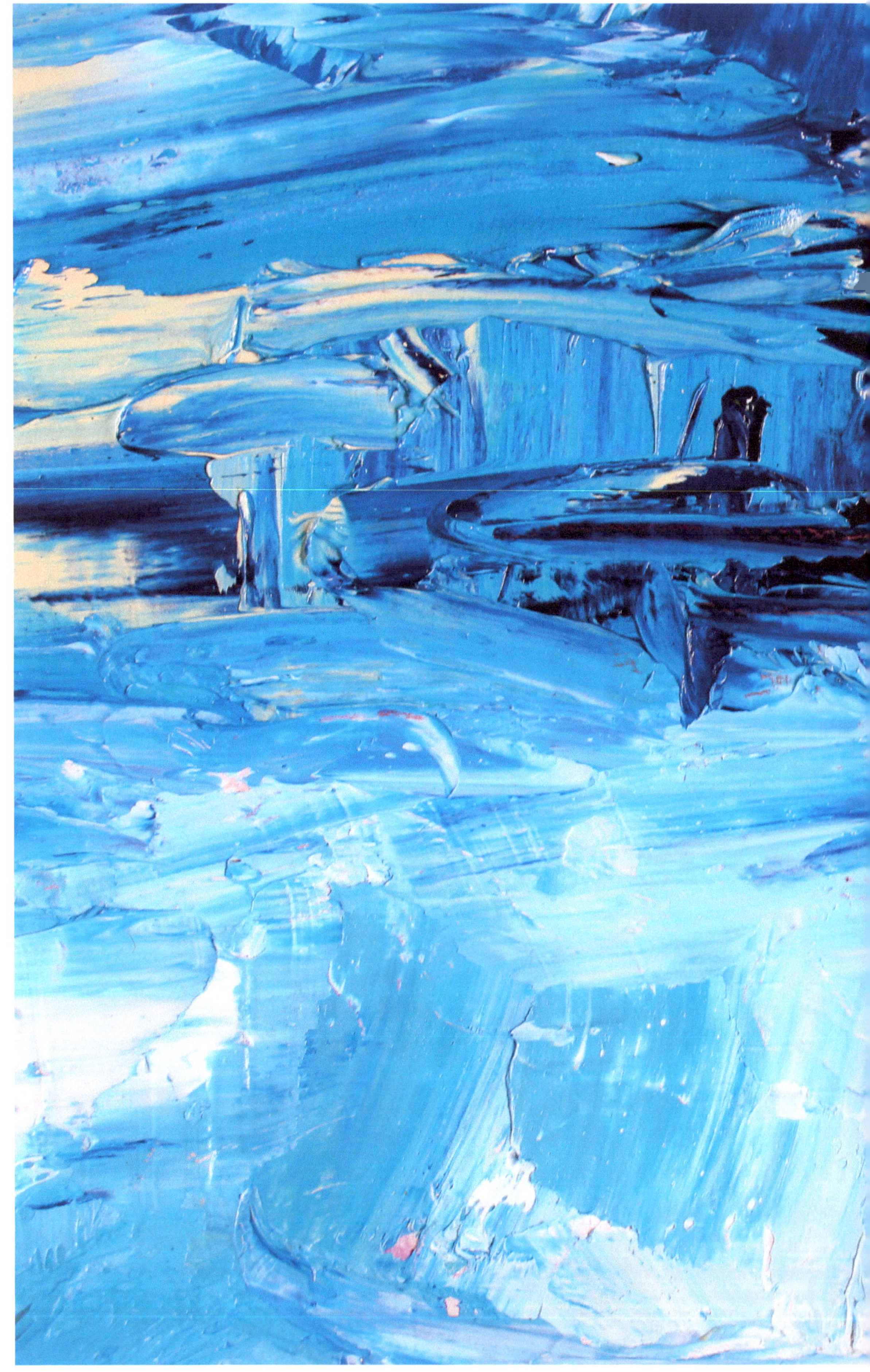

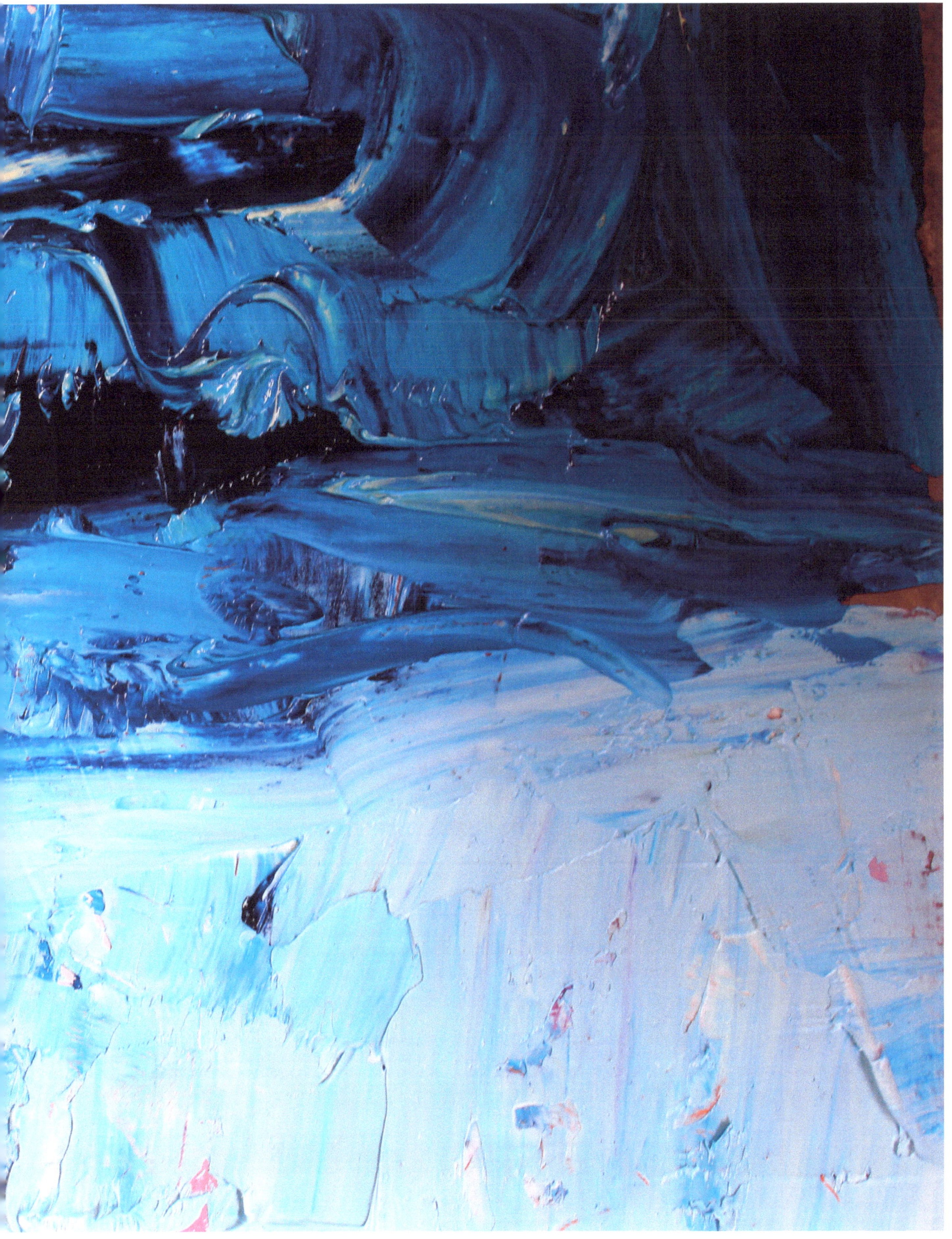

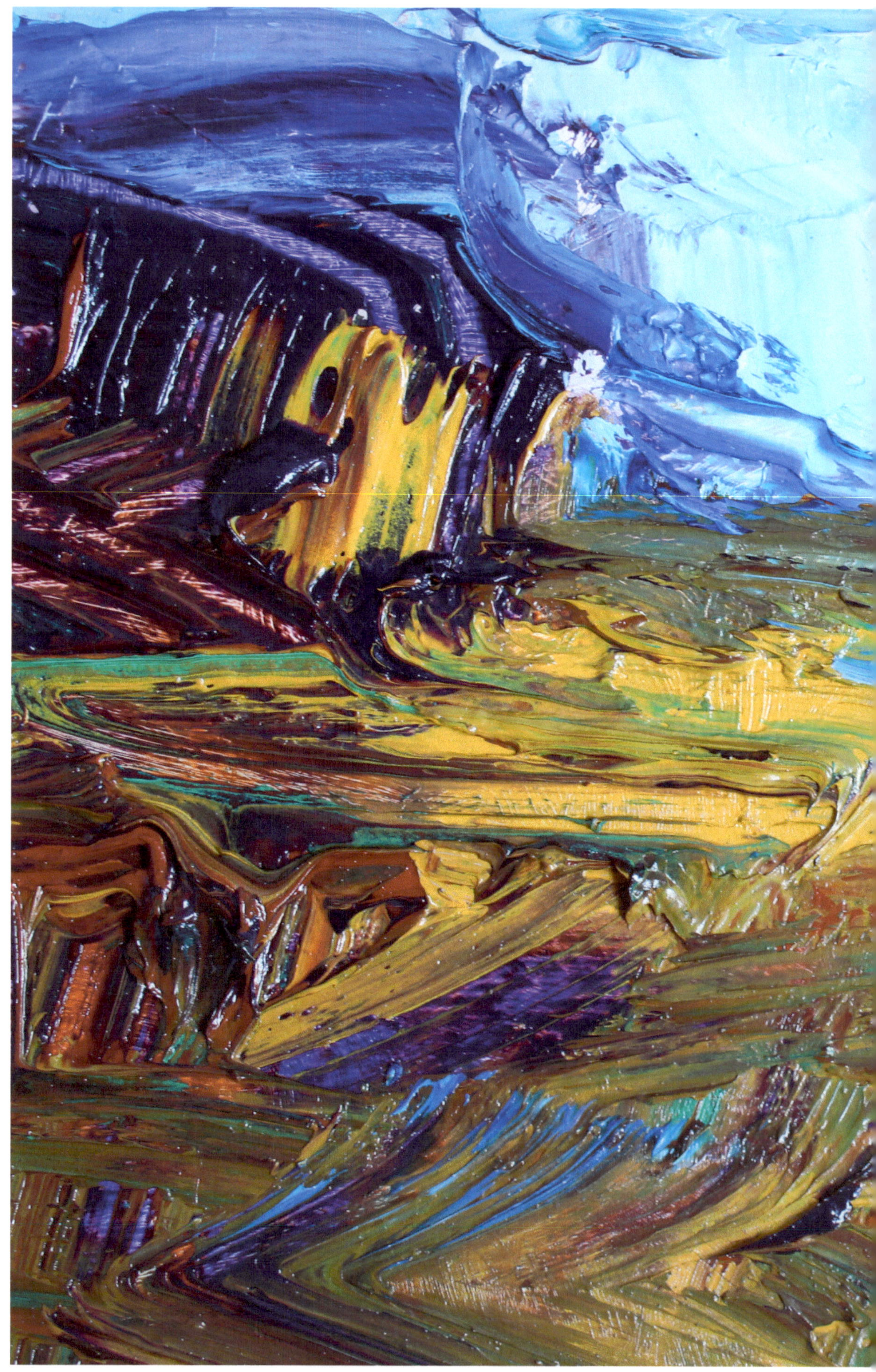

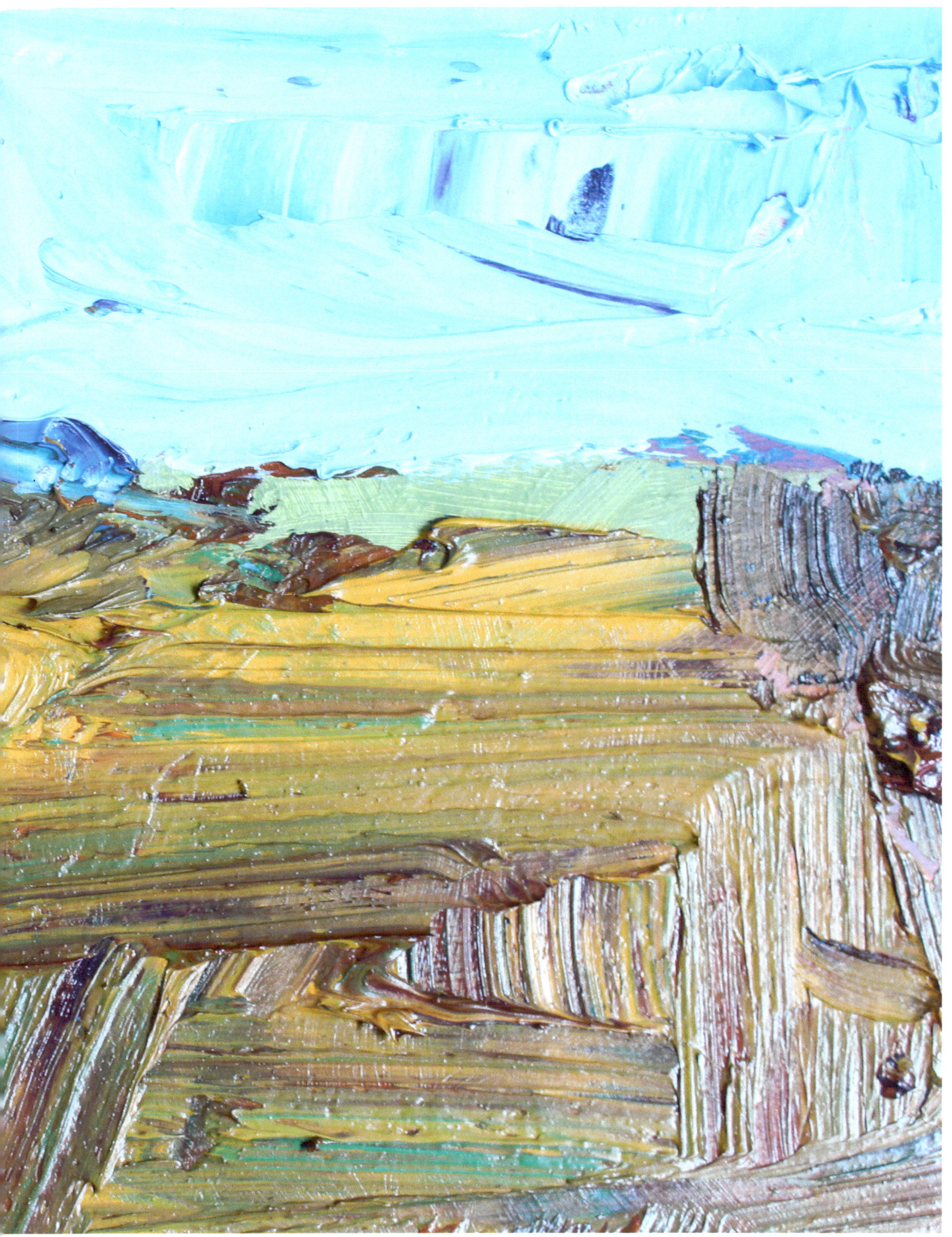

Detail 5

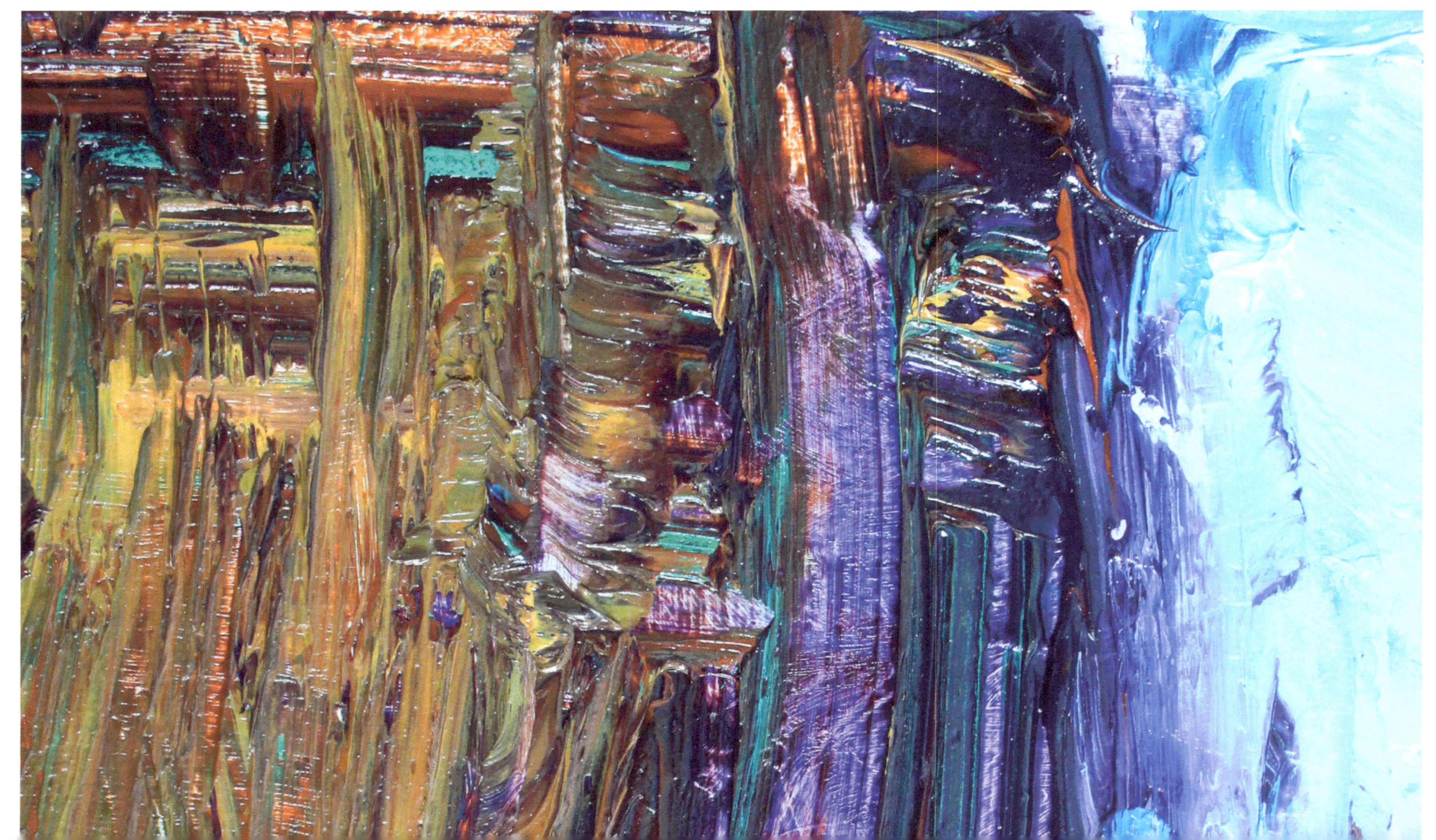

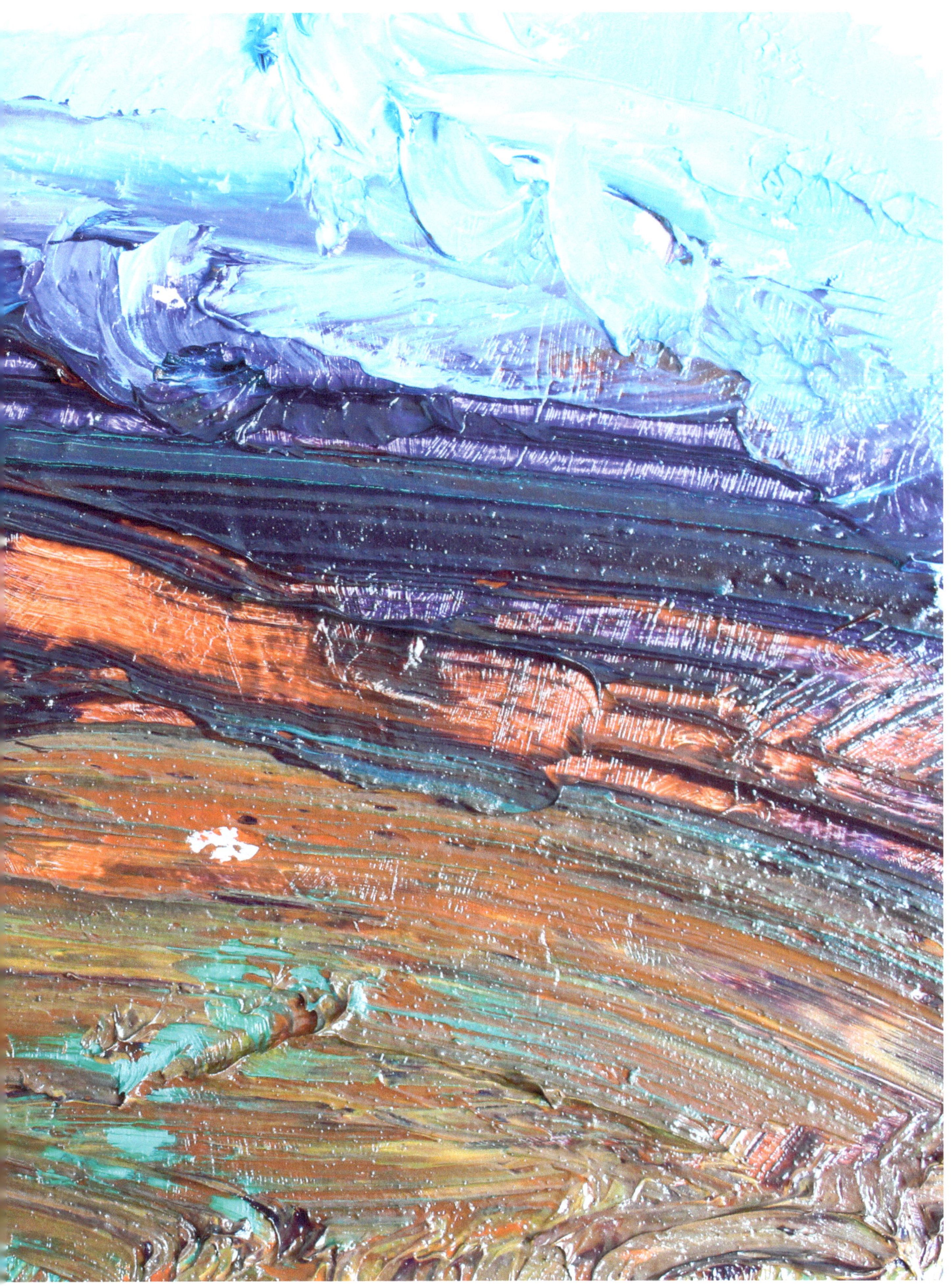

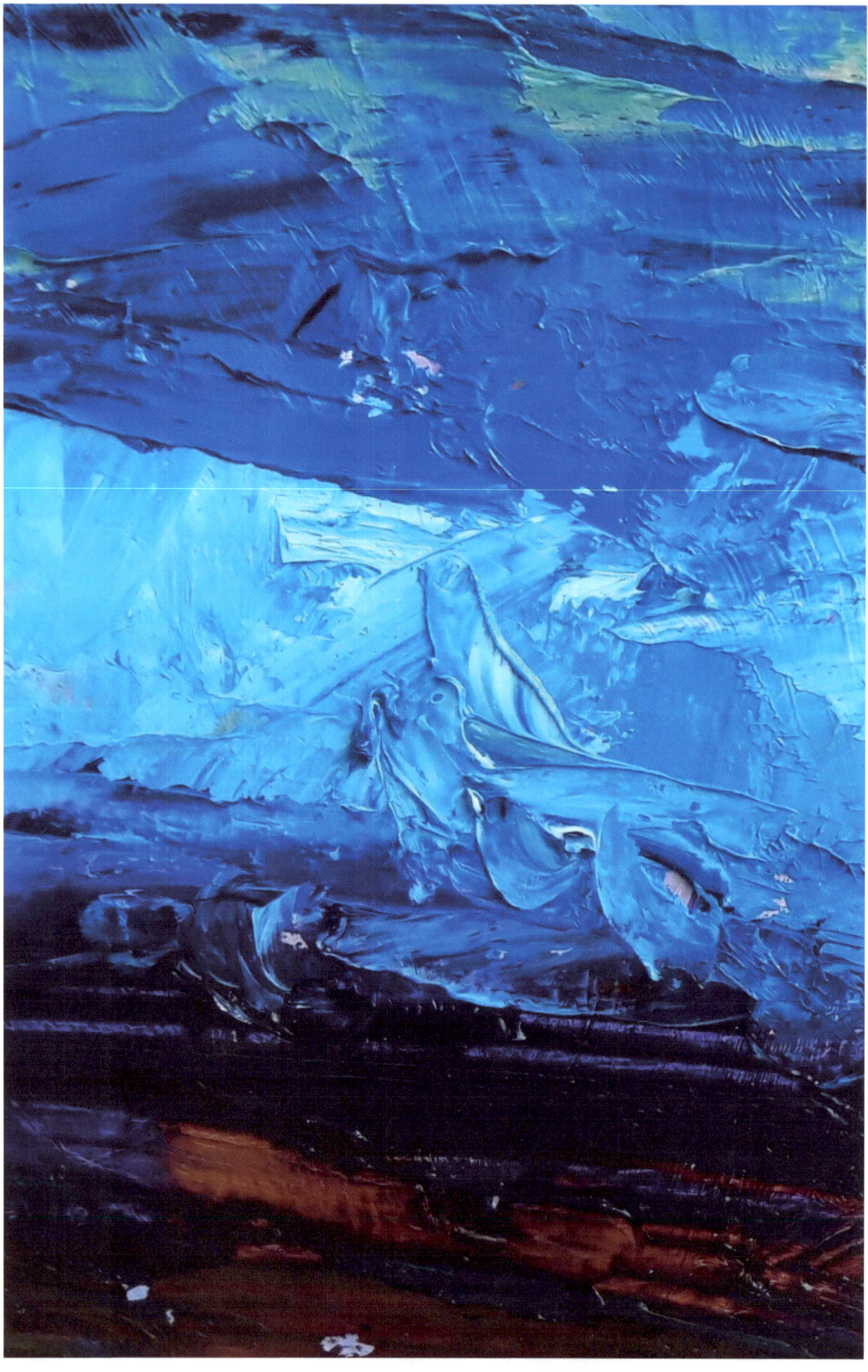

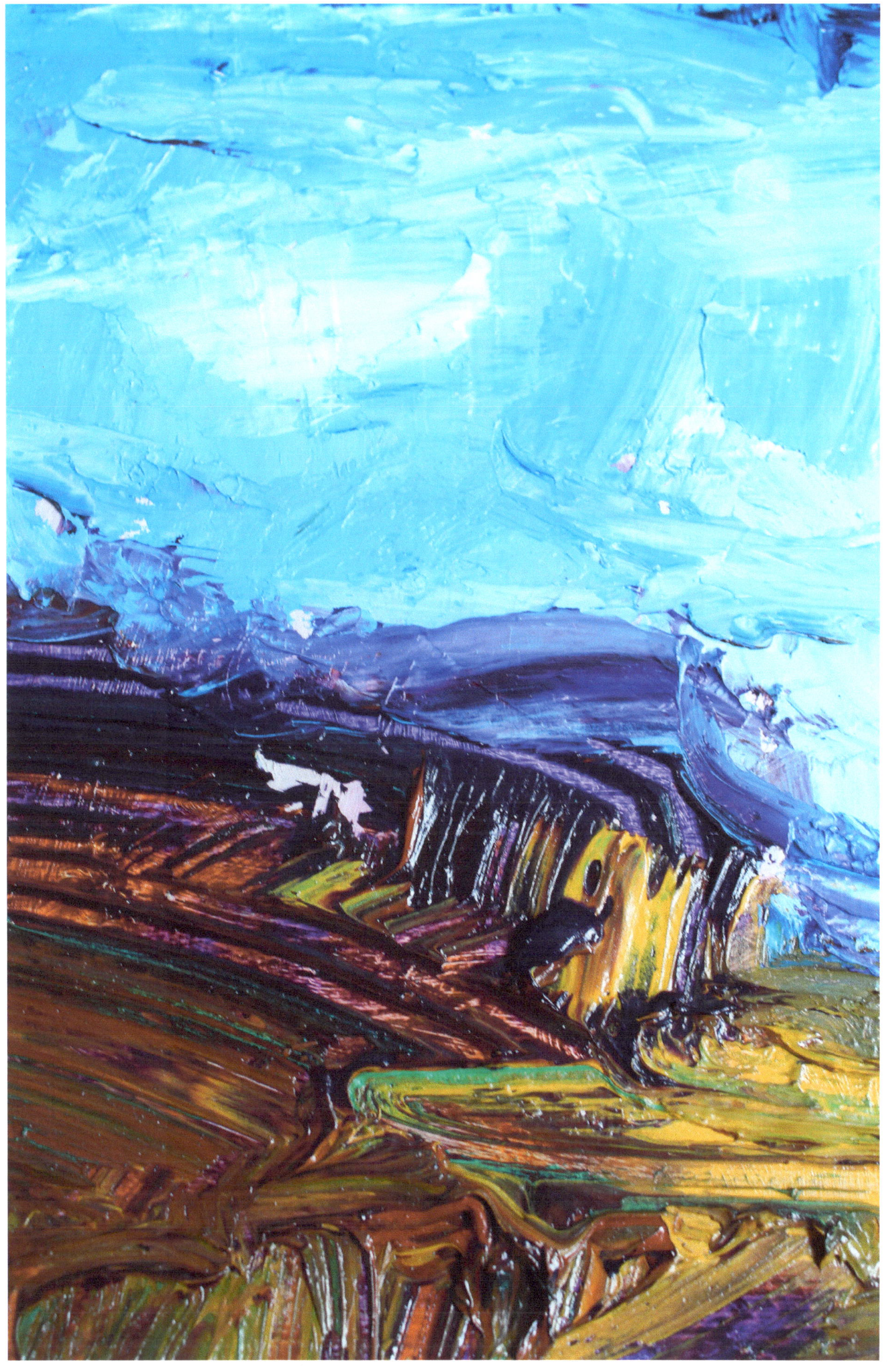

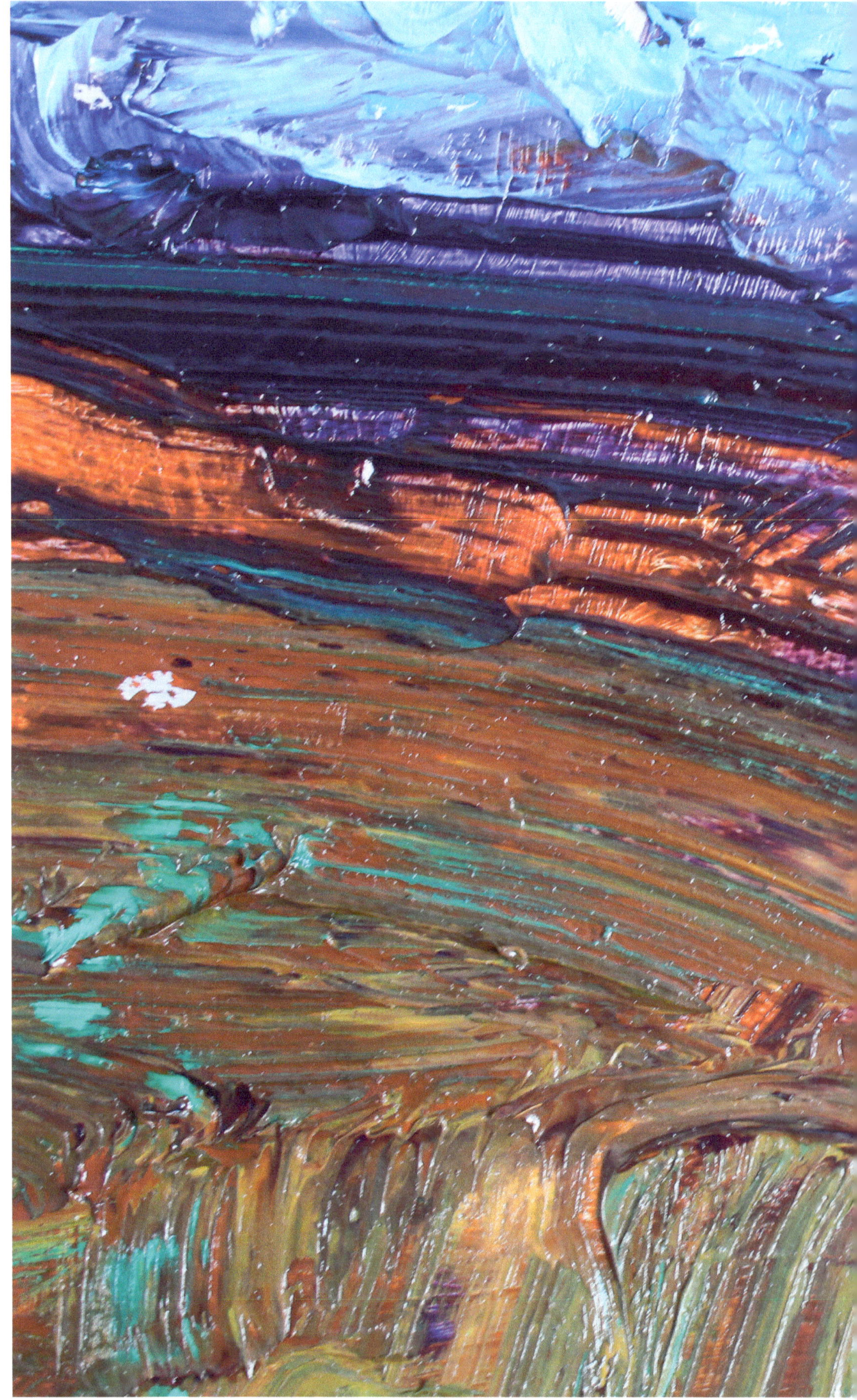

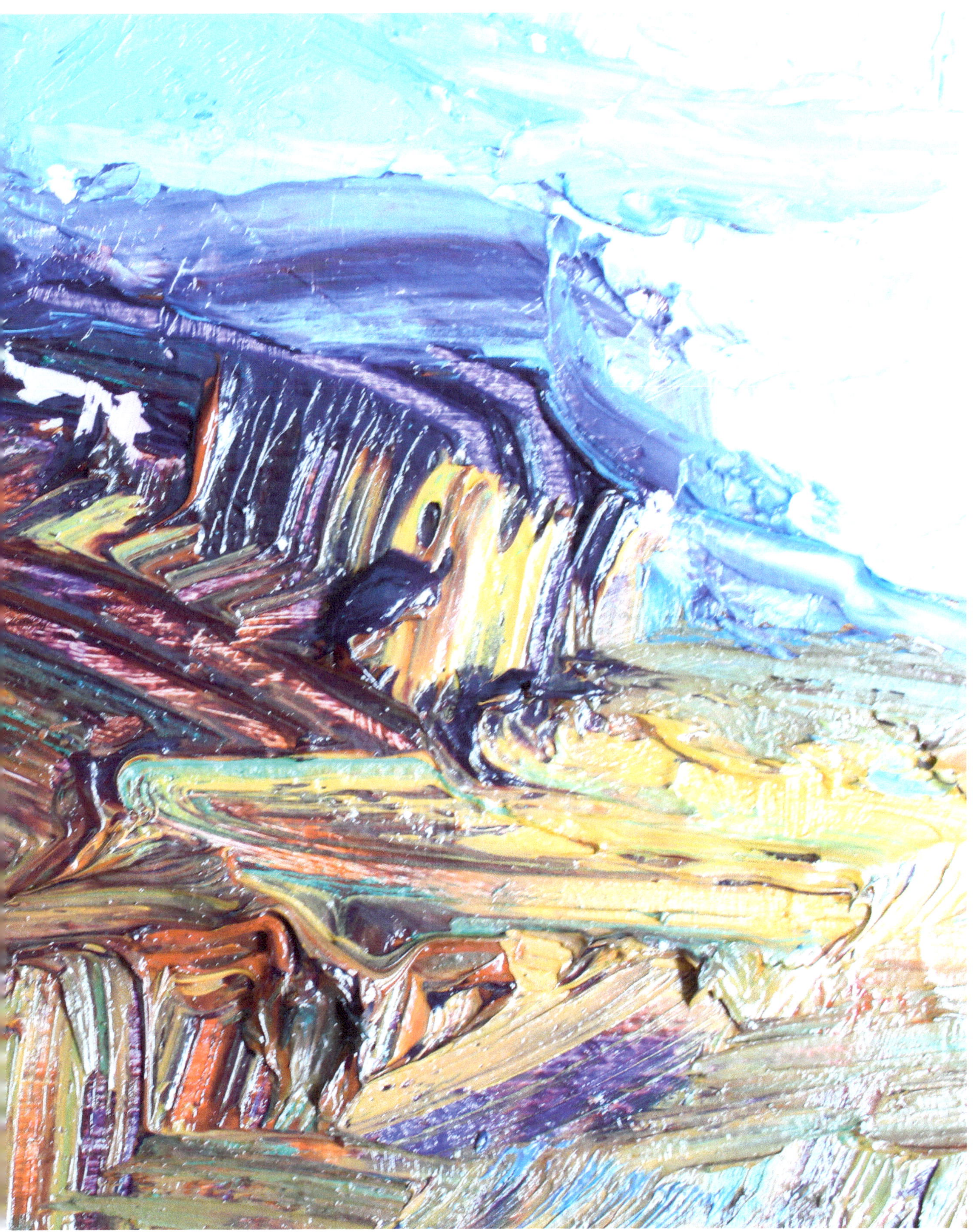

“CARN BHAC FROM GLEN EY, CAIRNGORMS, SCOTLAND”

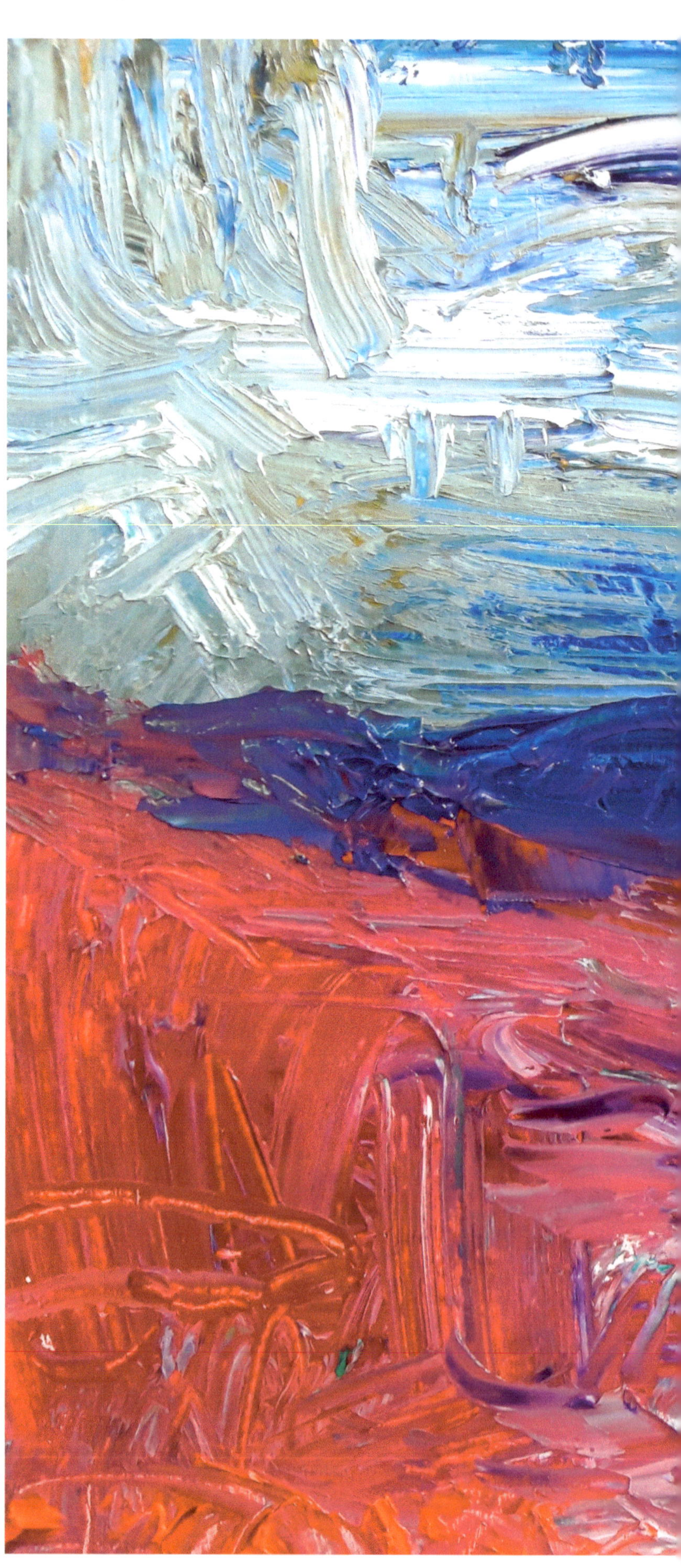

Technique: **Oil painting on canvas** - Size: **45 cm x 40 cm** - Year: **2018**

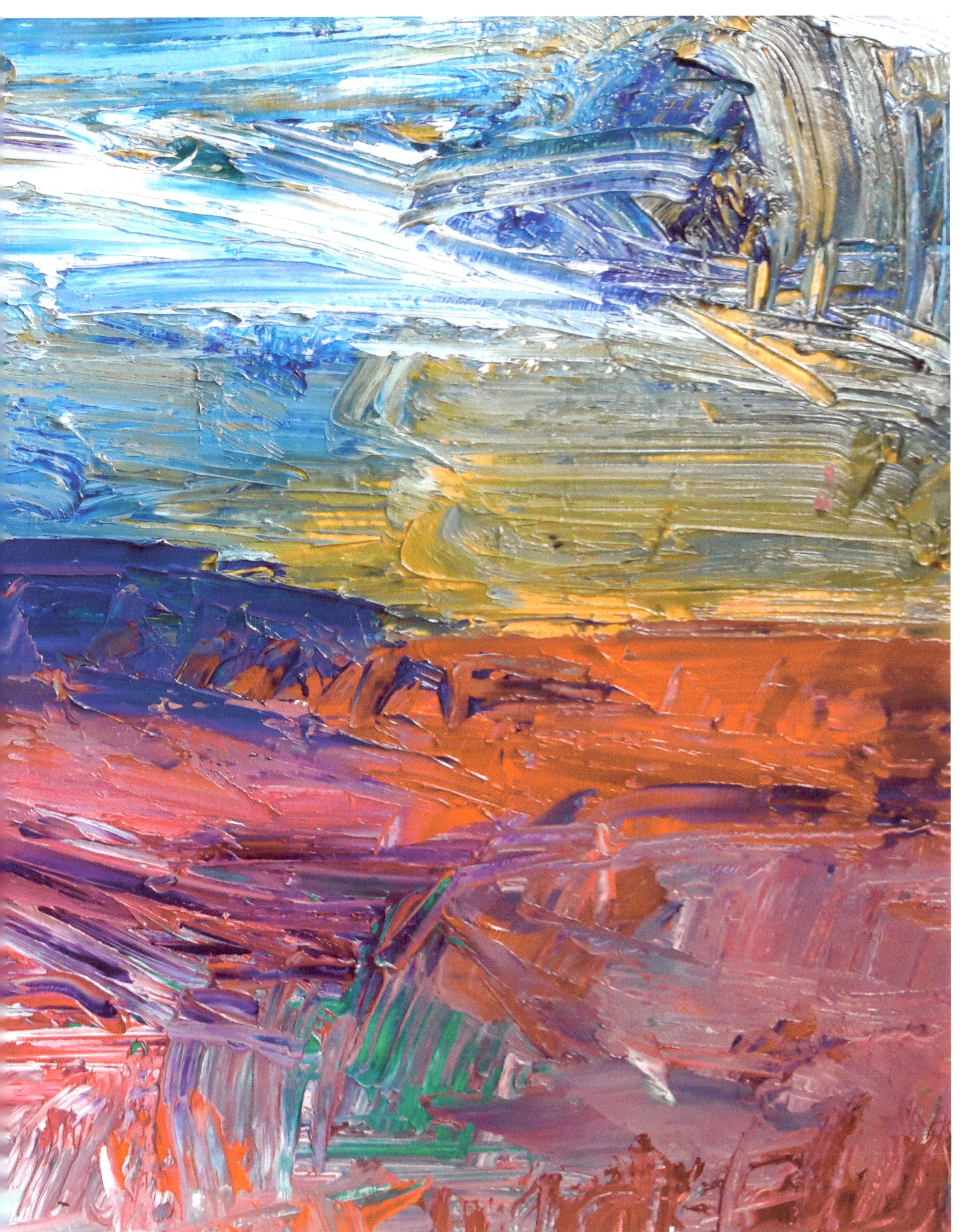

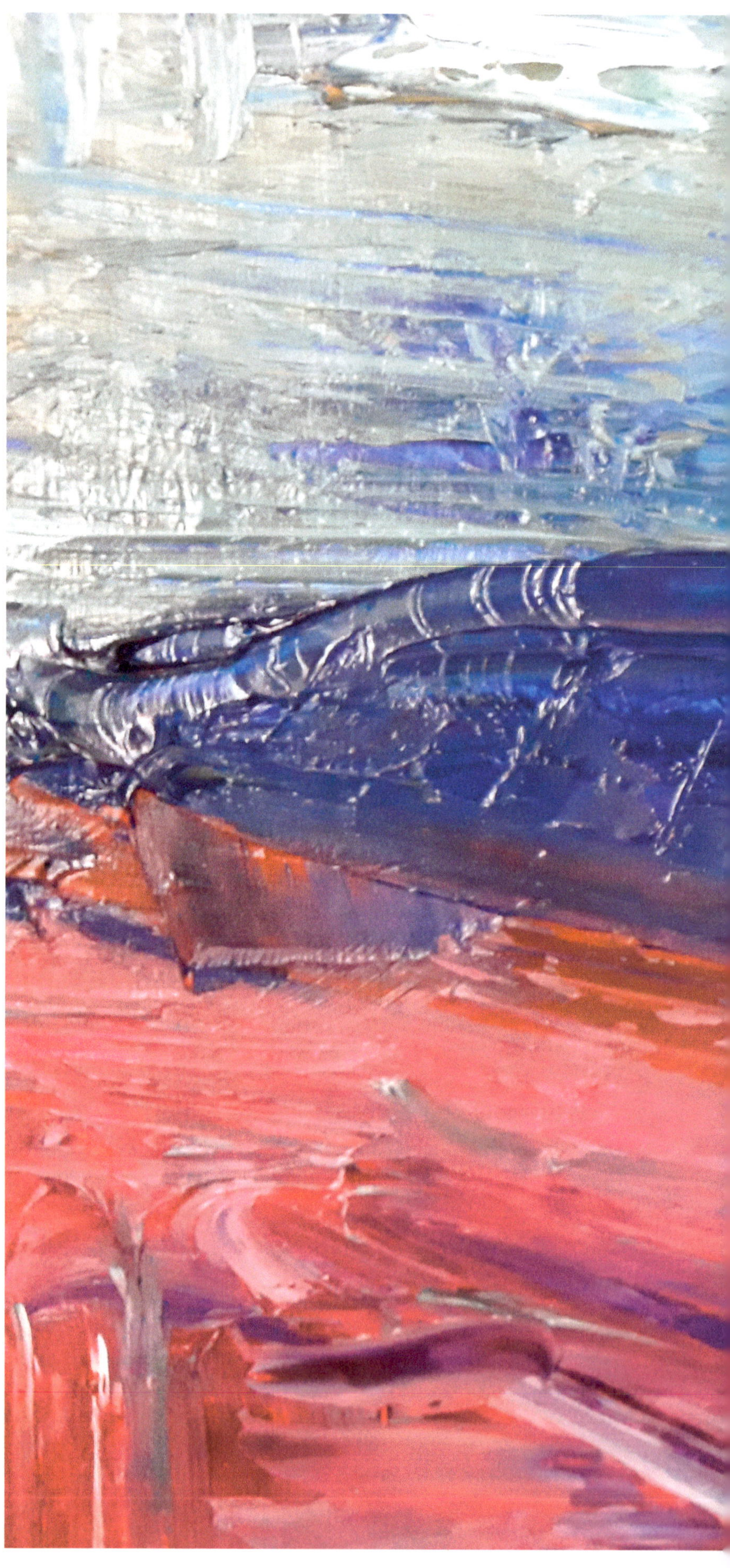

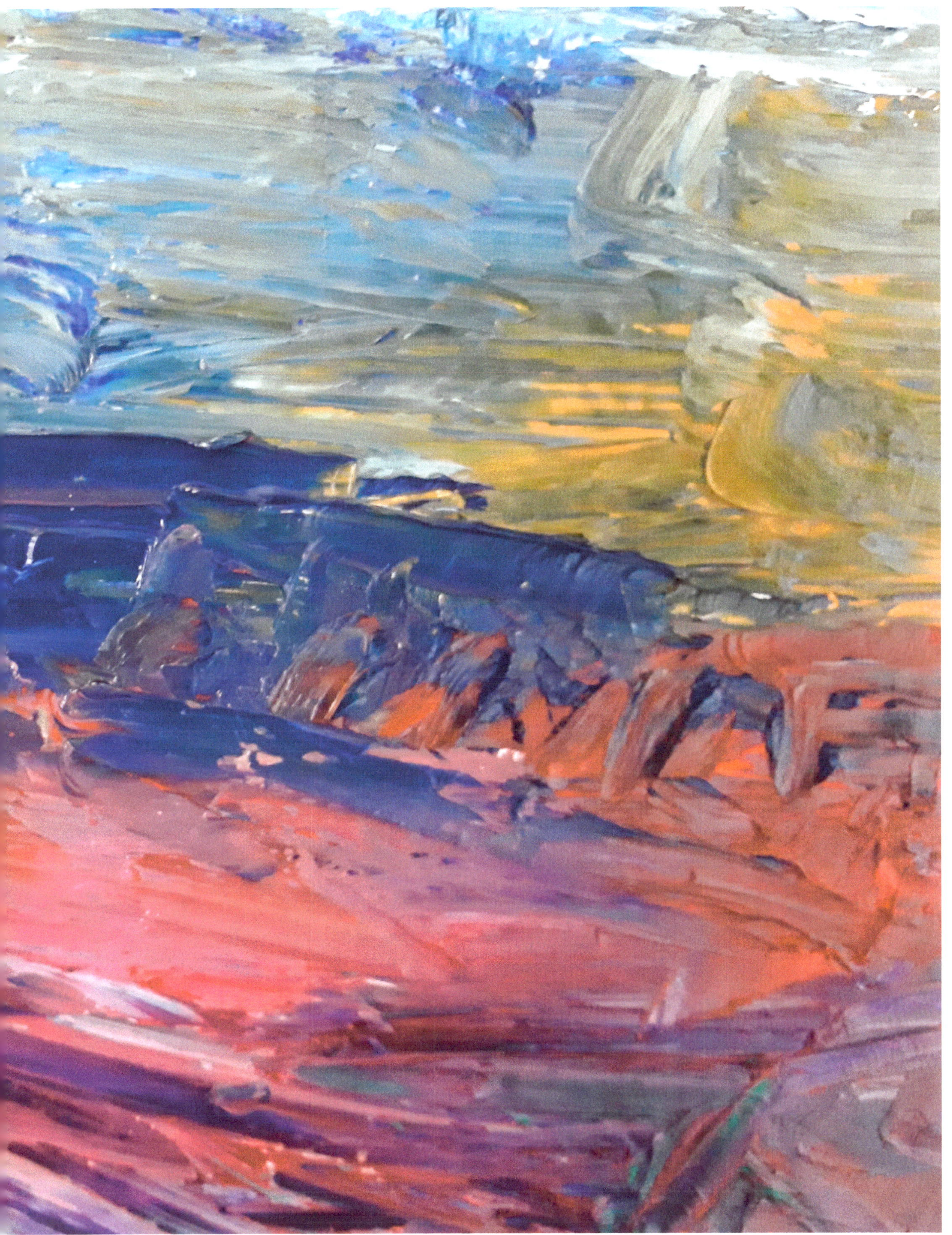

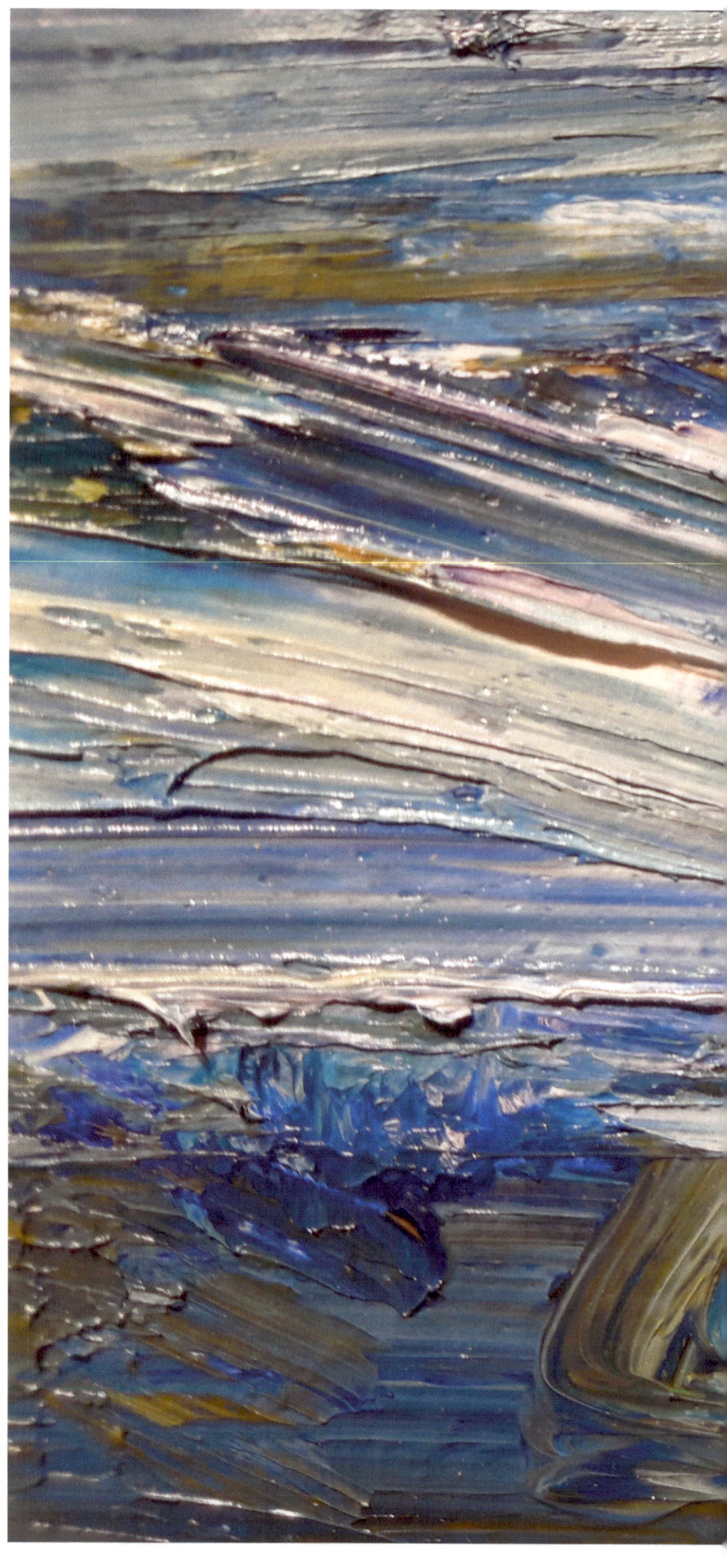

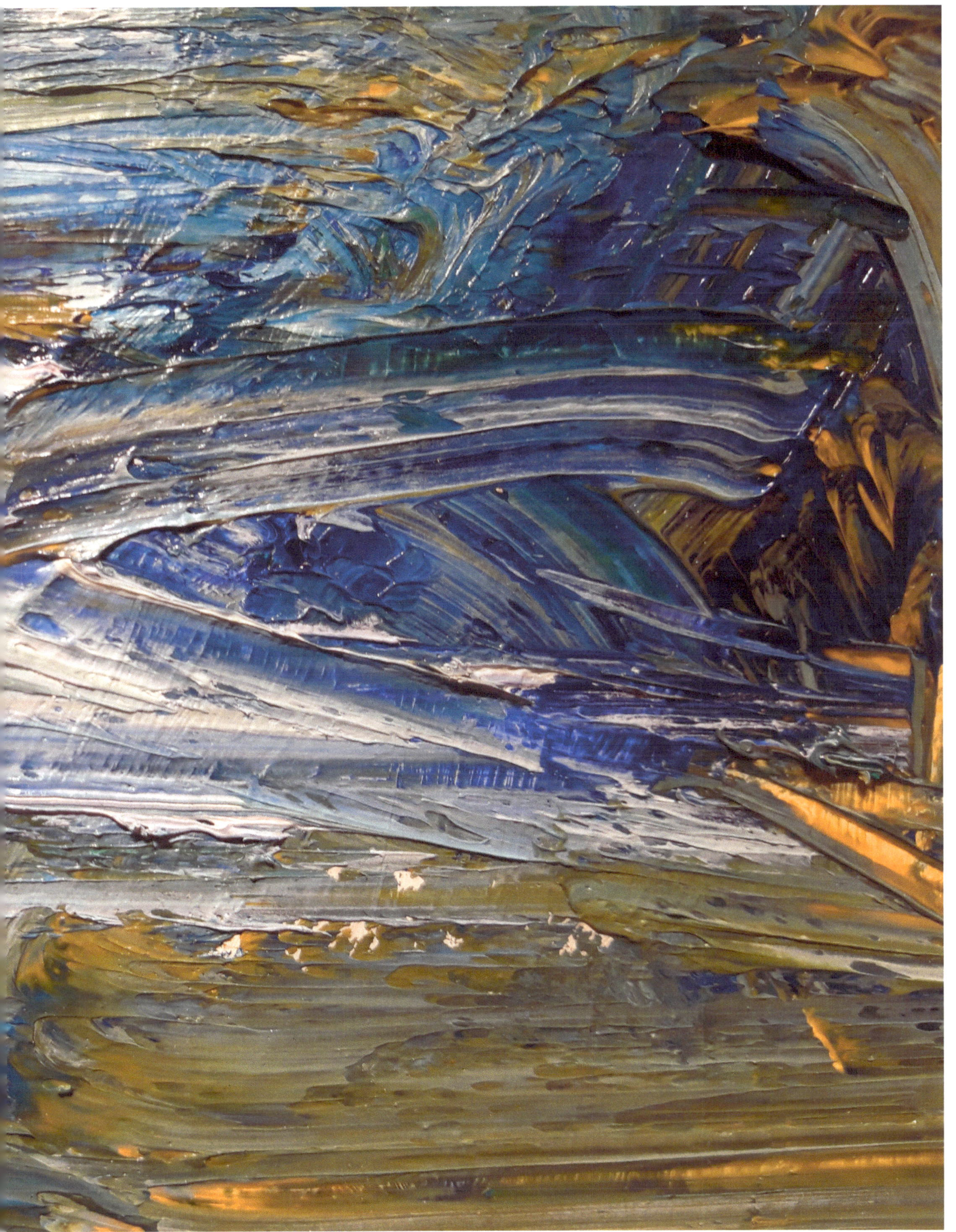

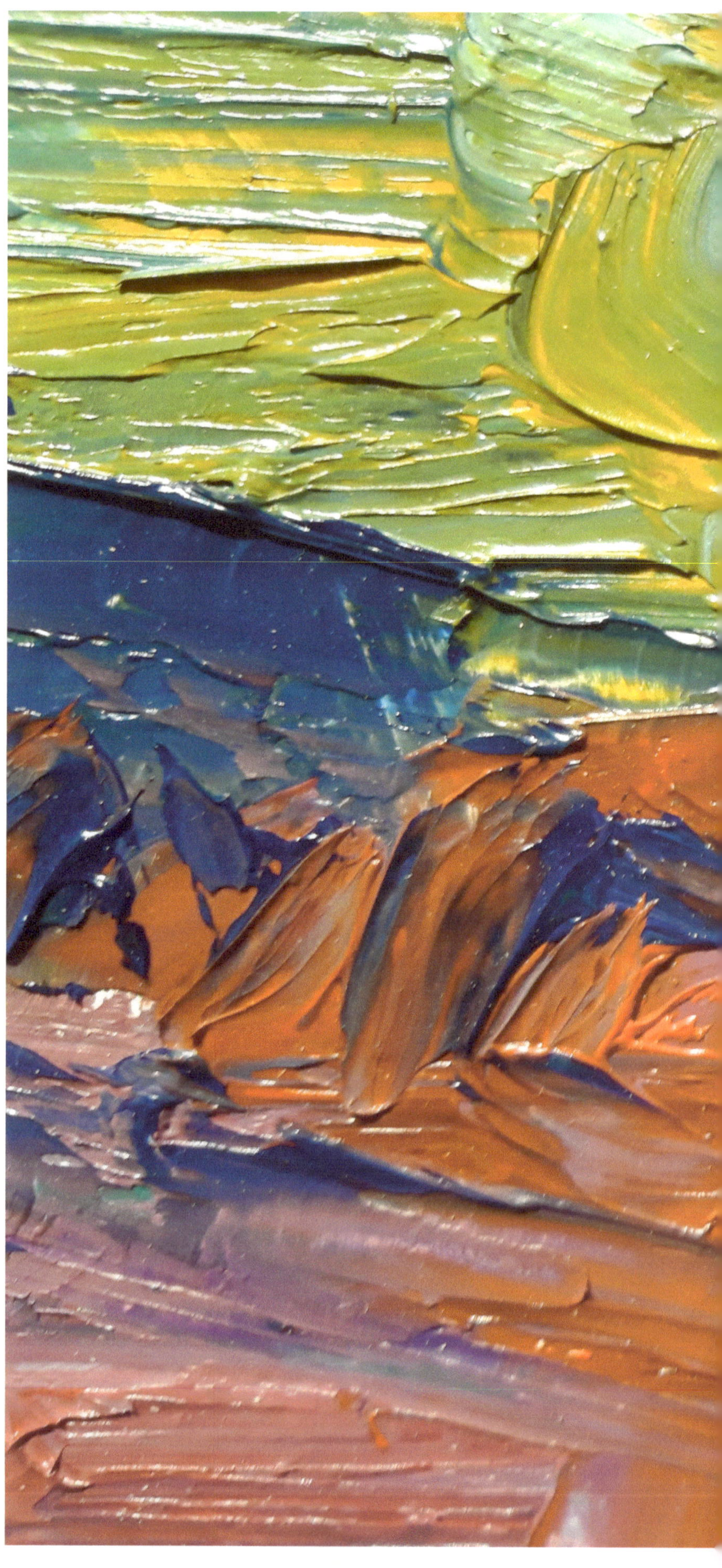

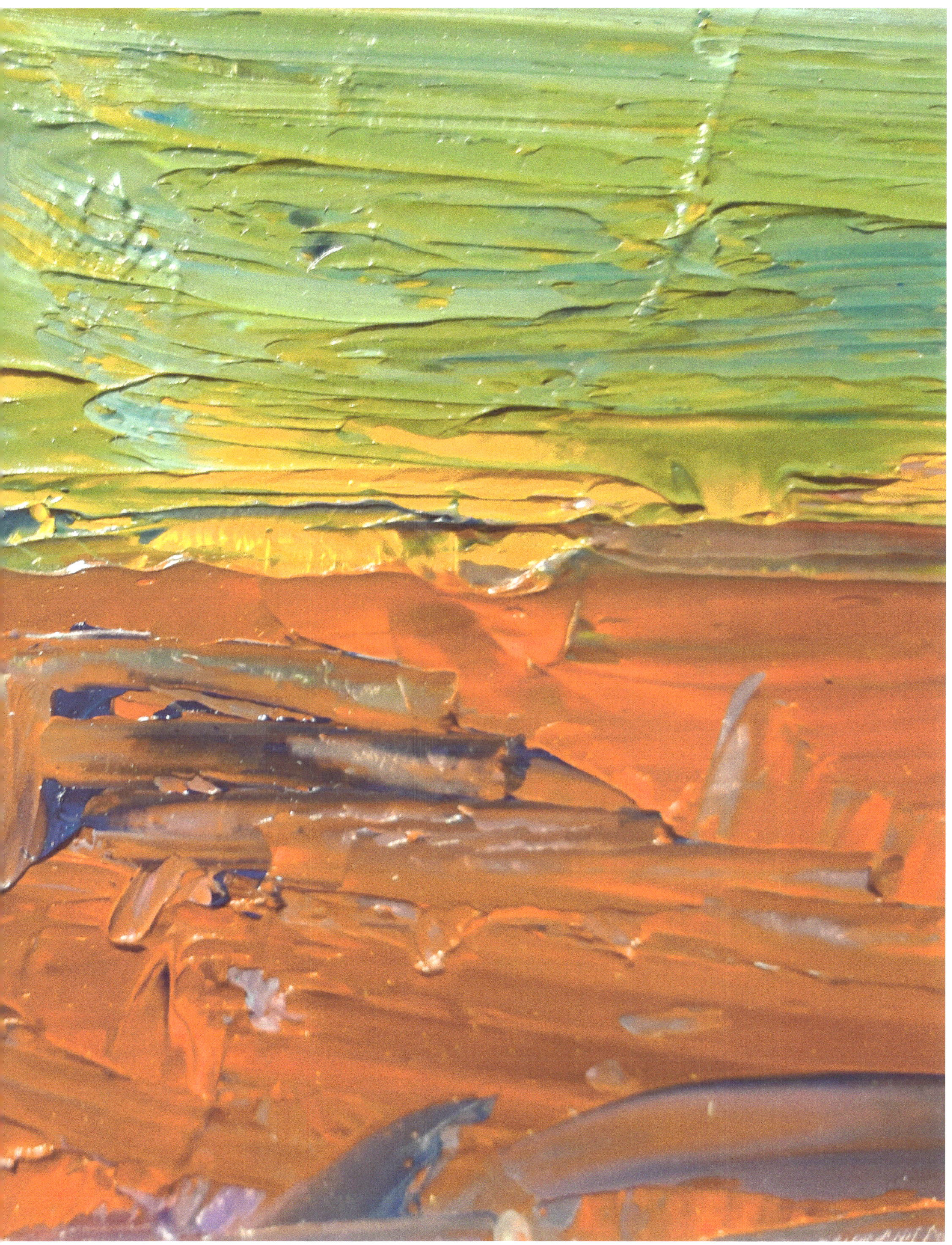

Detail 4

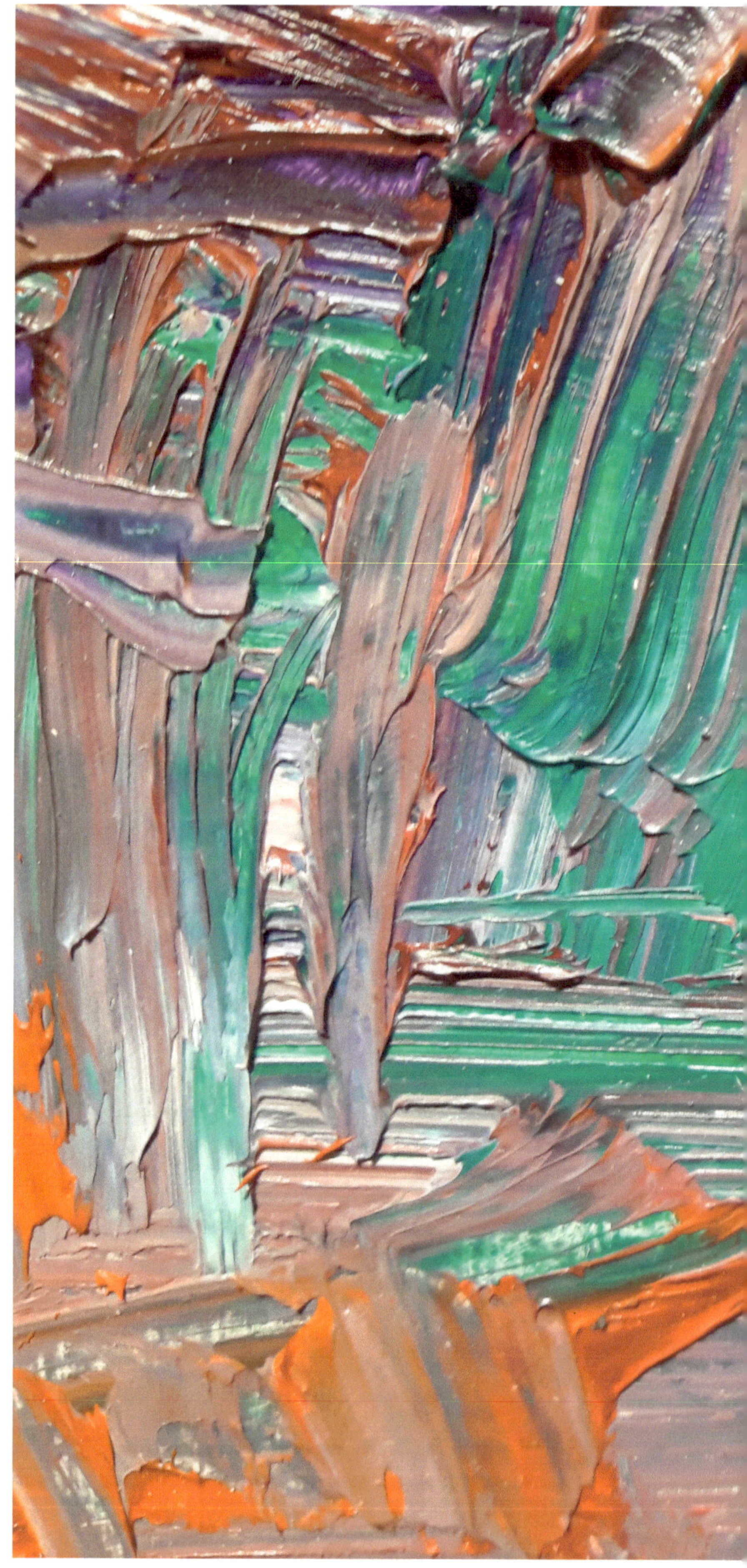

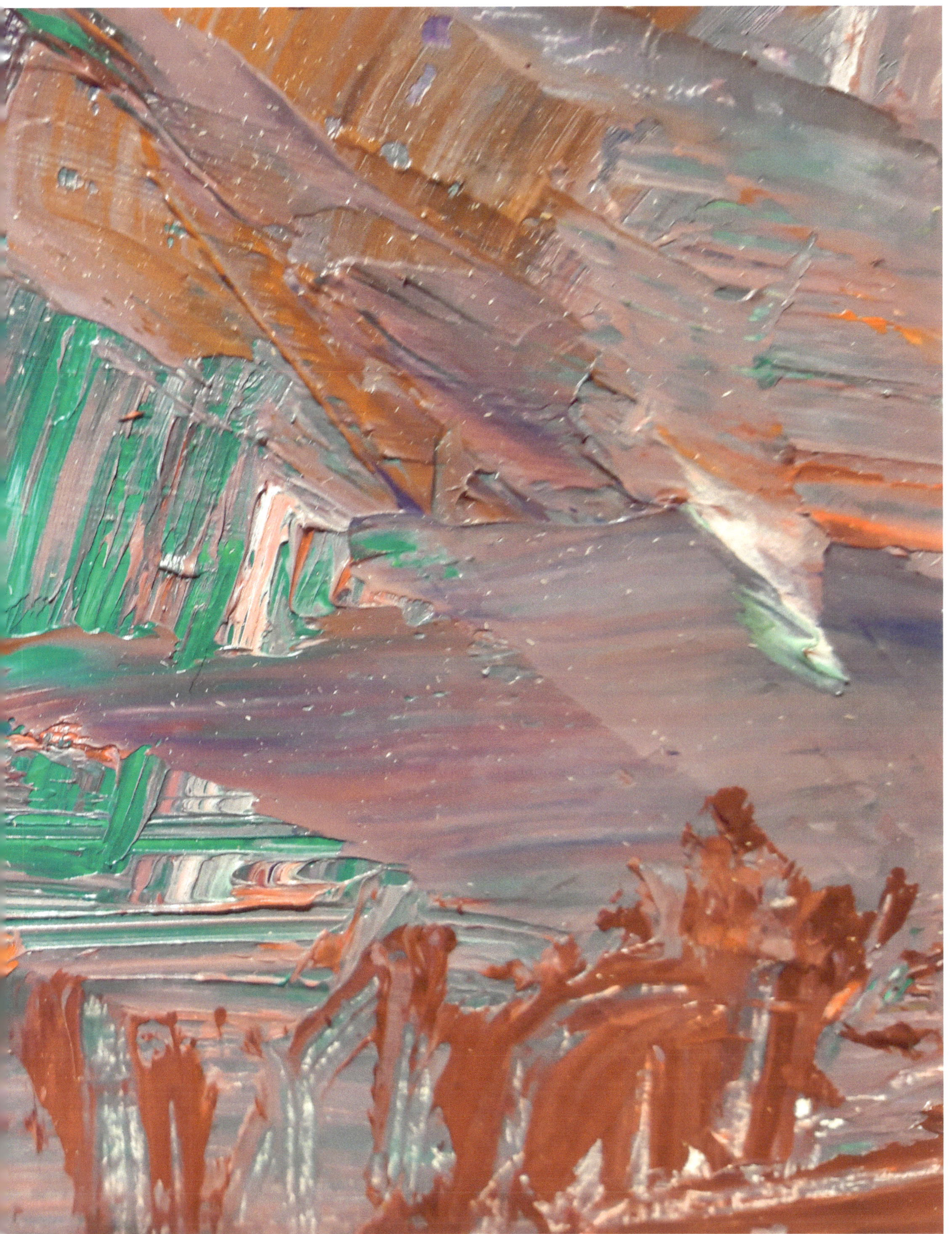

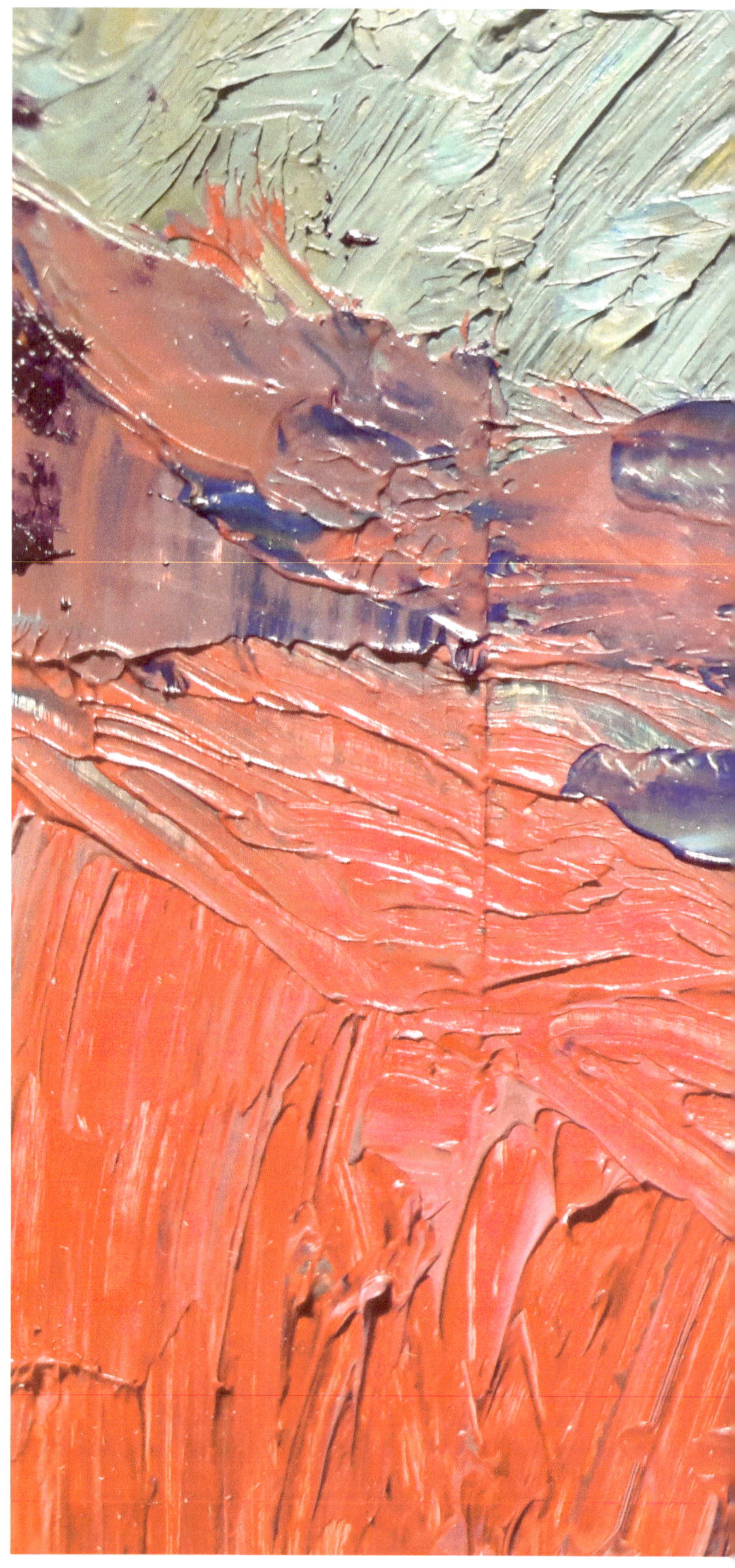

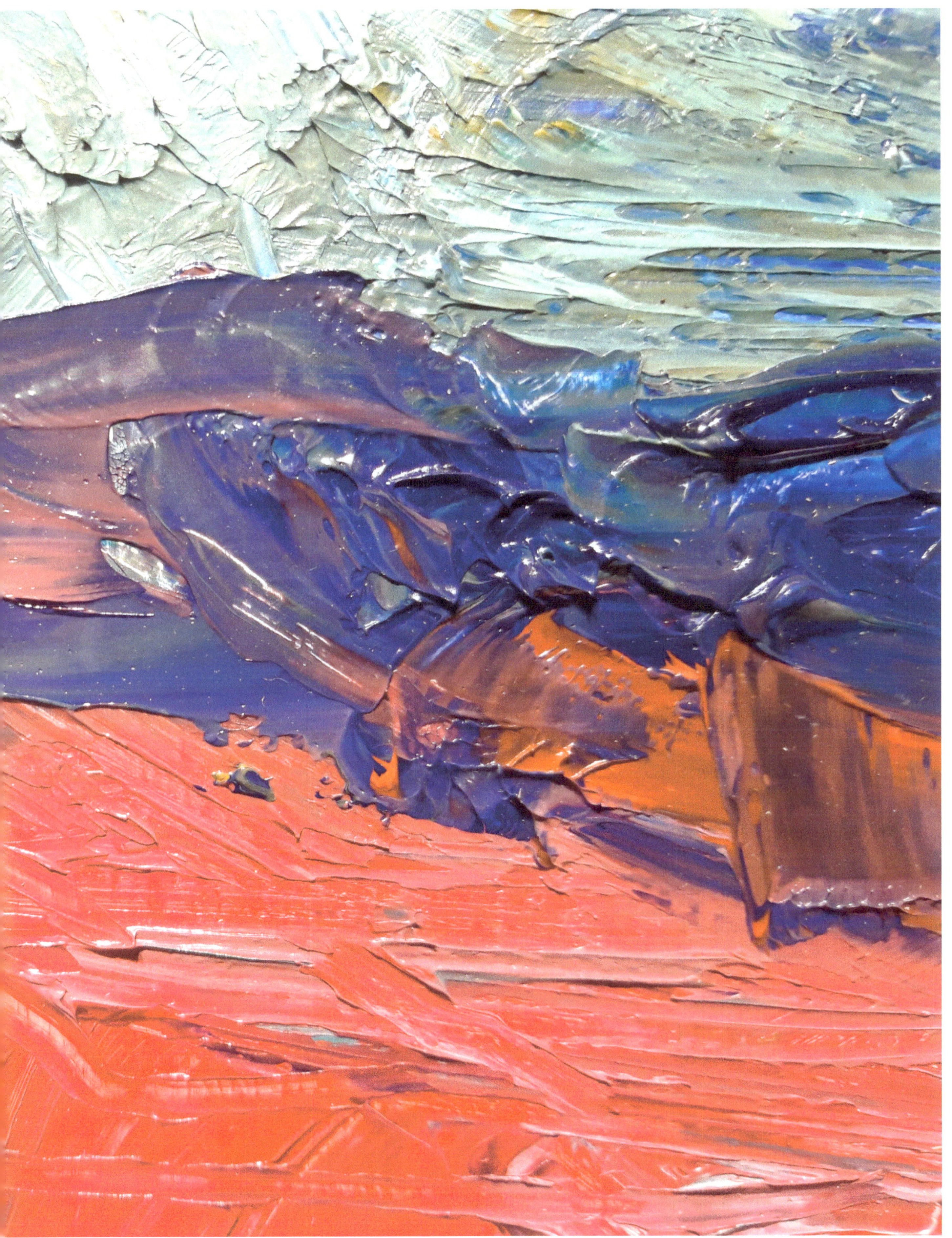

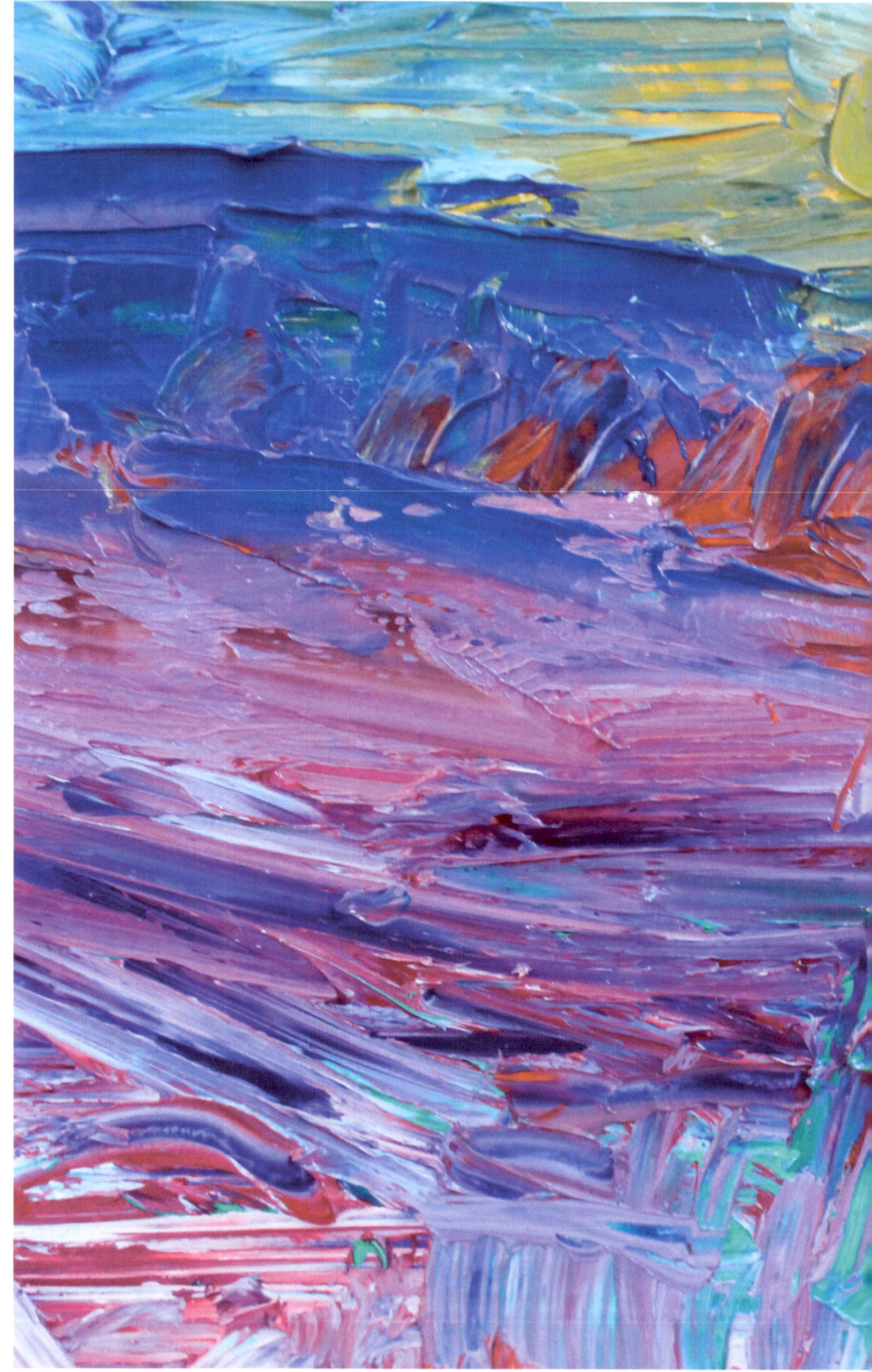

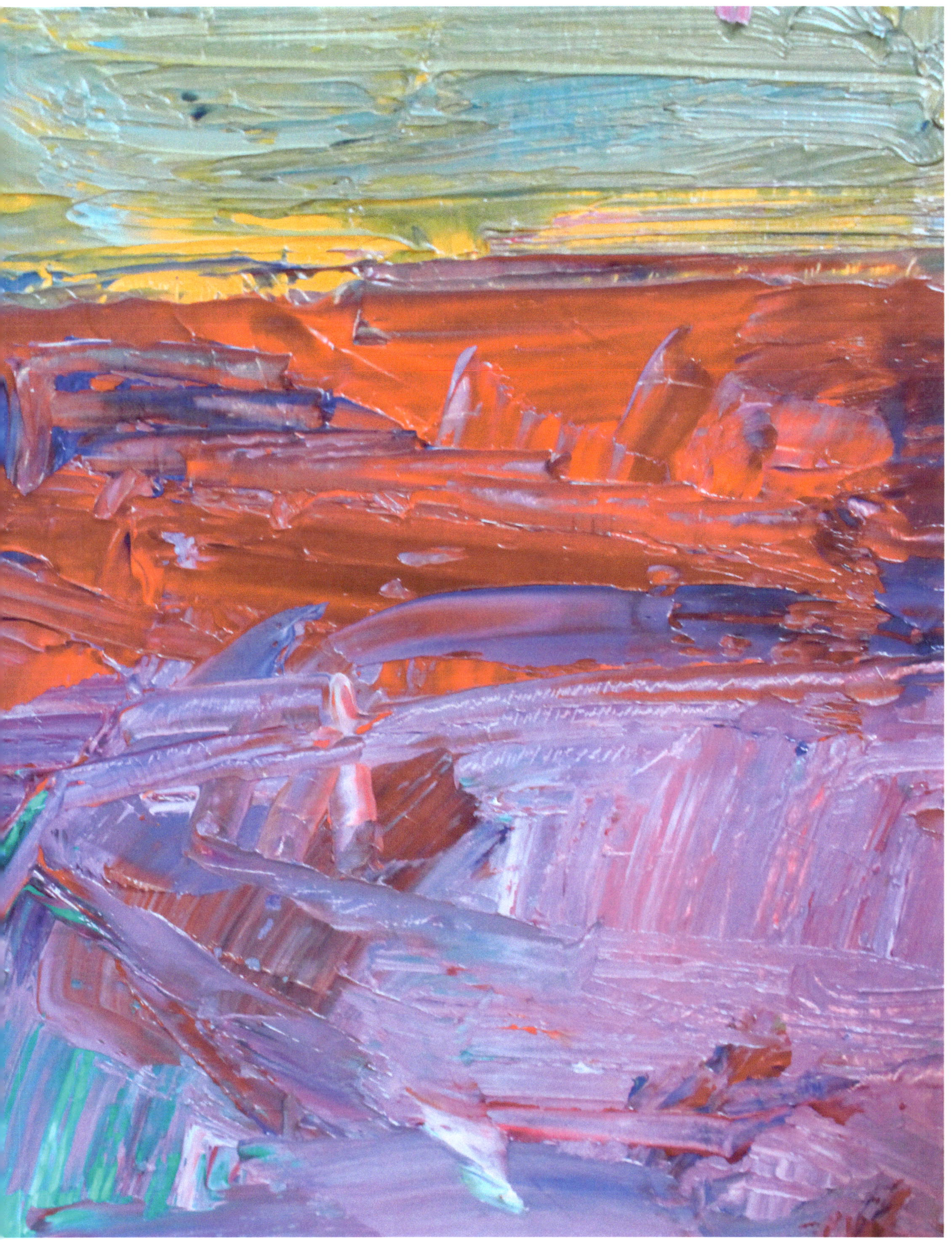

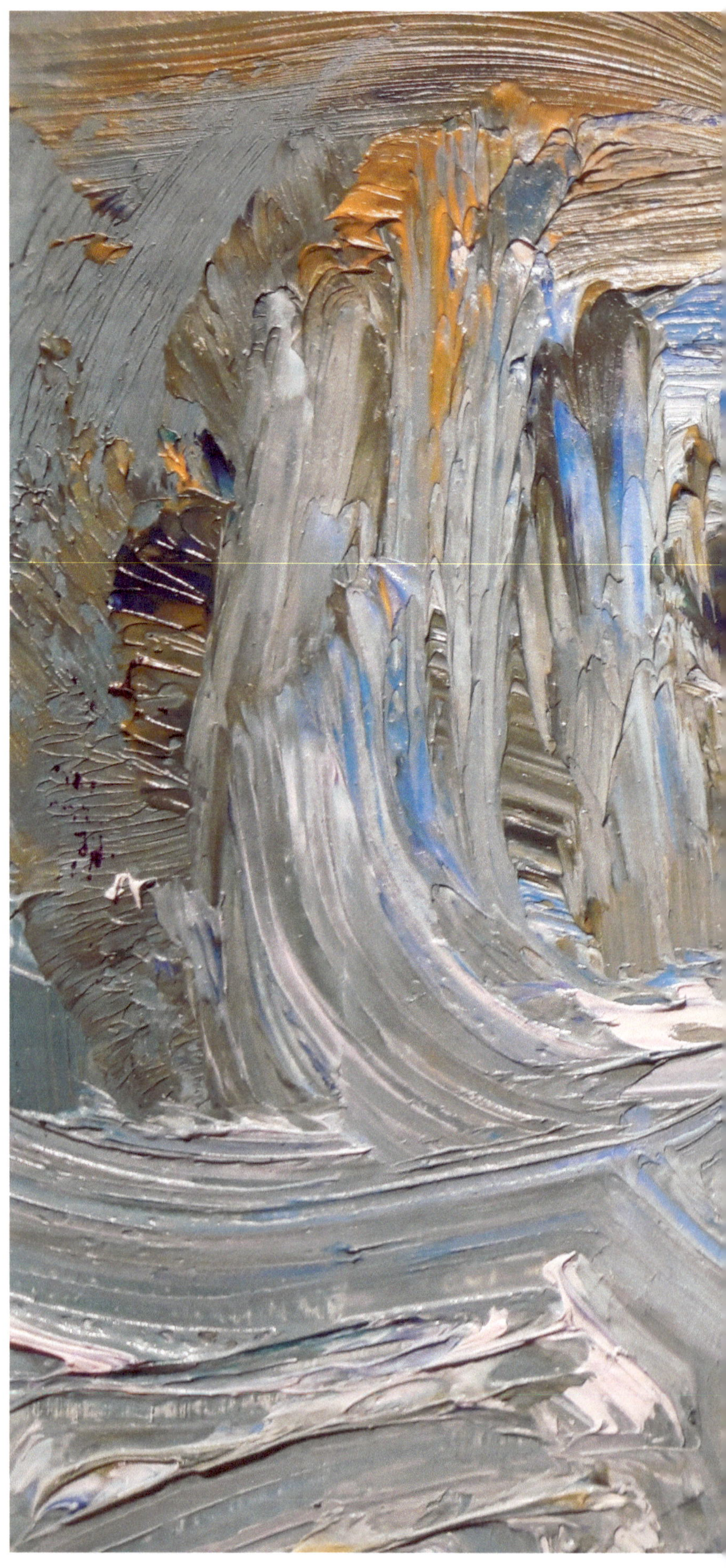

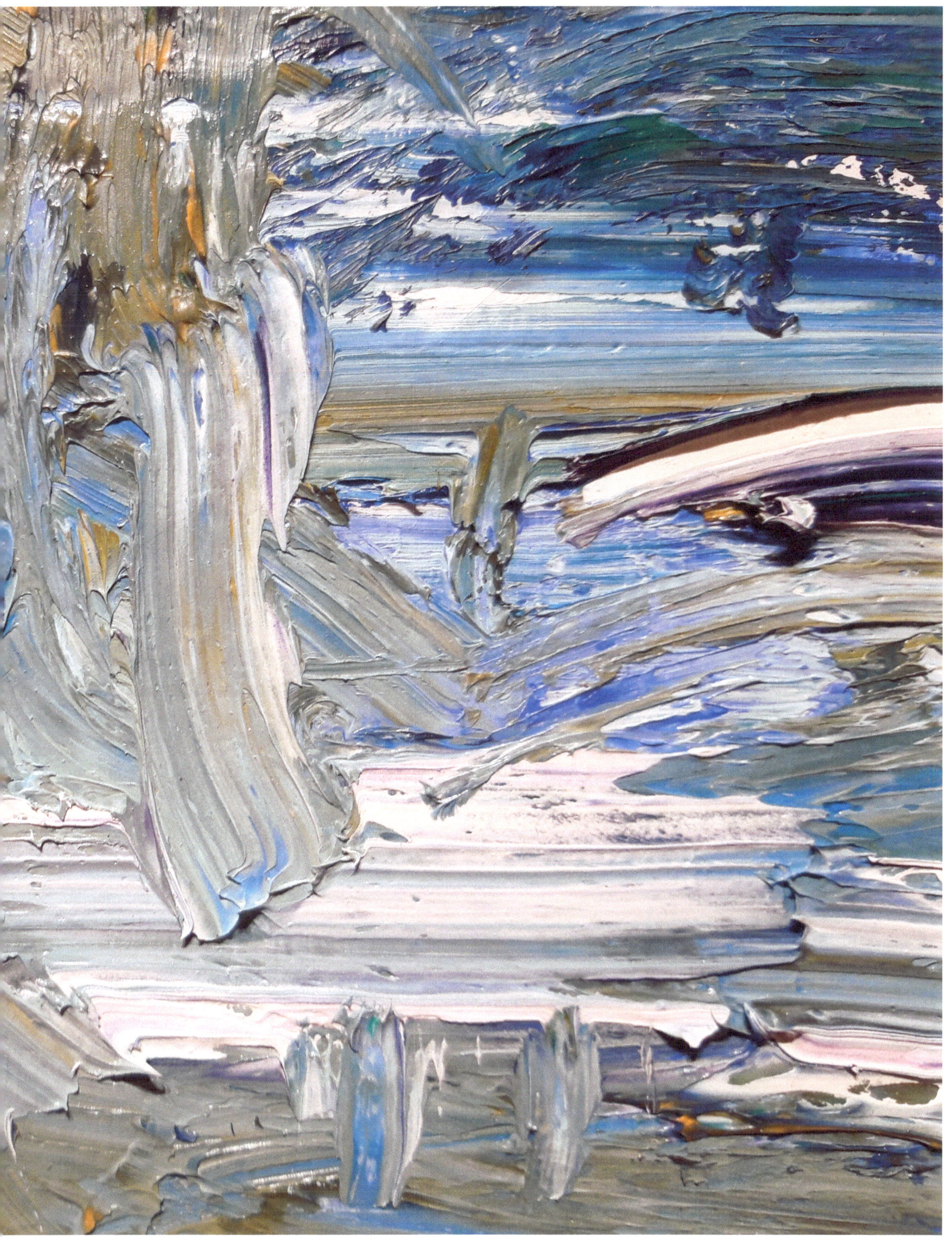

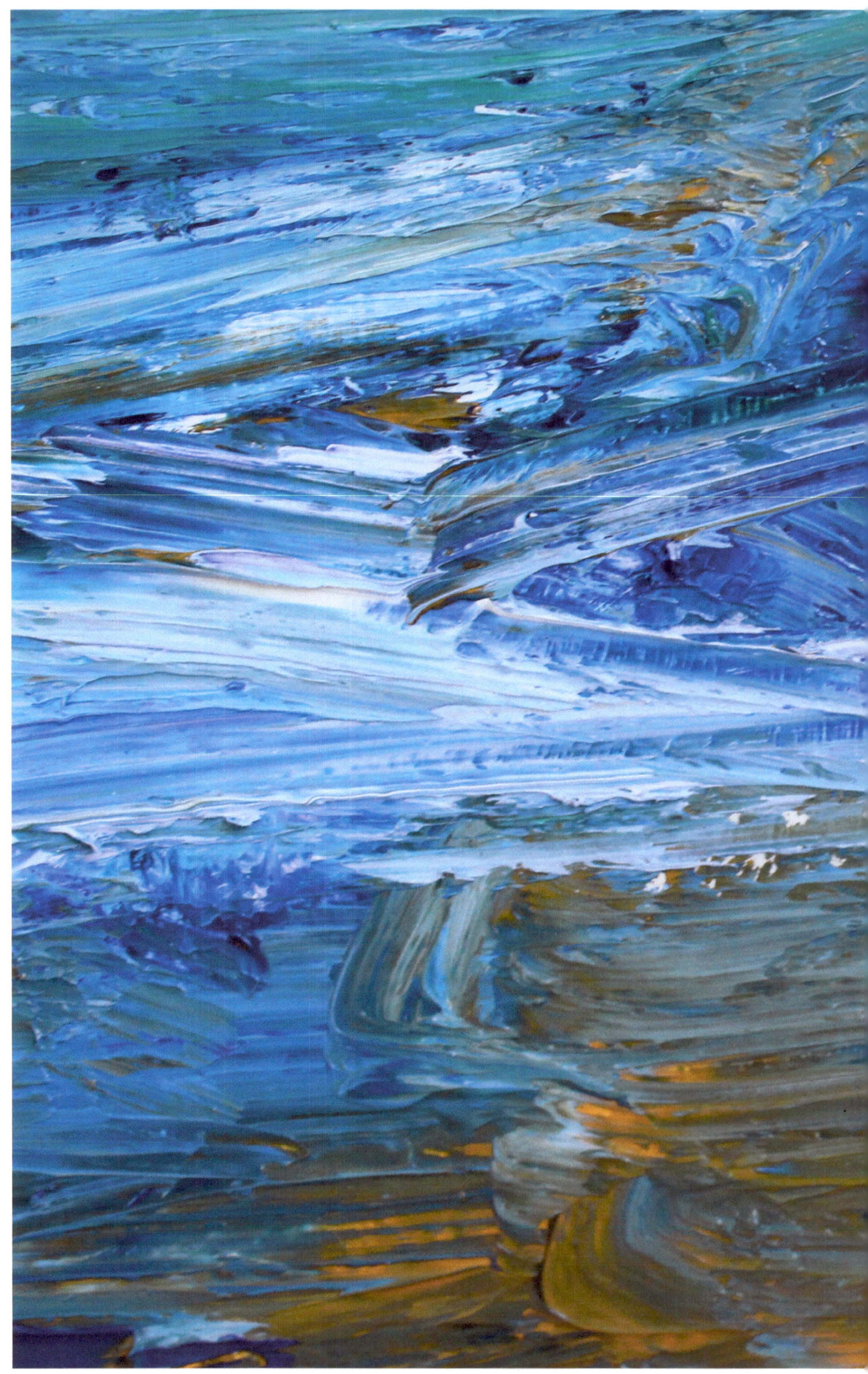

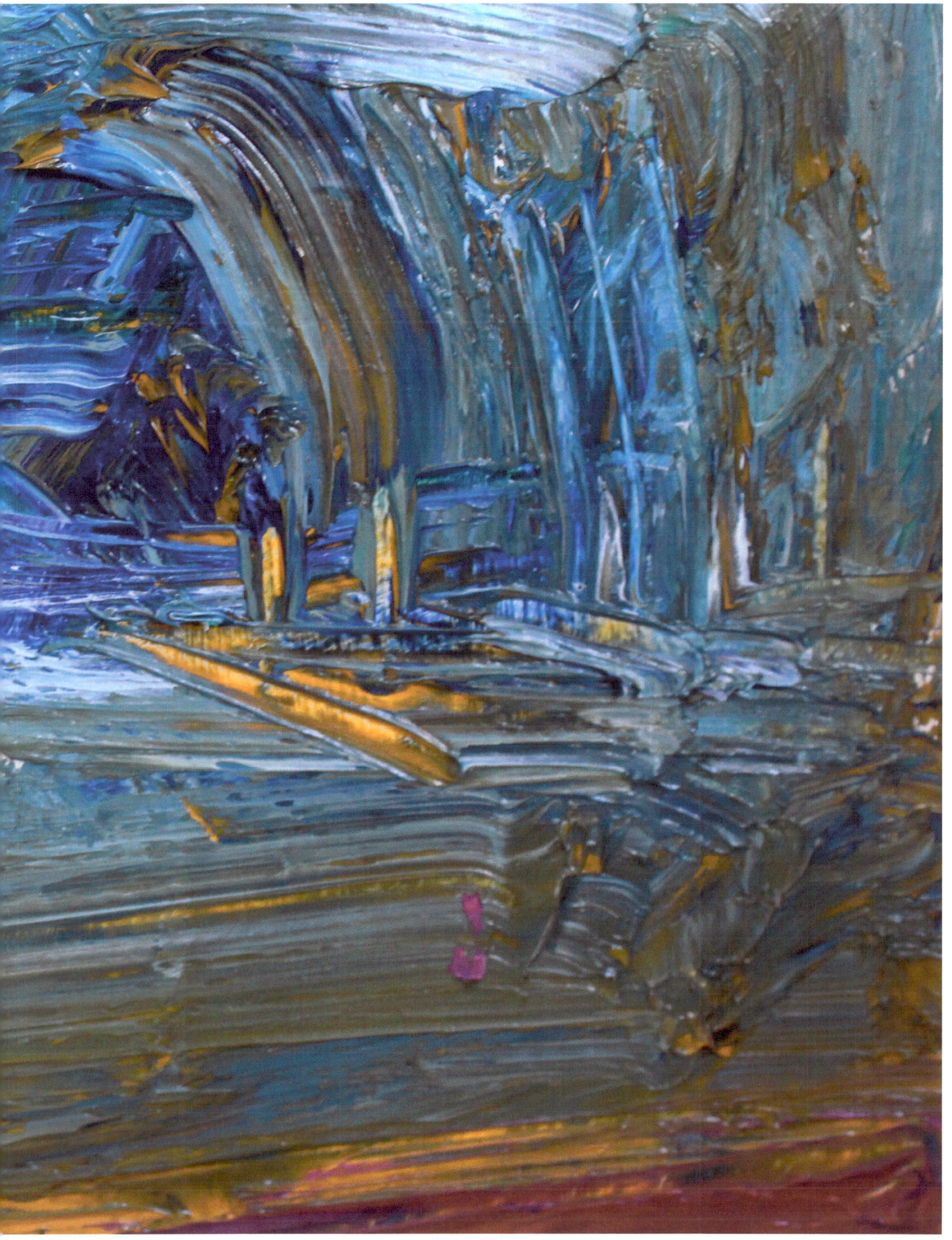

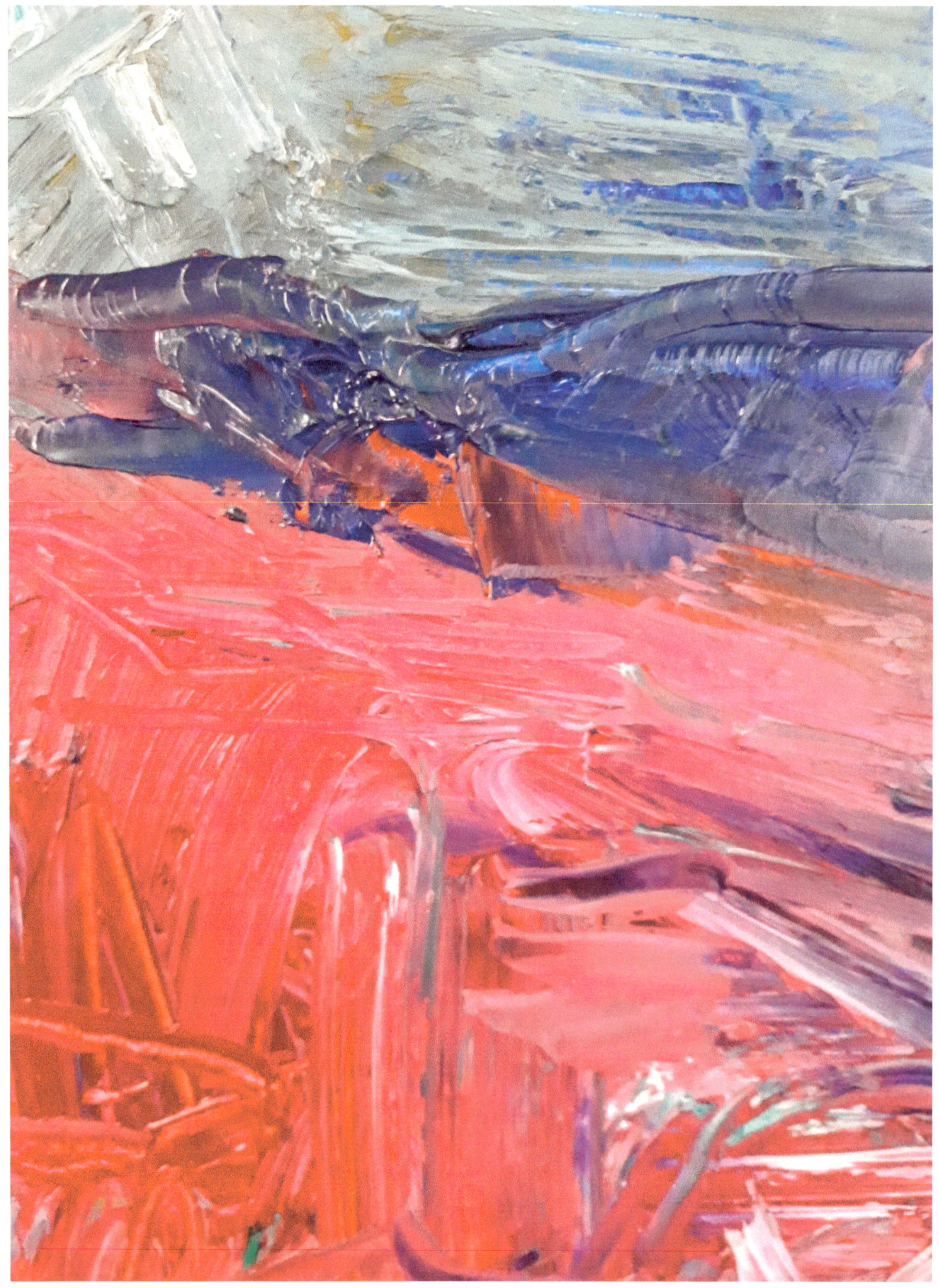

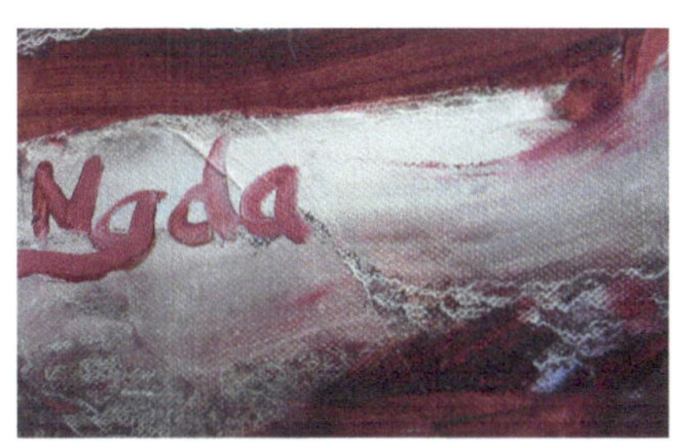

PHOTO GALLERY

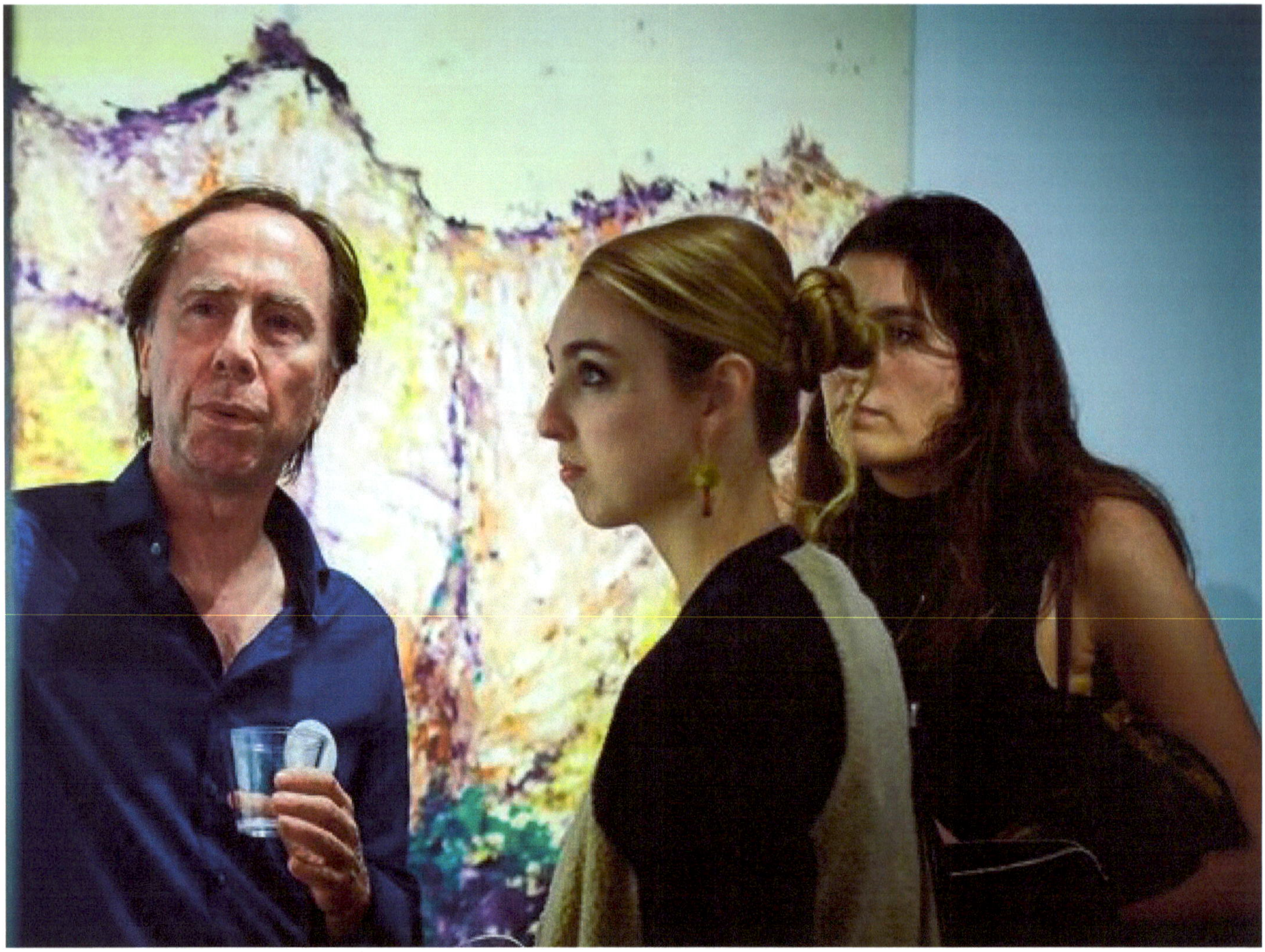

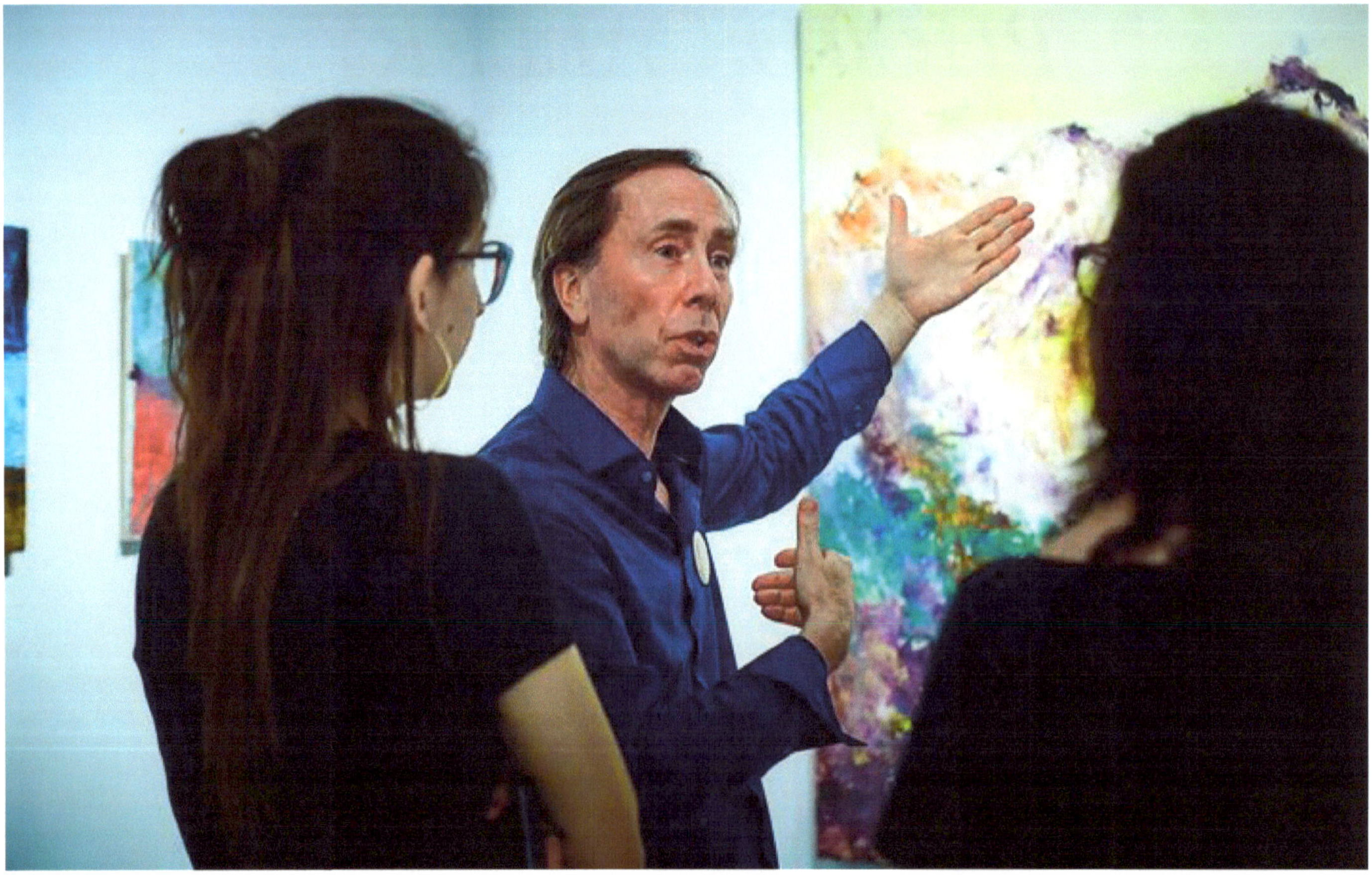

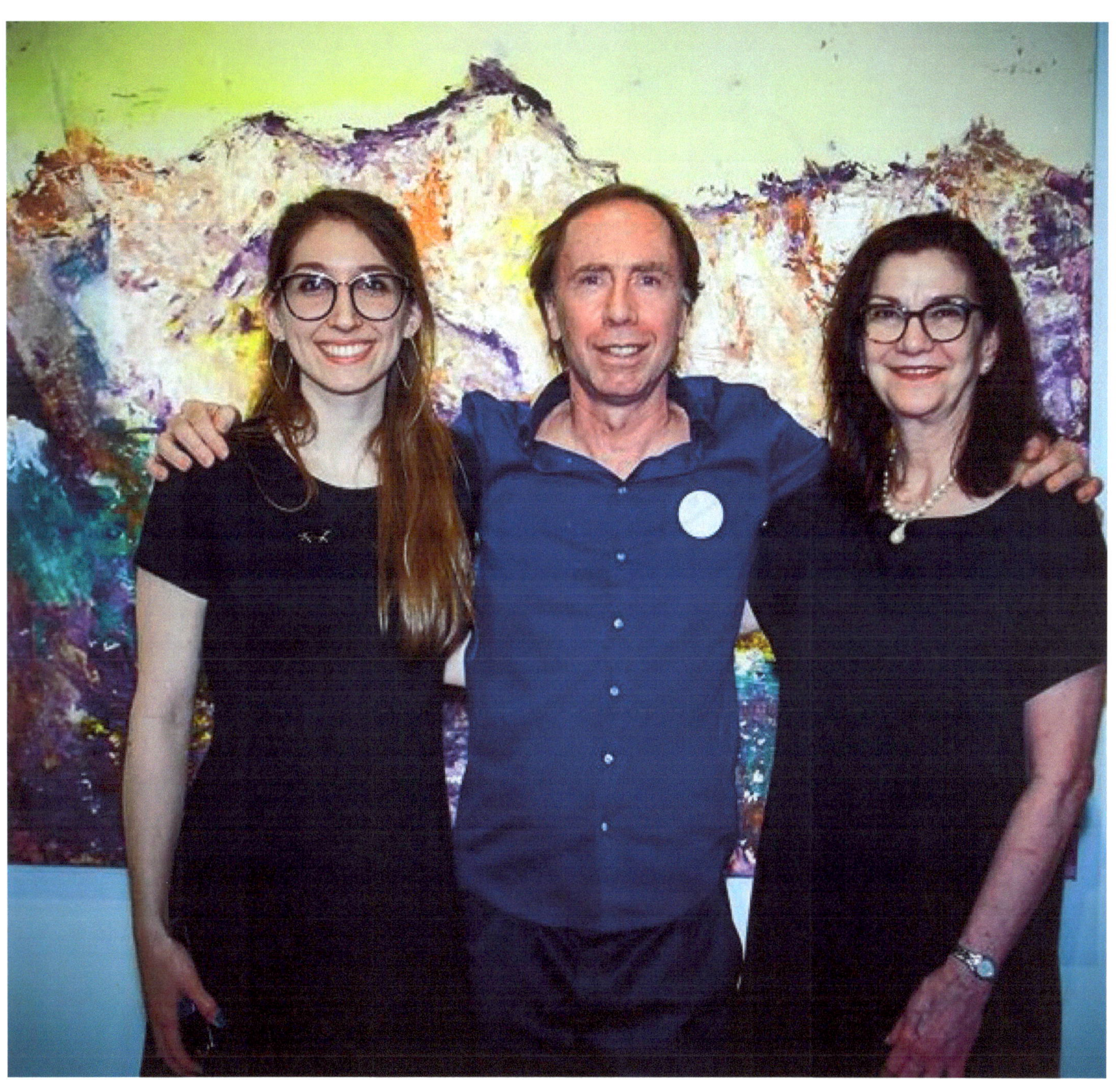

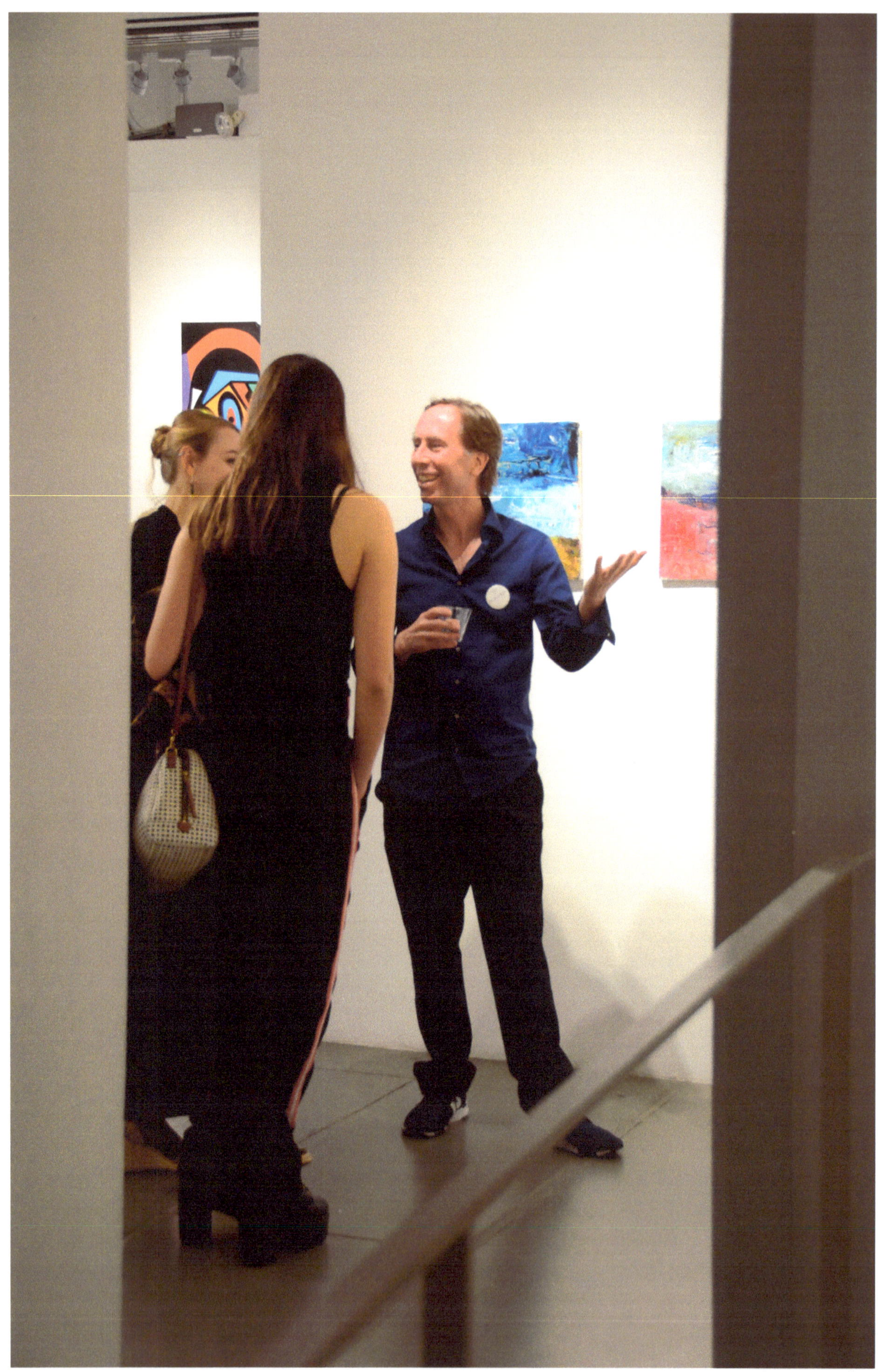

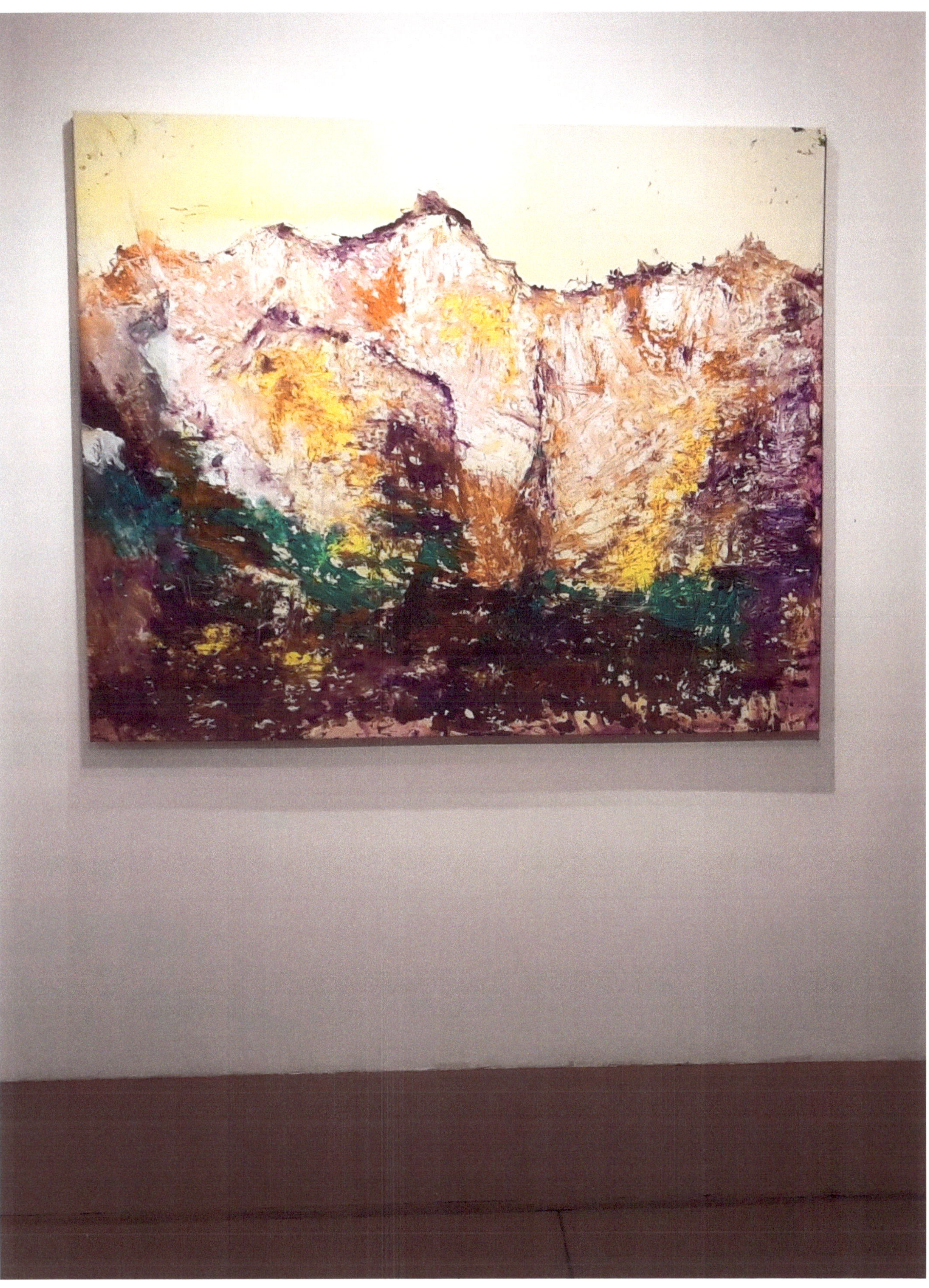

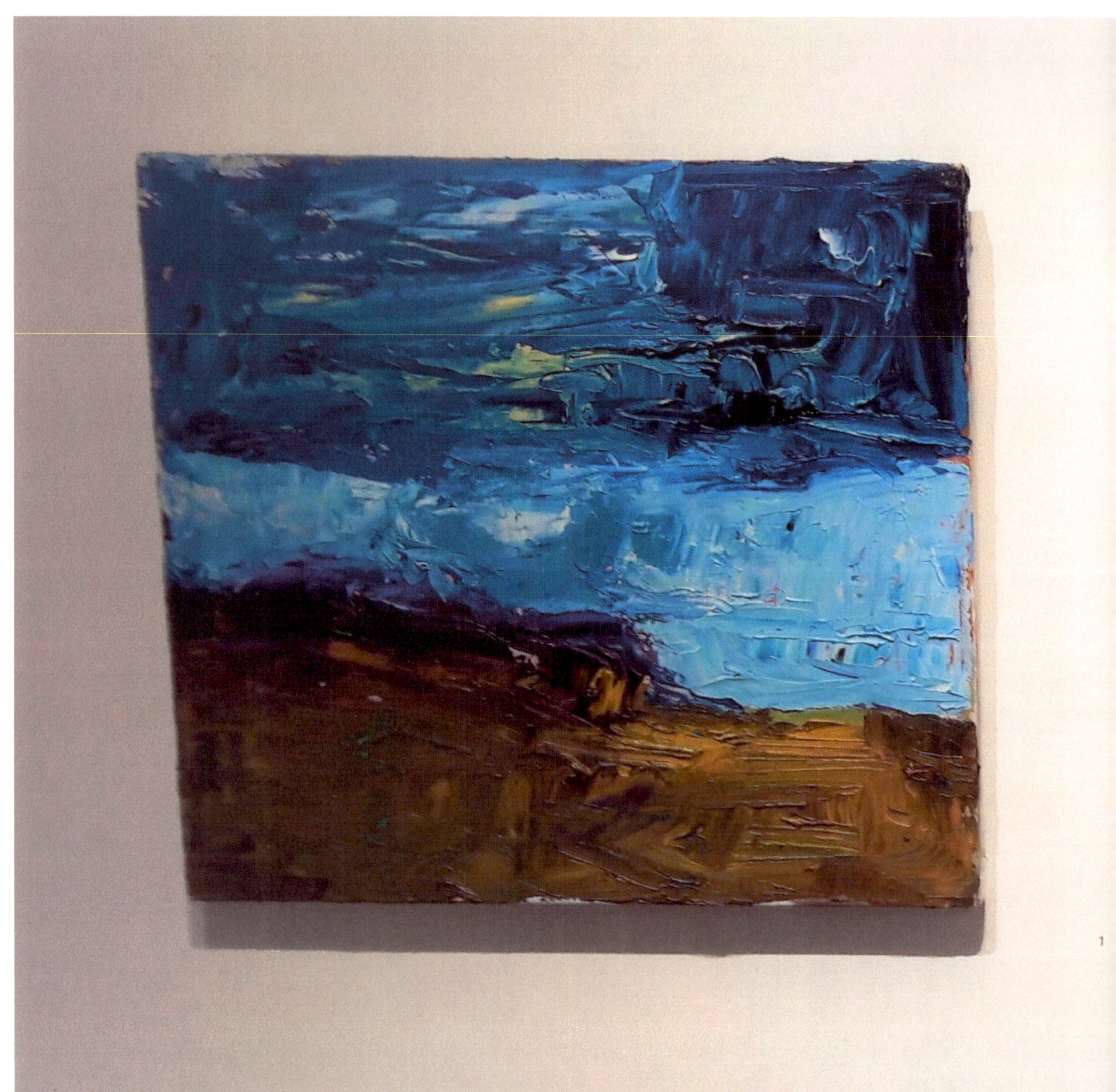

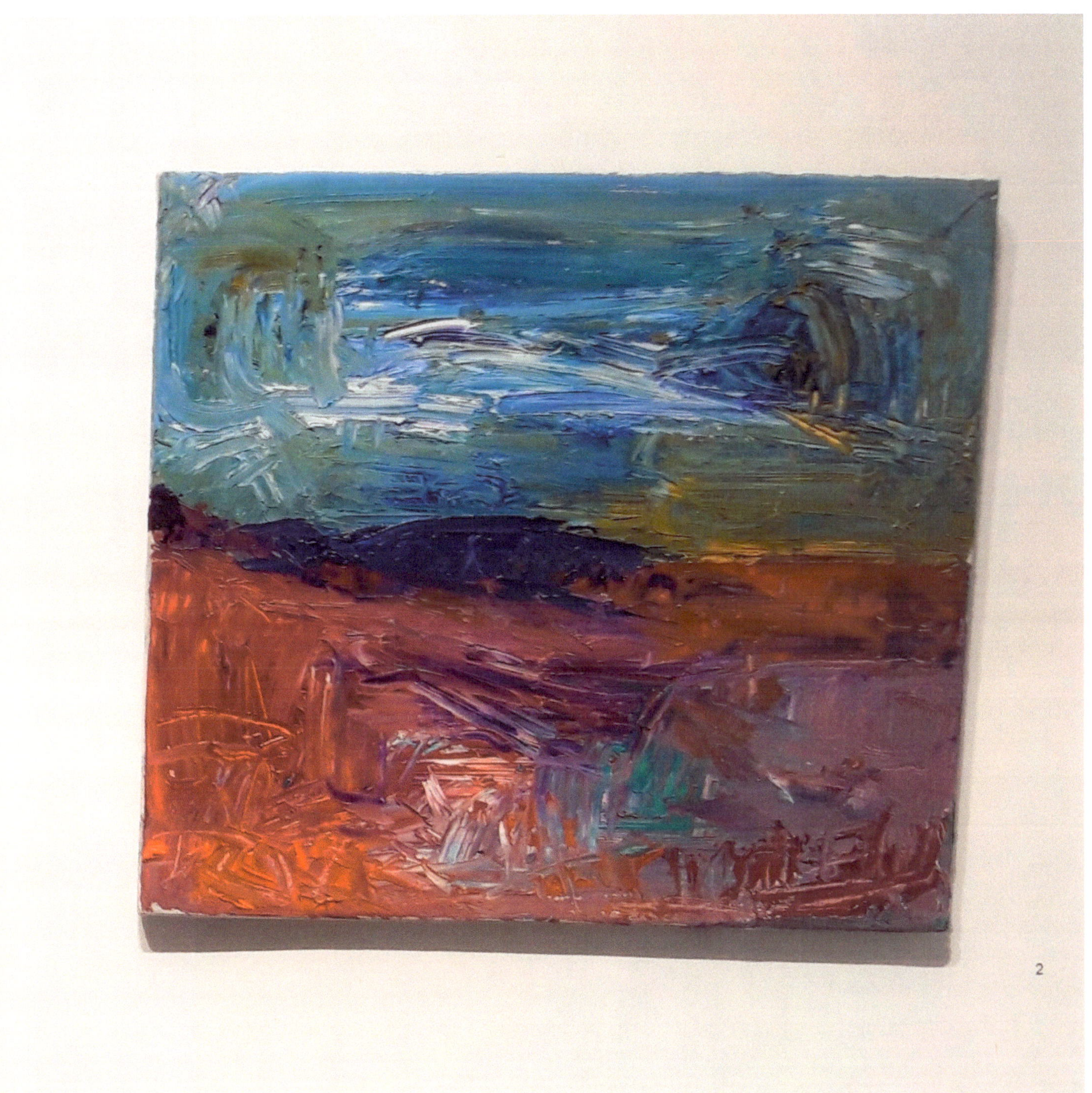

2

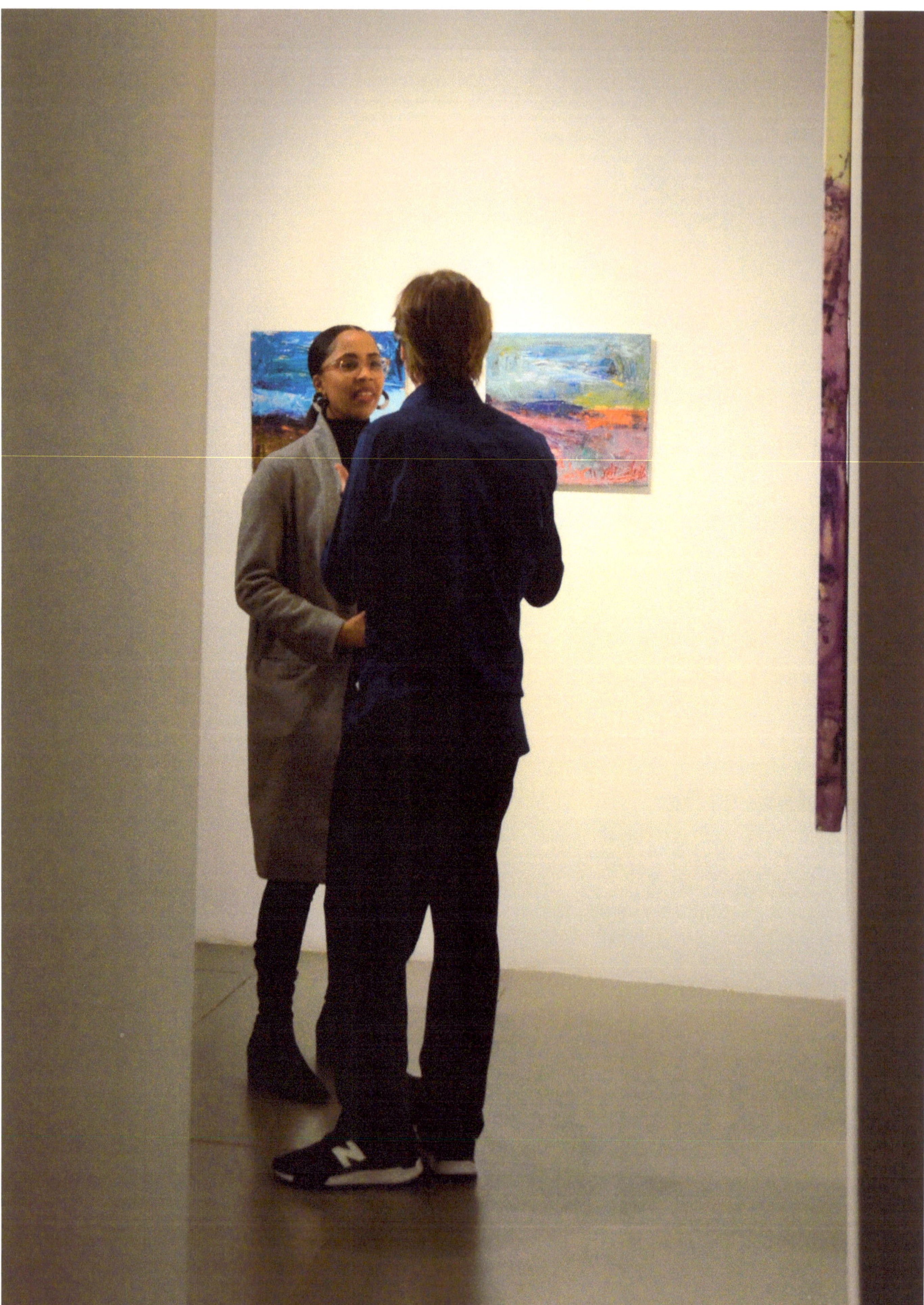

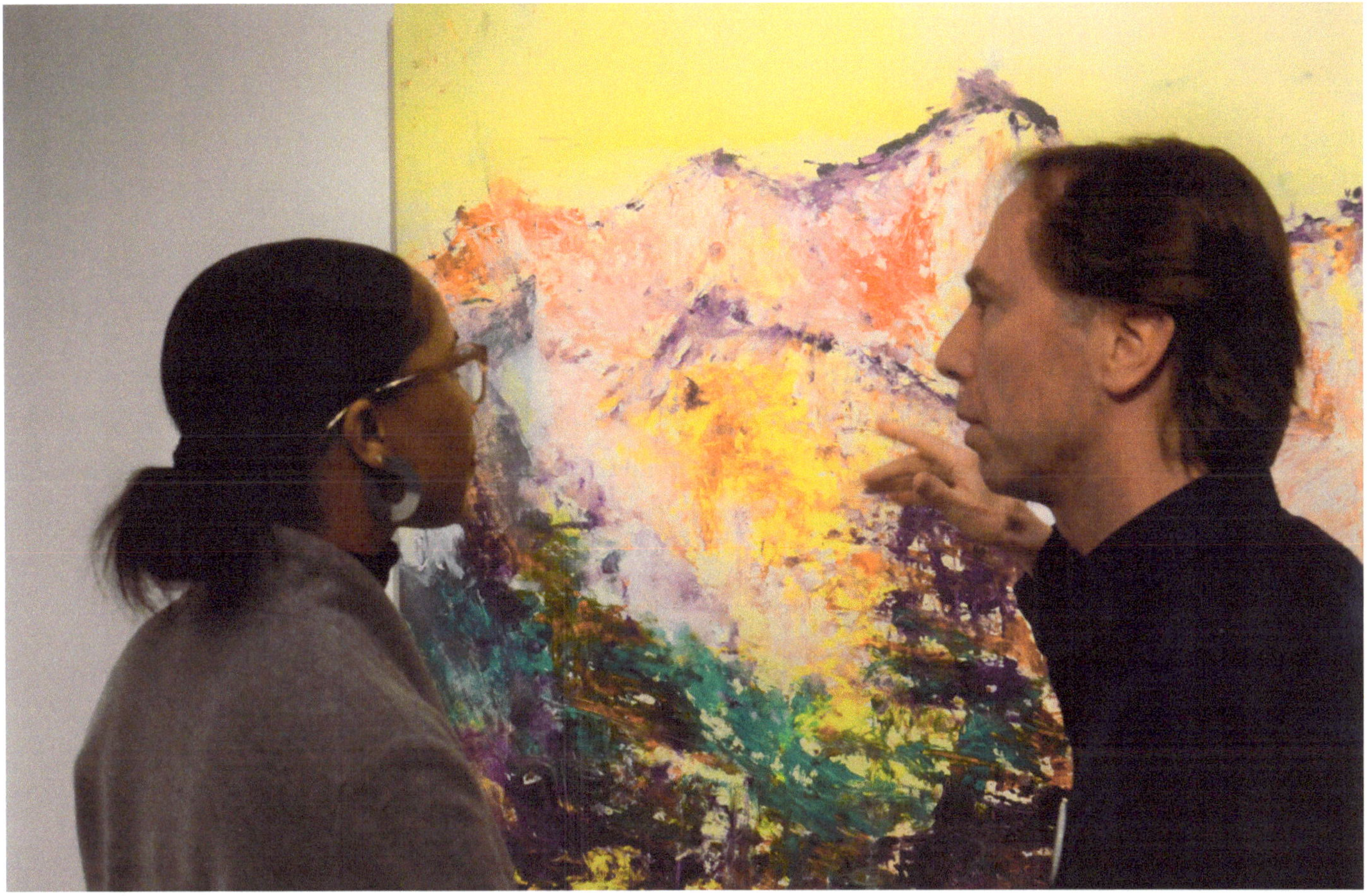

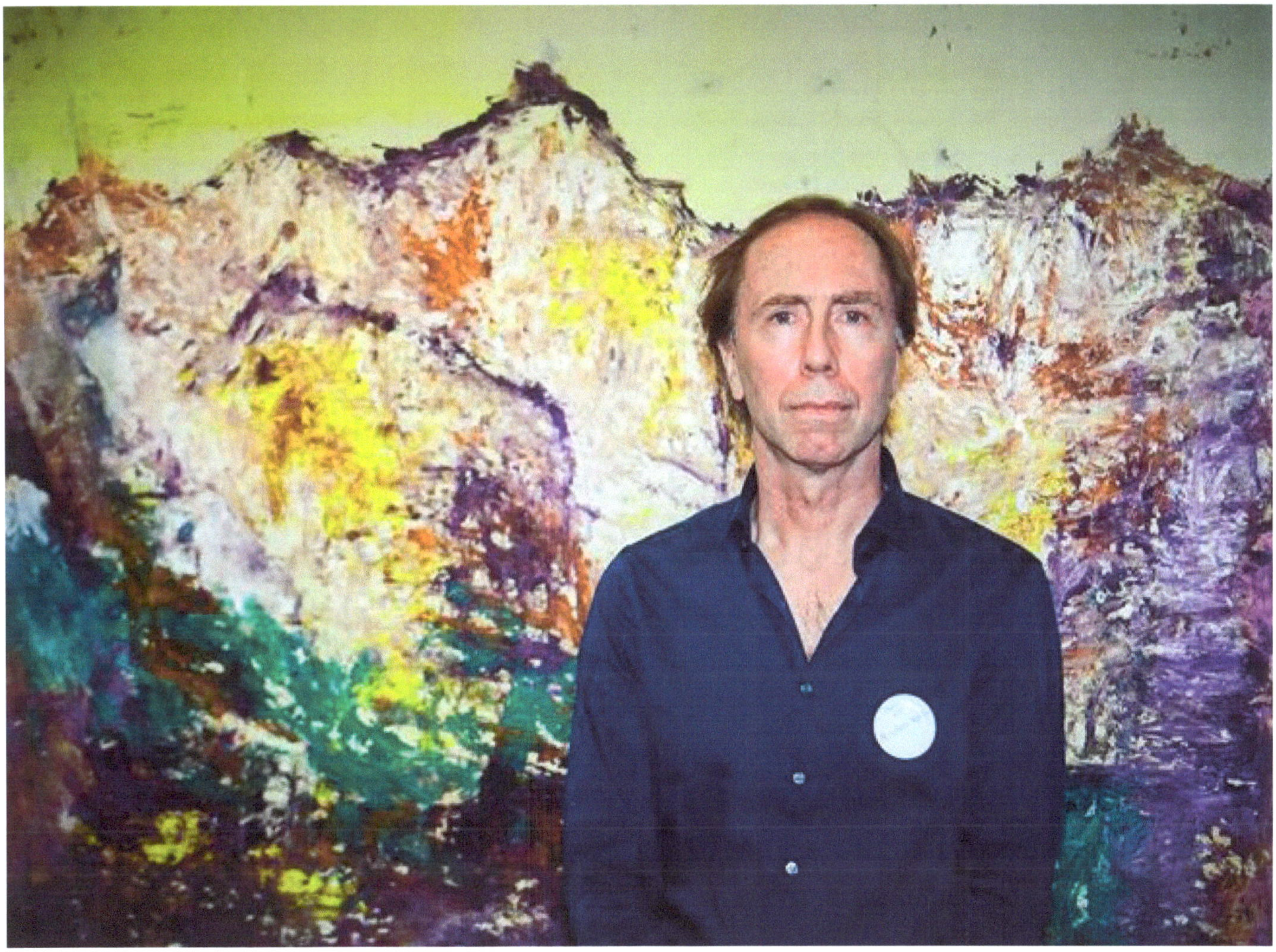

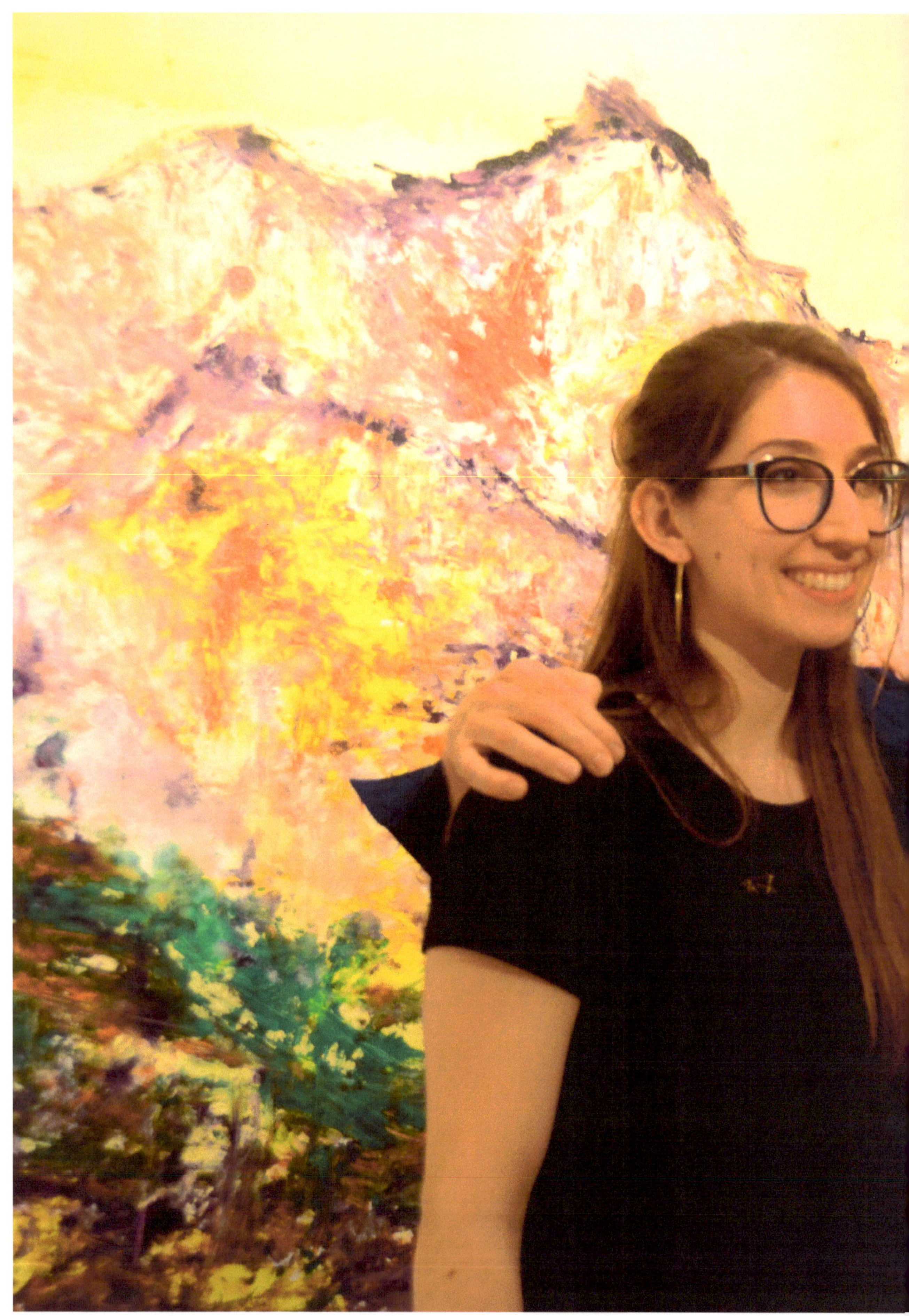

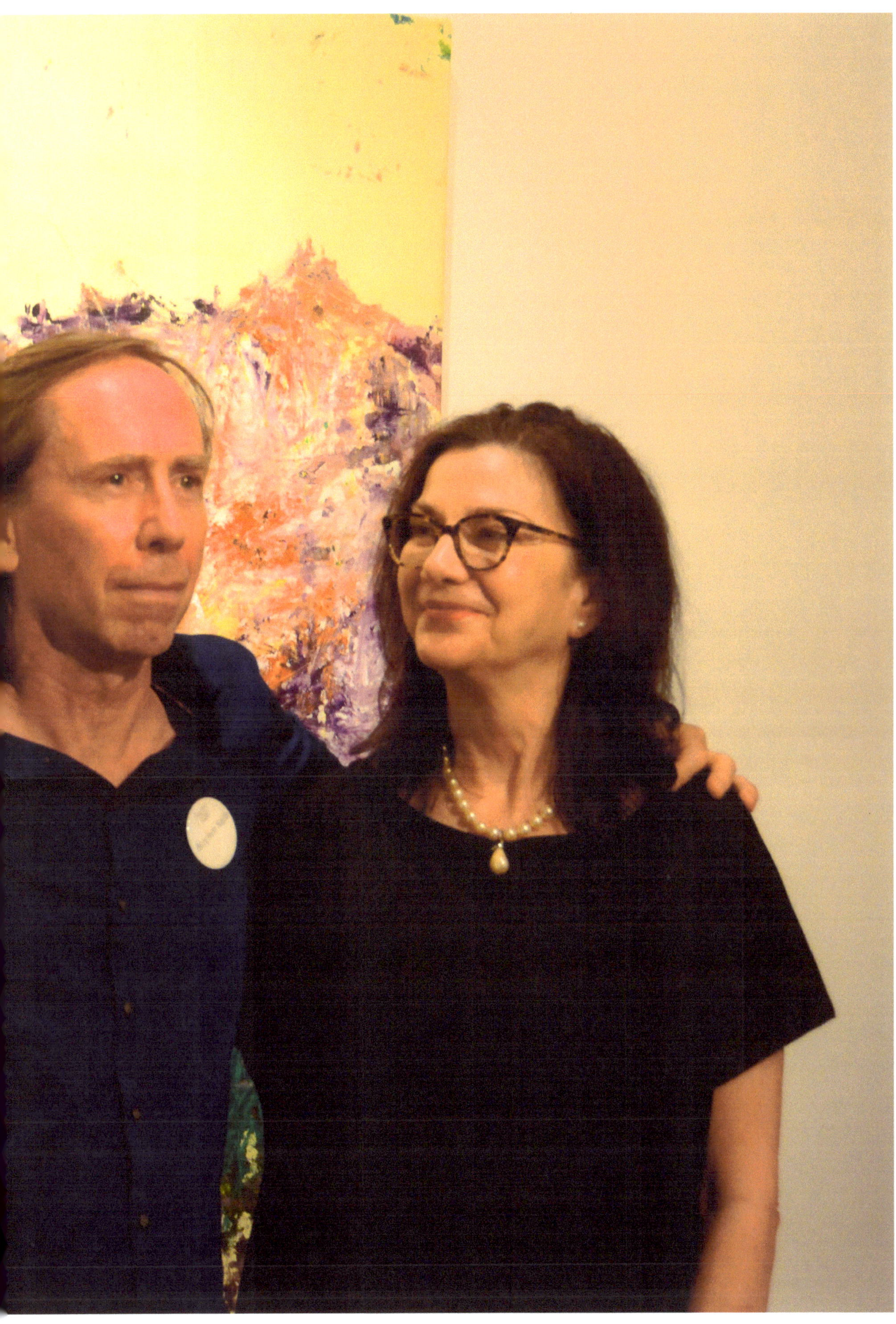

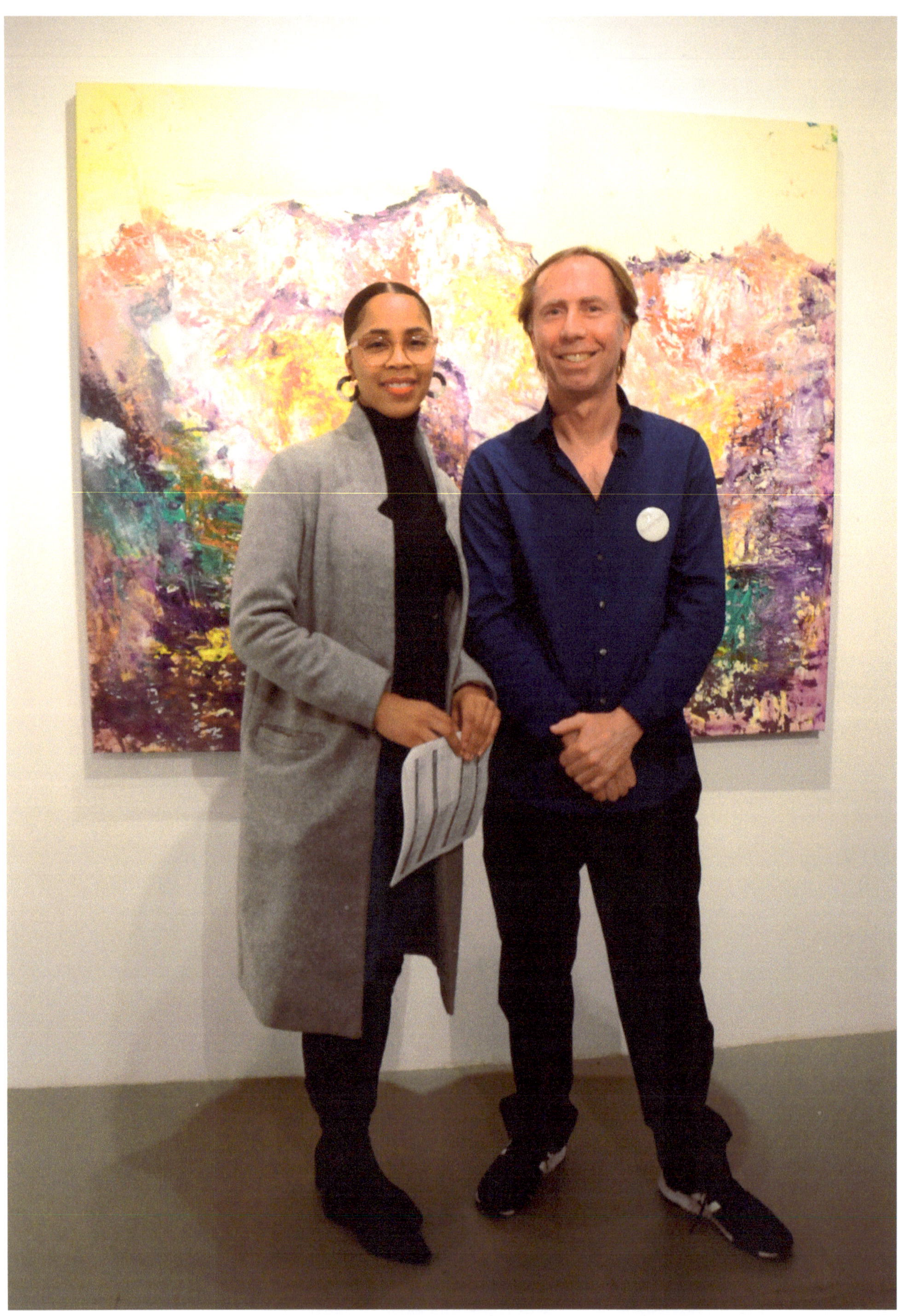

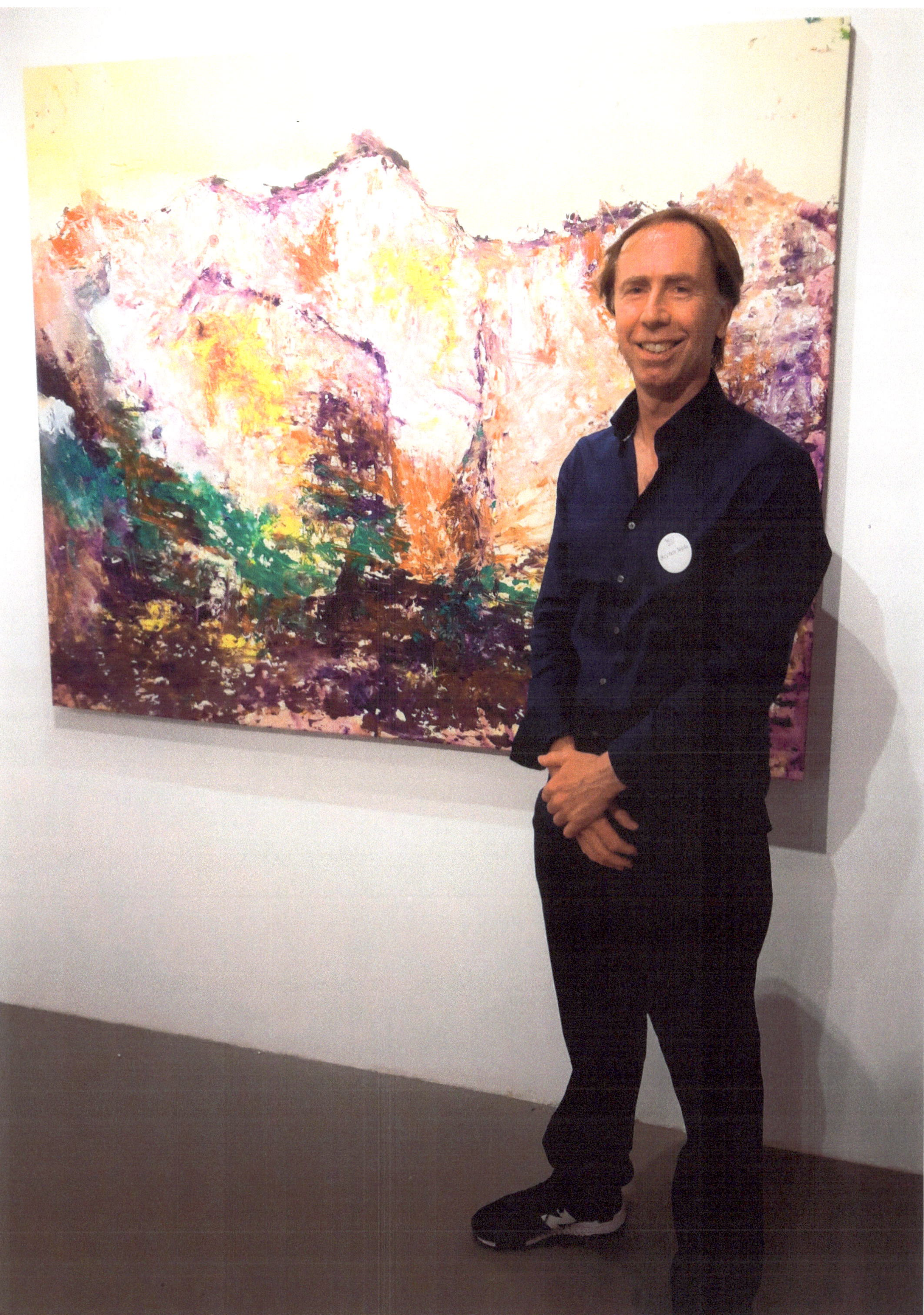

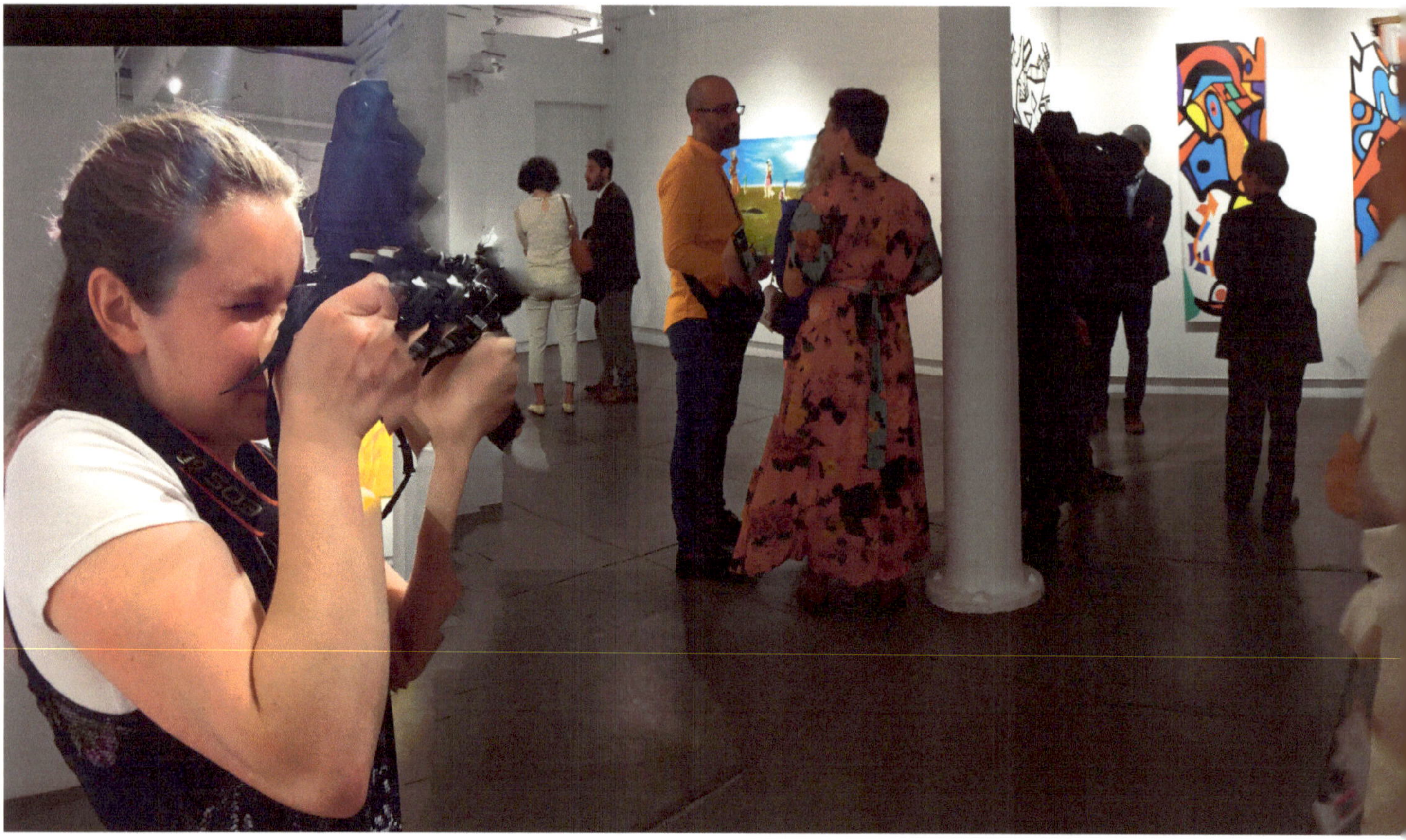

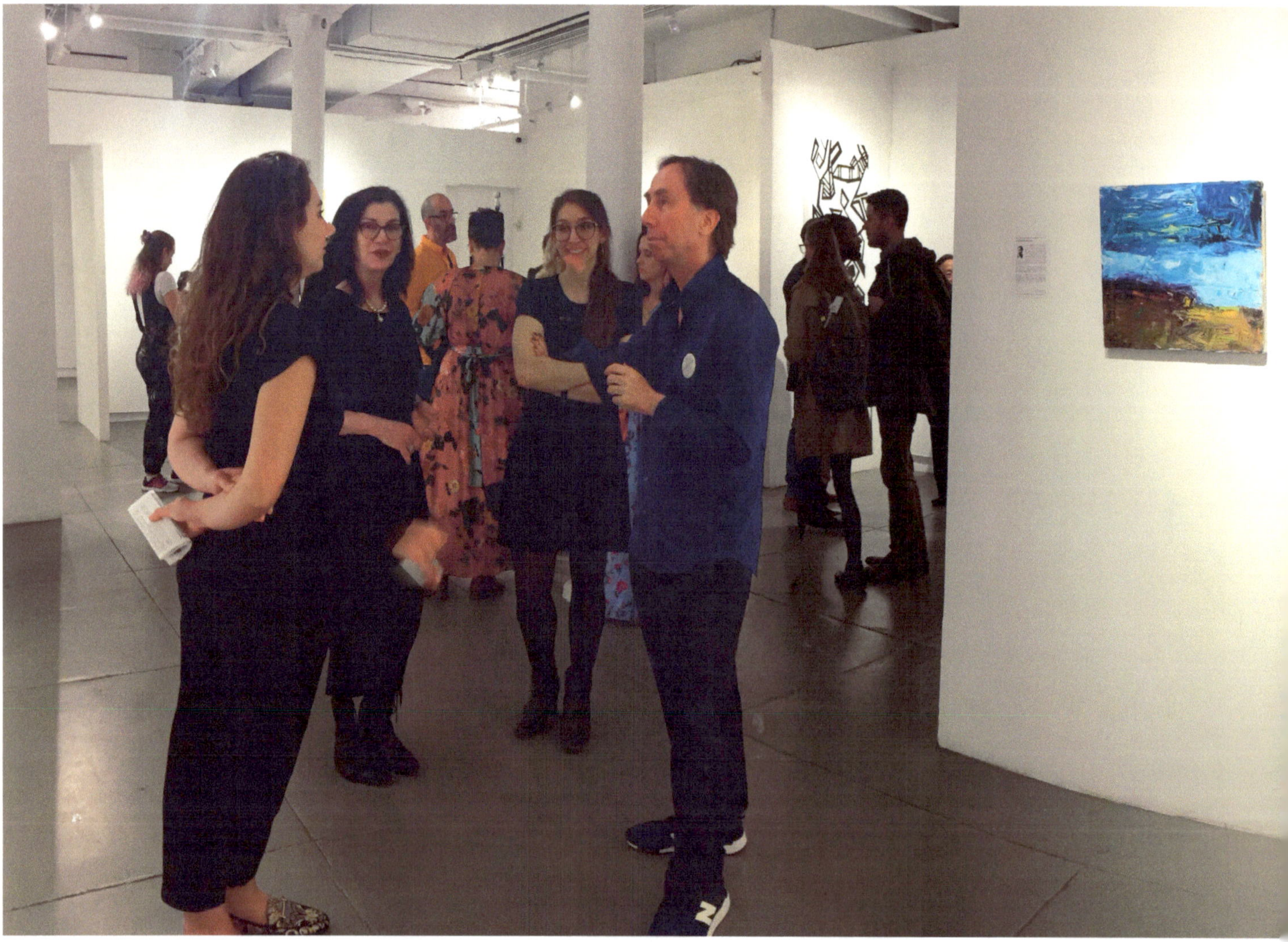

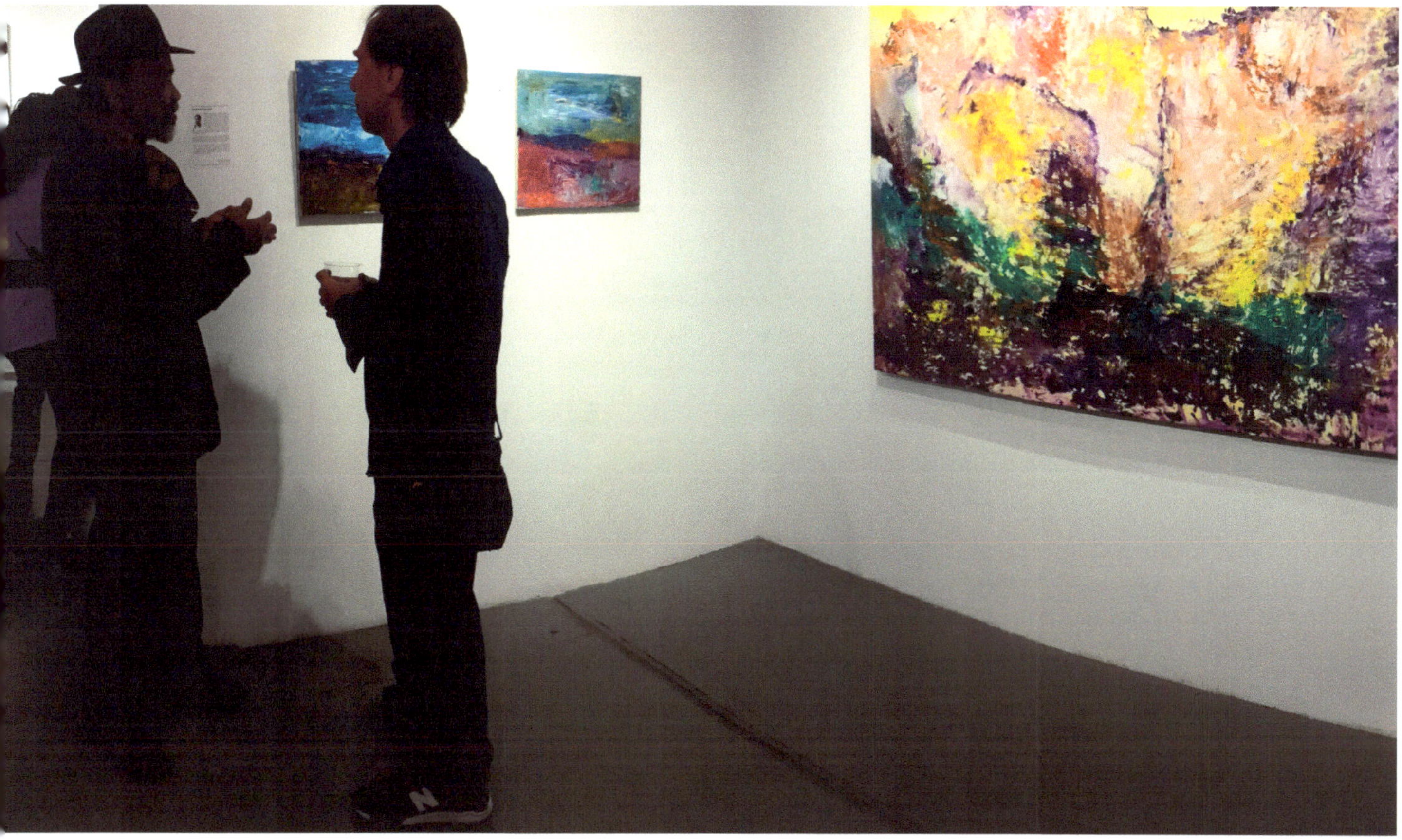

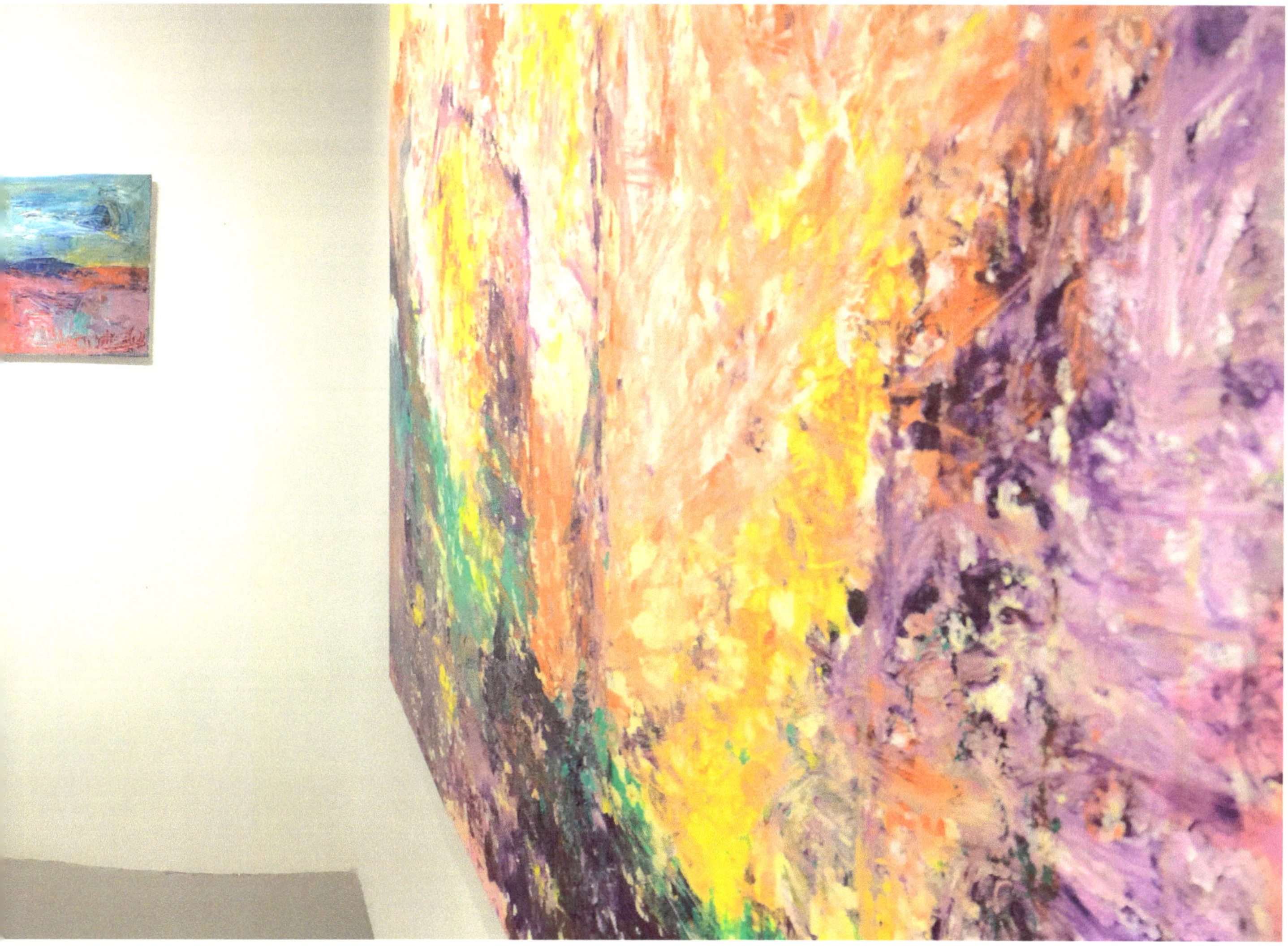

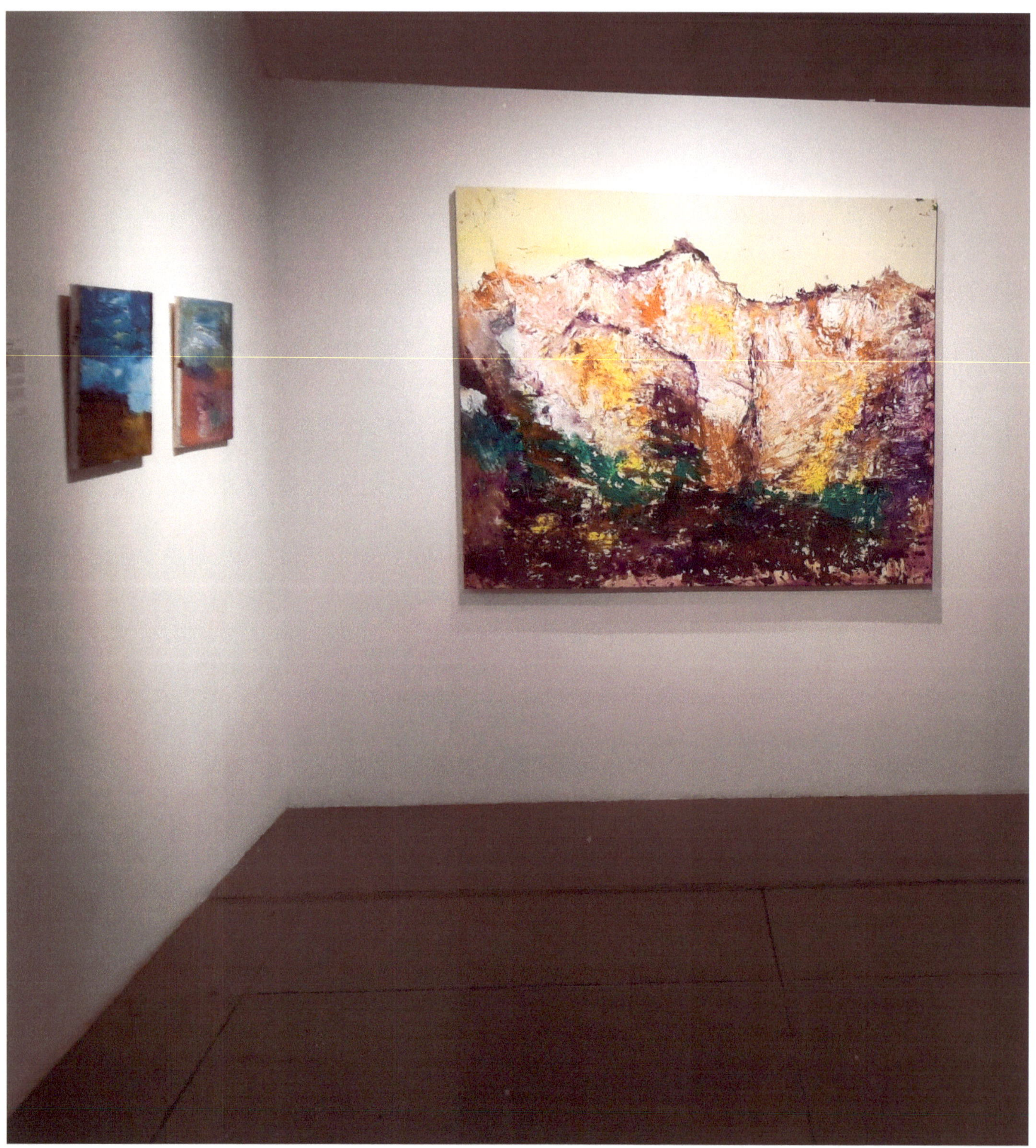

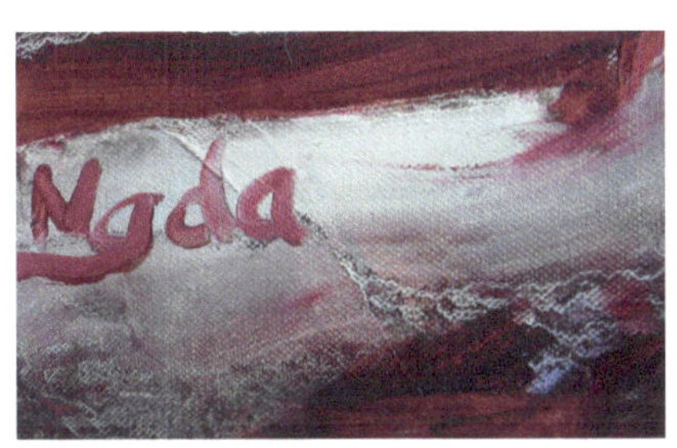

OTHER WORKS

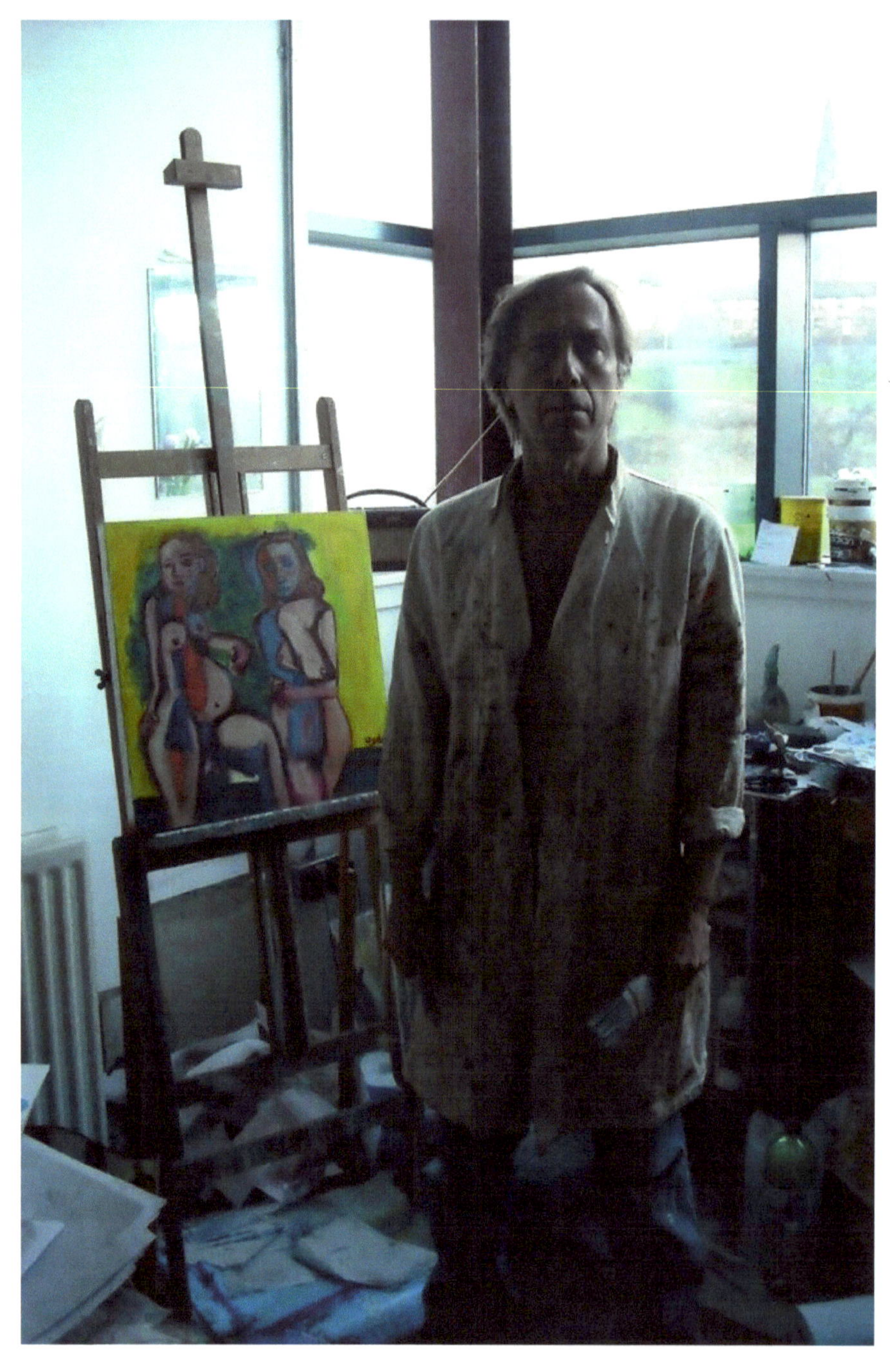

Photo with painting **"TREE IN THE LOST VALLEY, GLENCOE, SCOTLAND"**

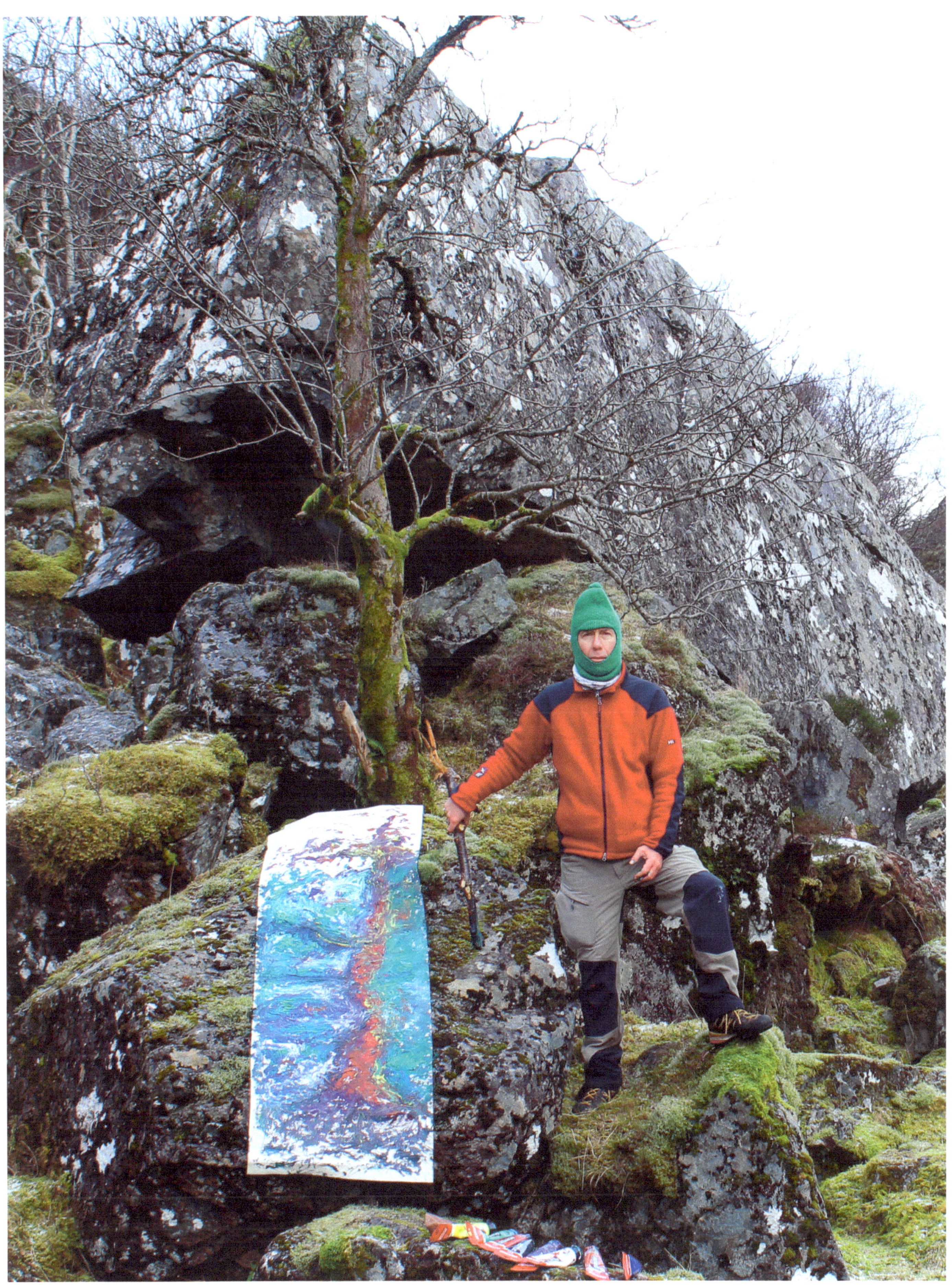

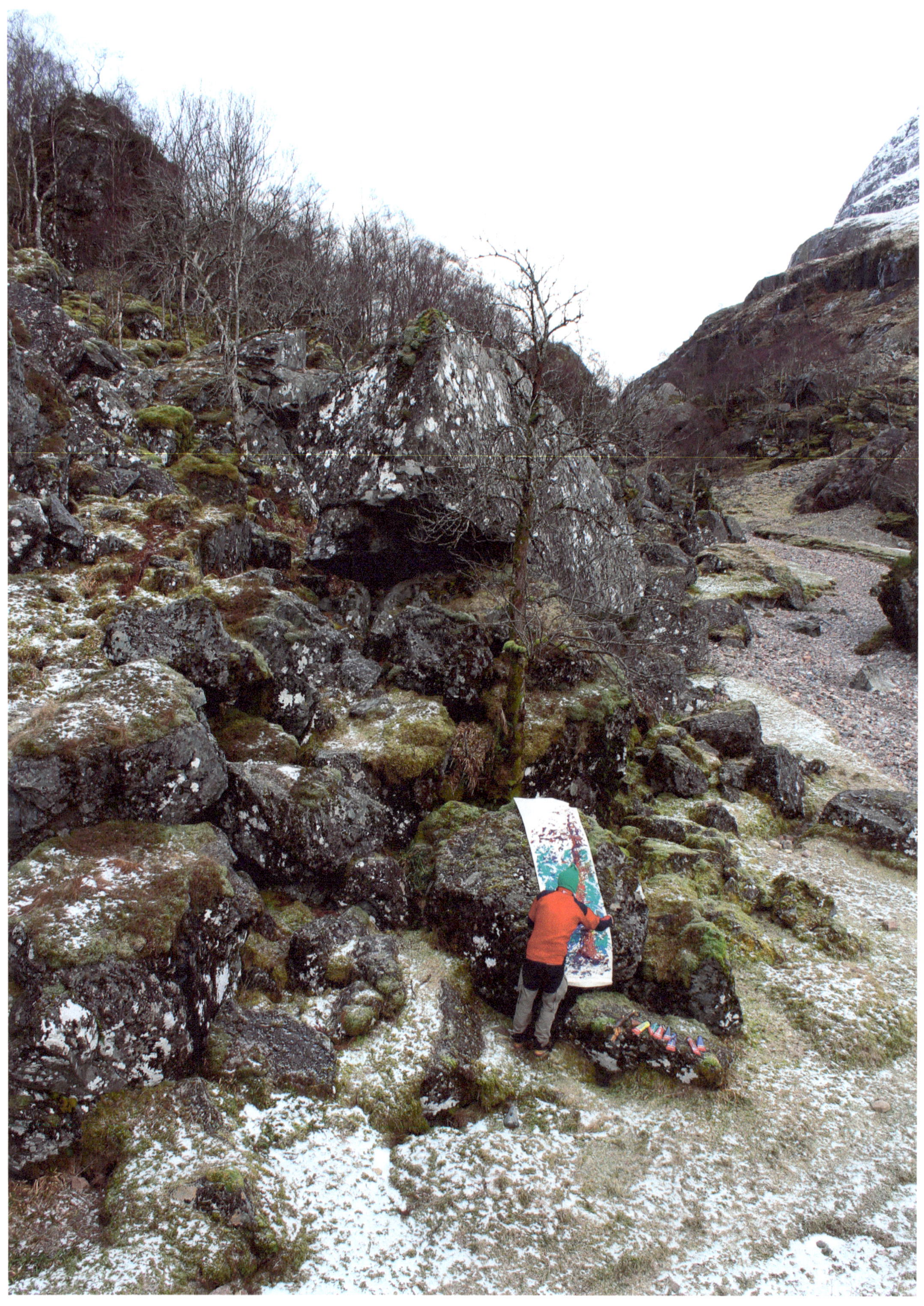

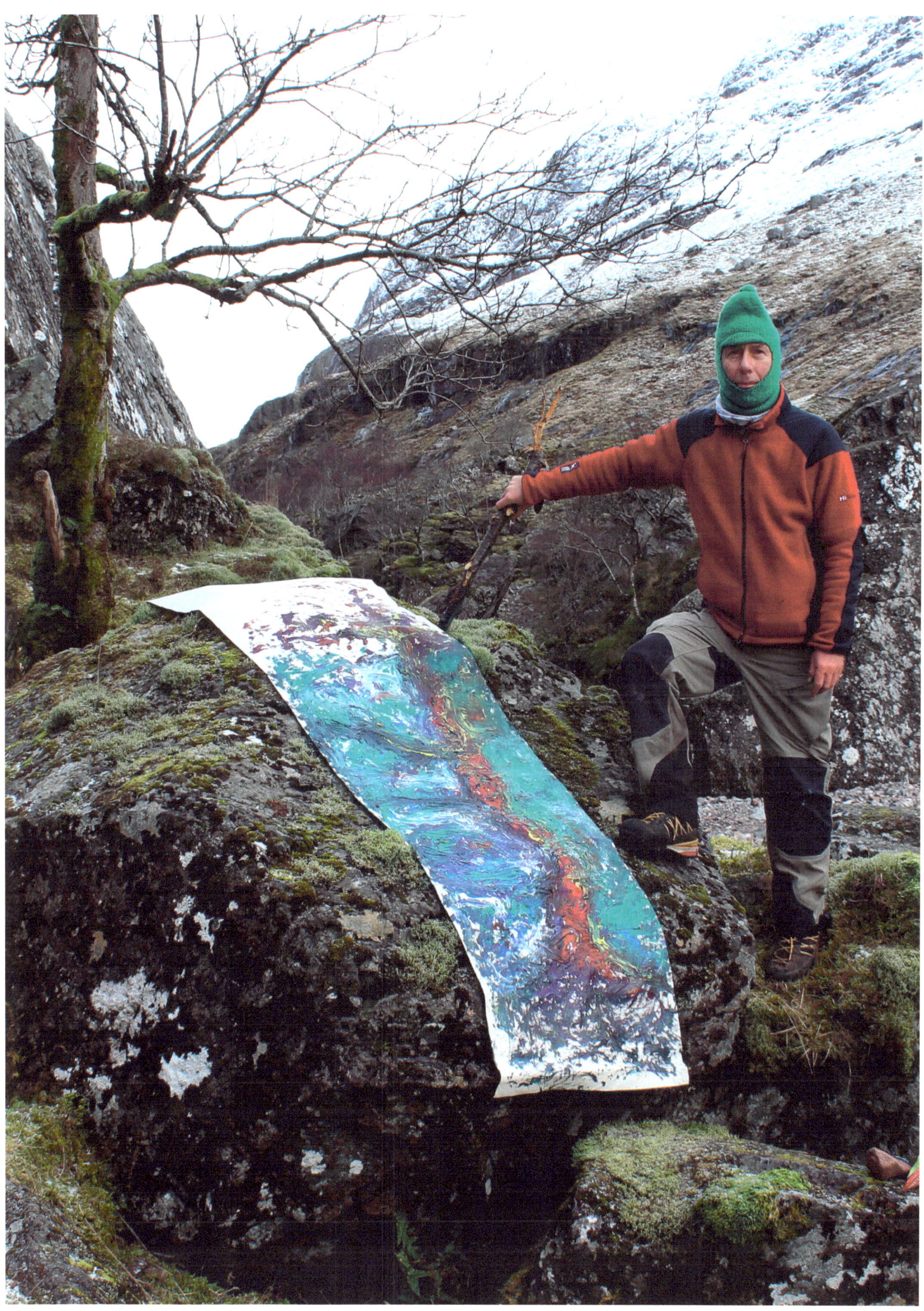

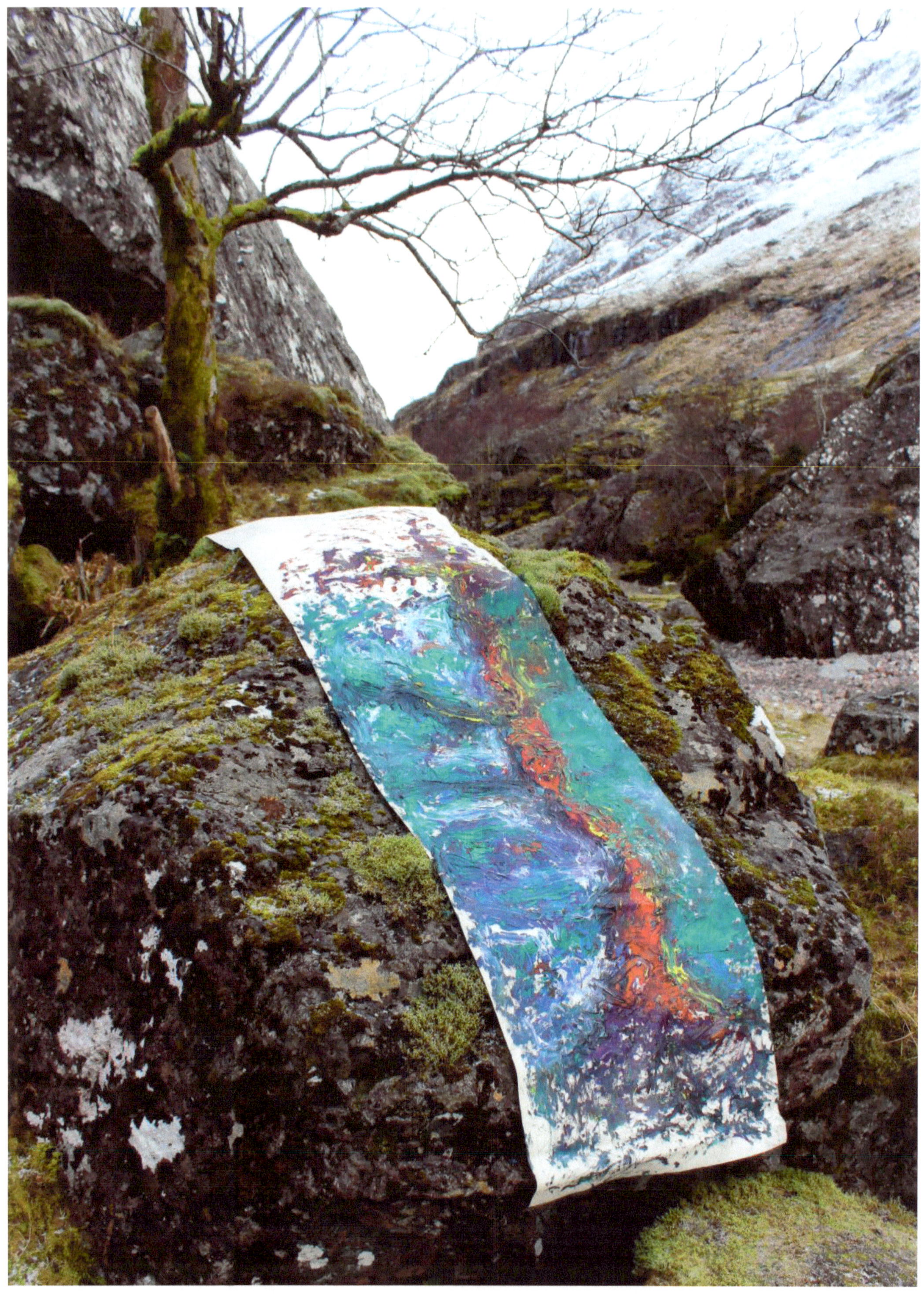

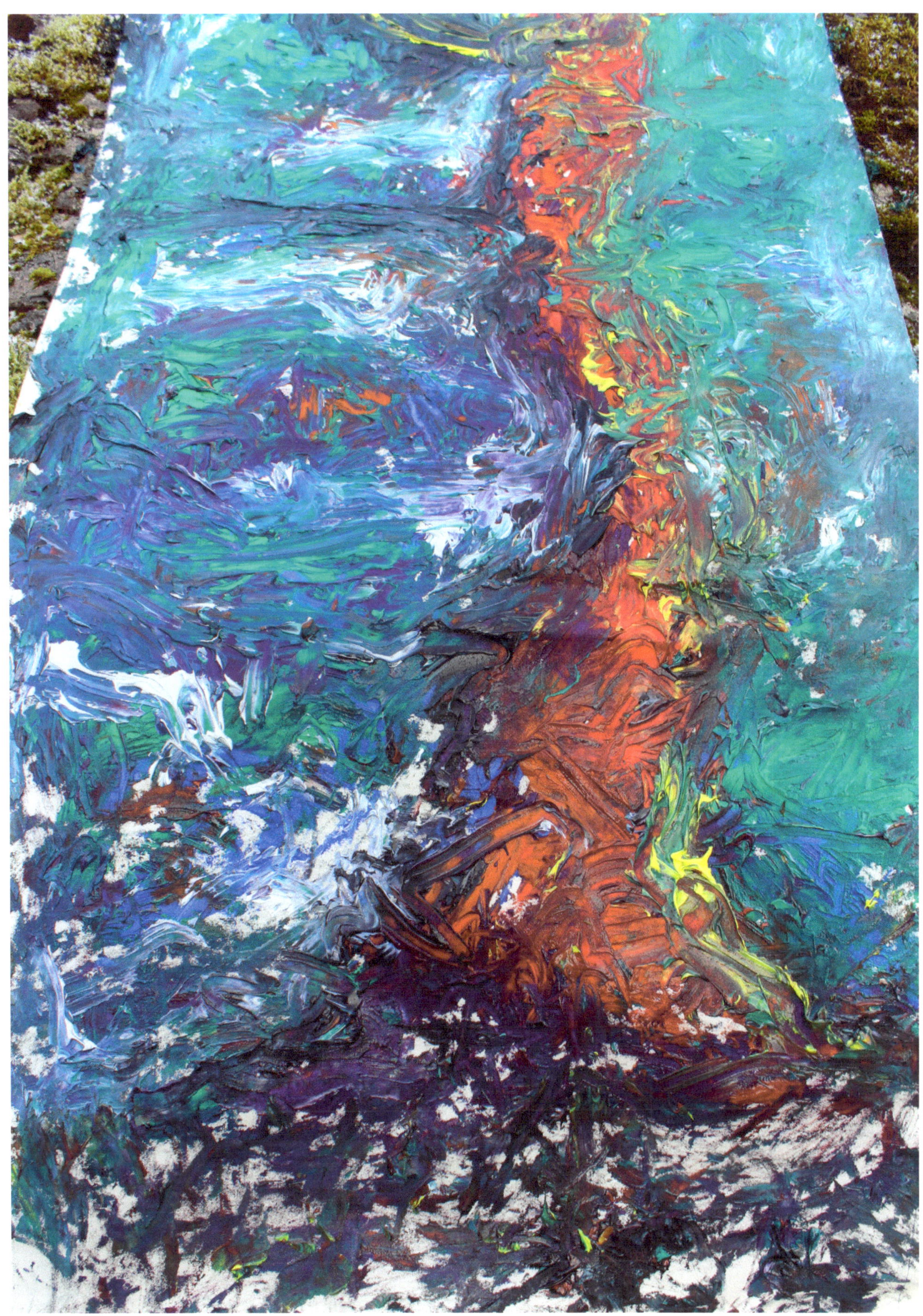

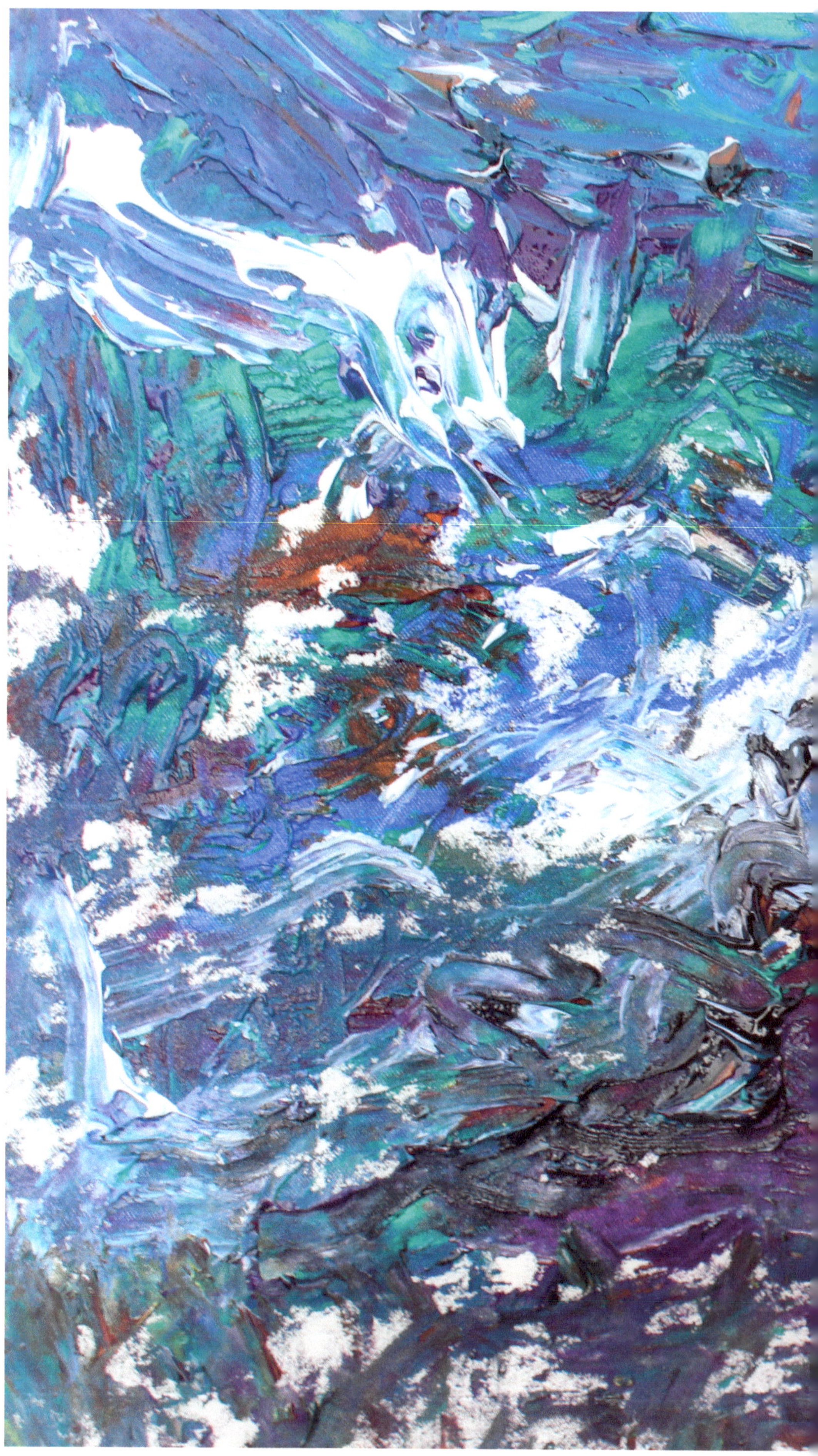

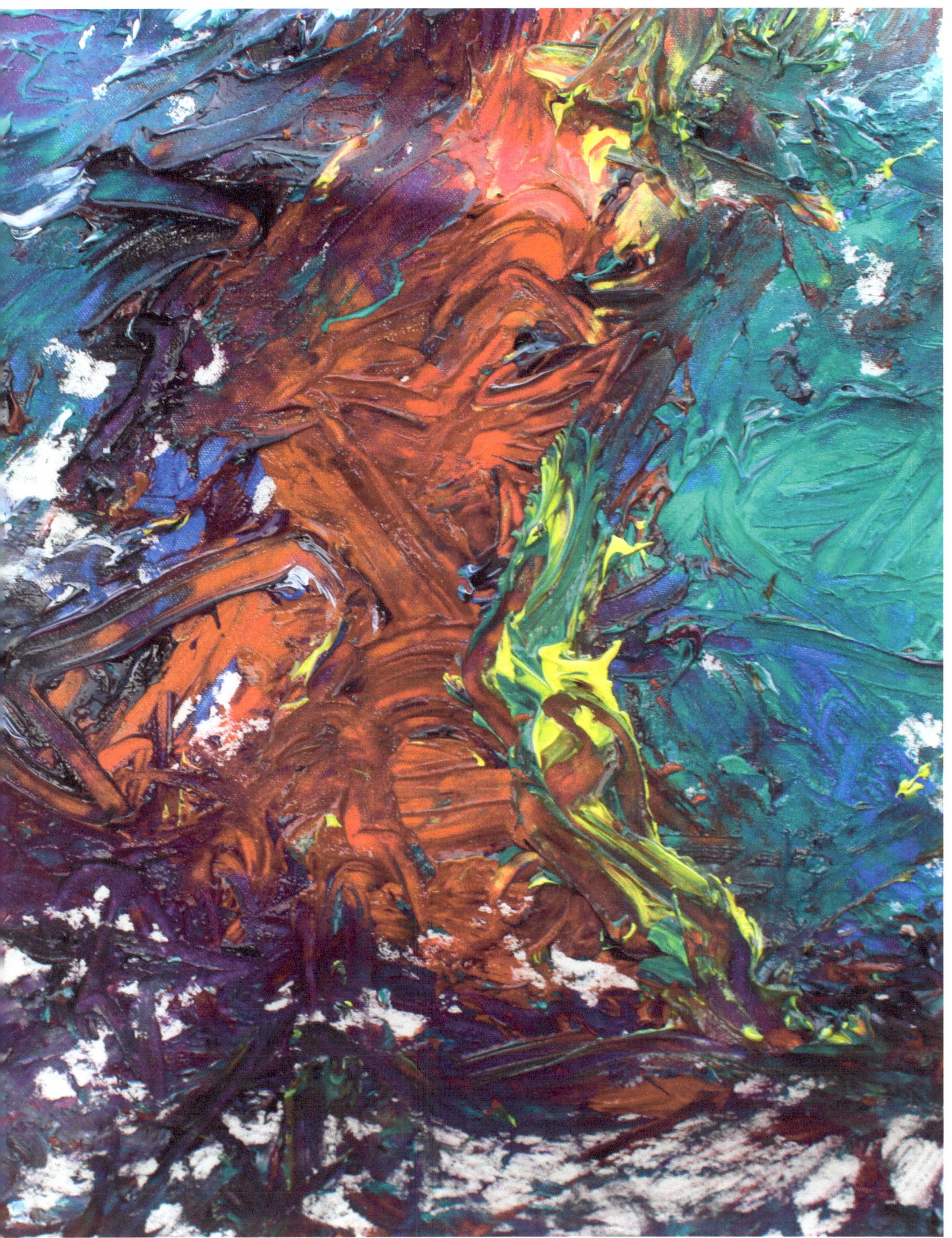

Detail 3

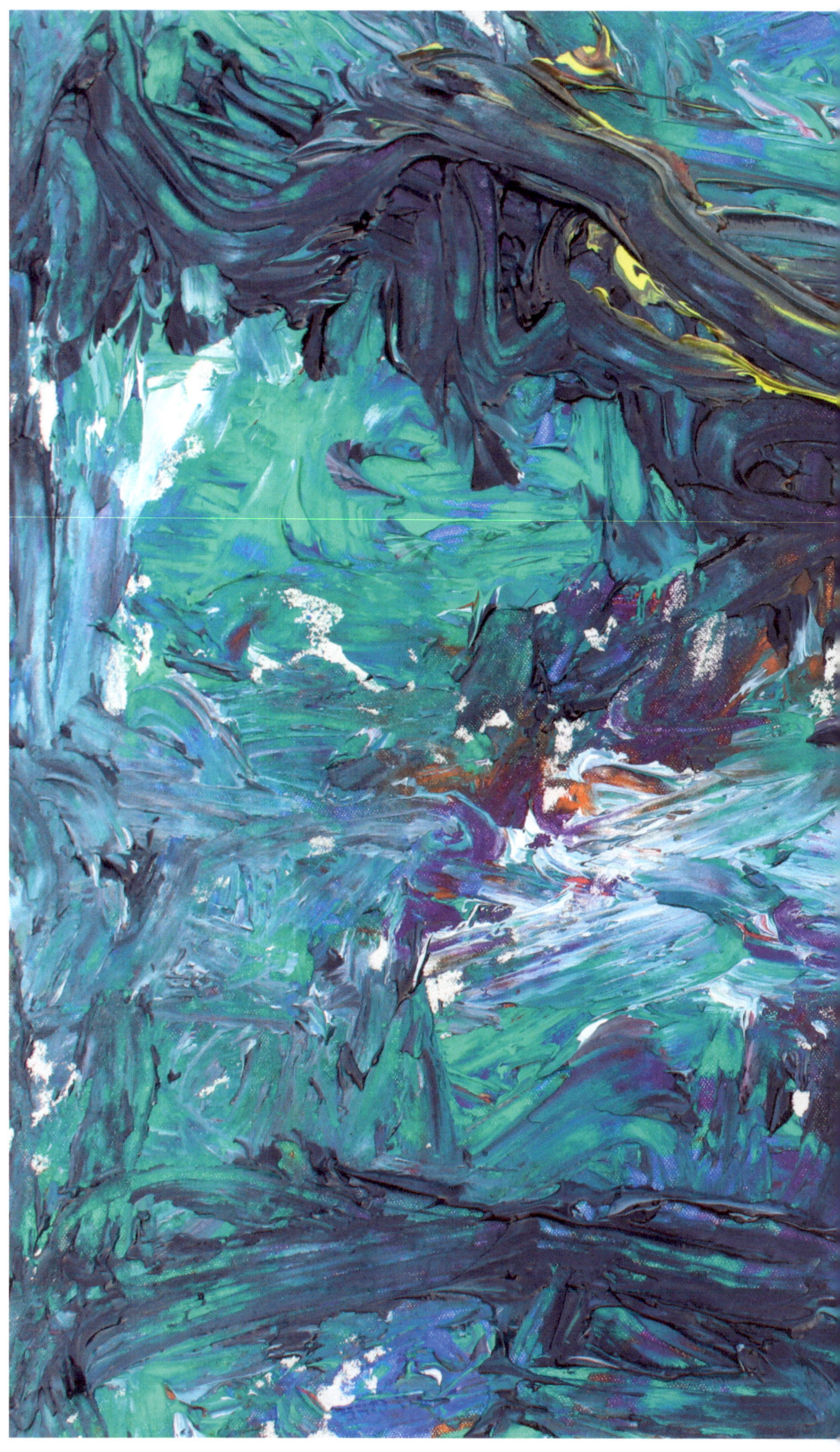

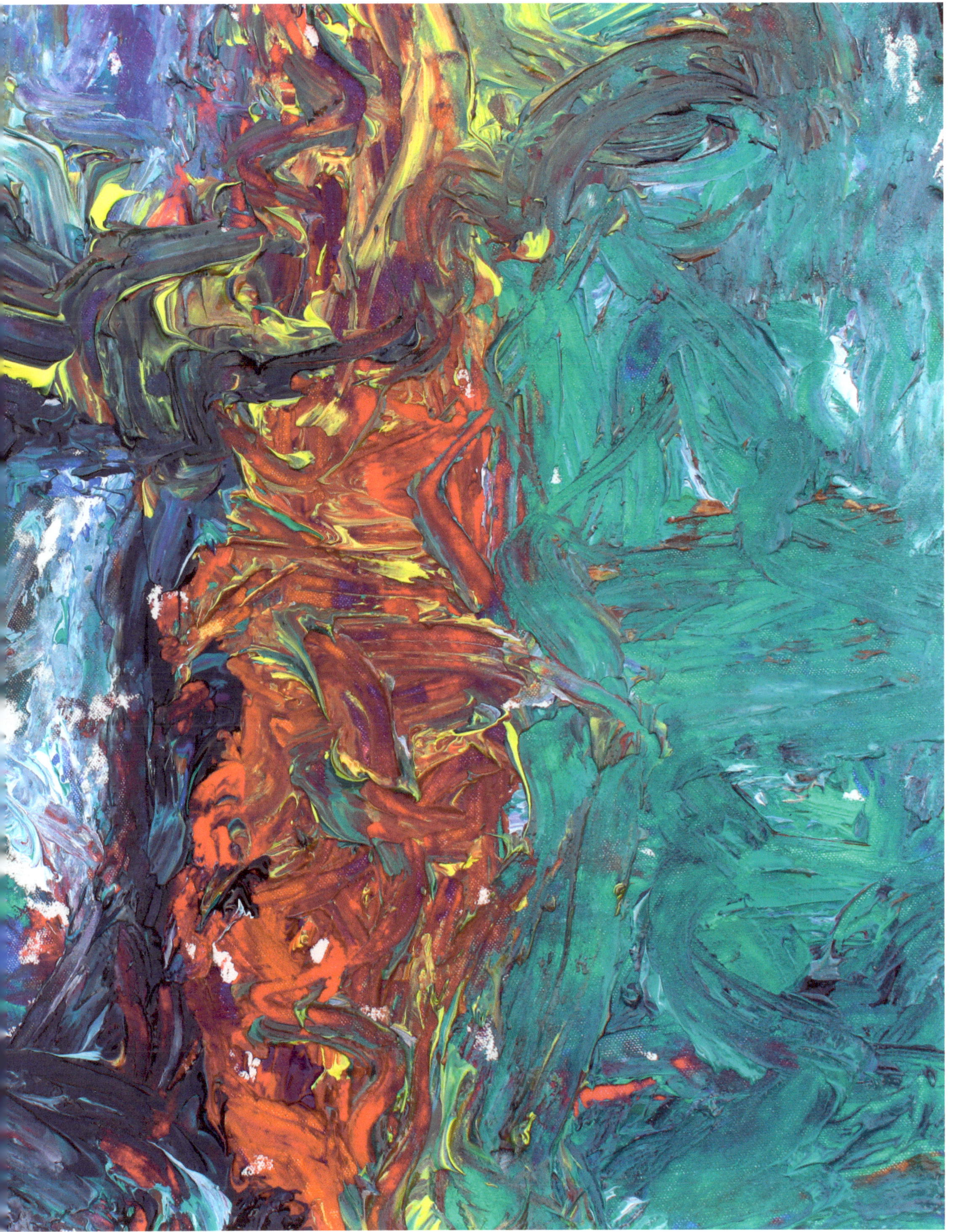

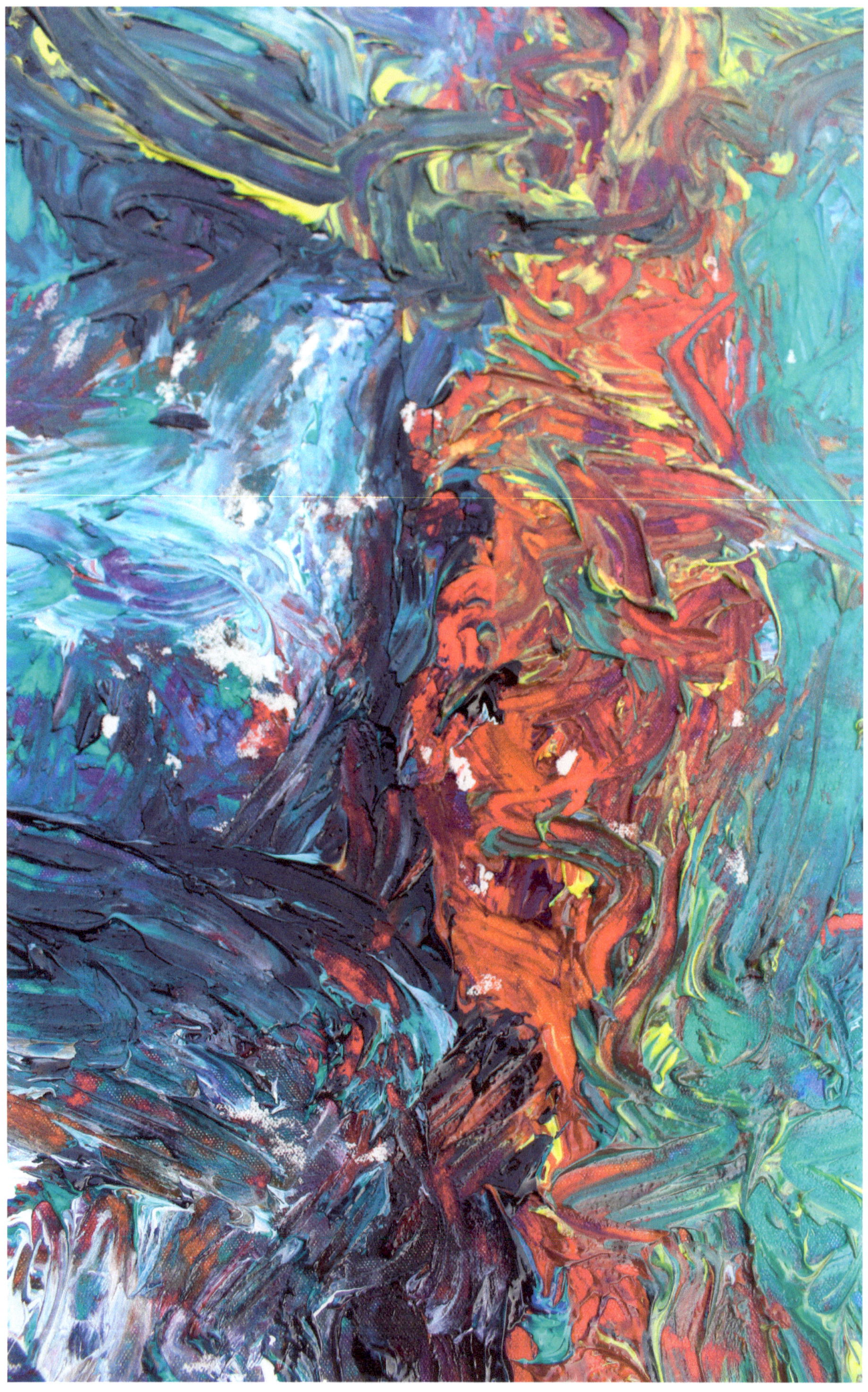

TREE IN THE LOST VALLEY, GLENCOE, SCOTLAND

(FULL IMAGE OF BACKSIDE CANVAS)

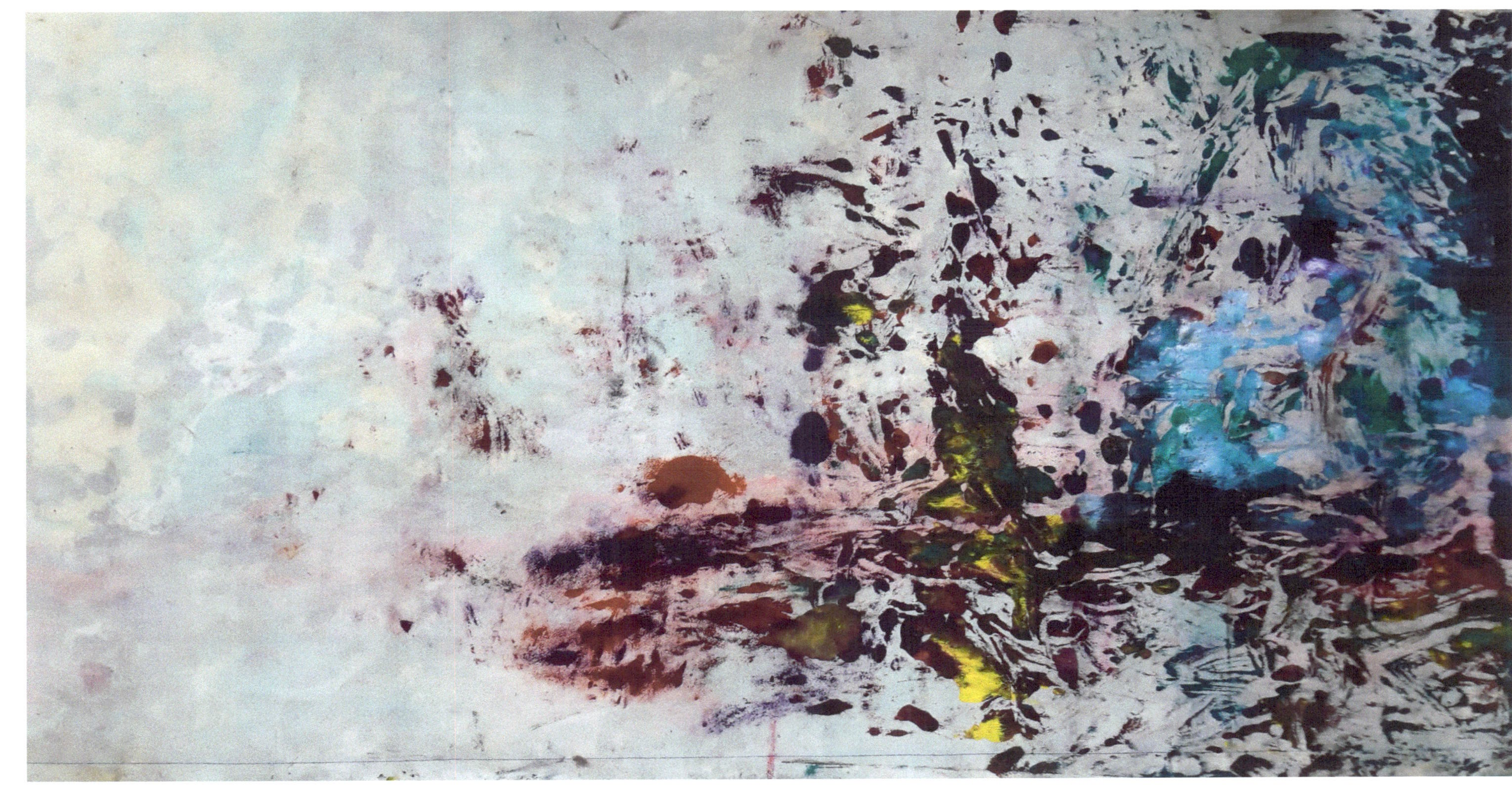

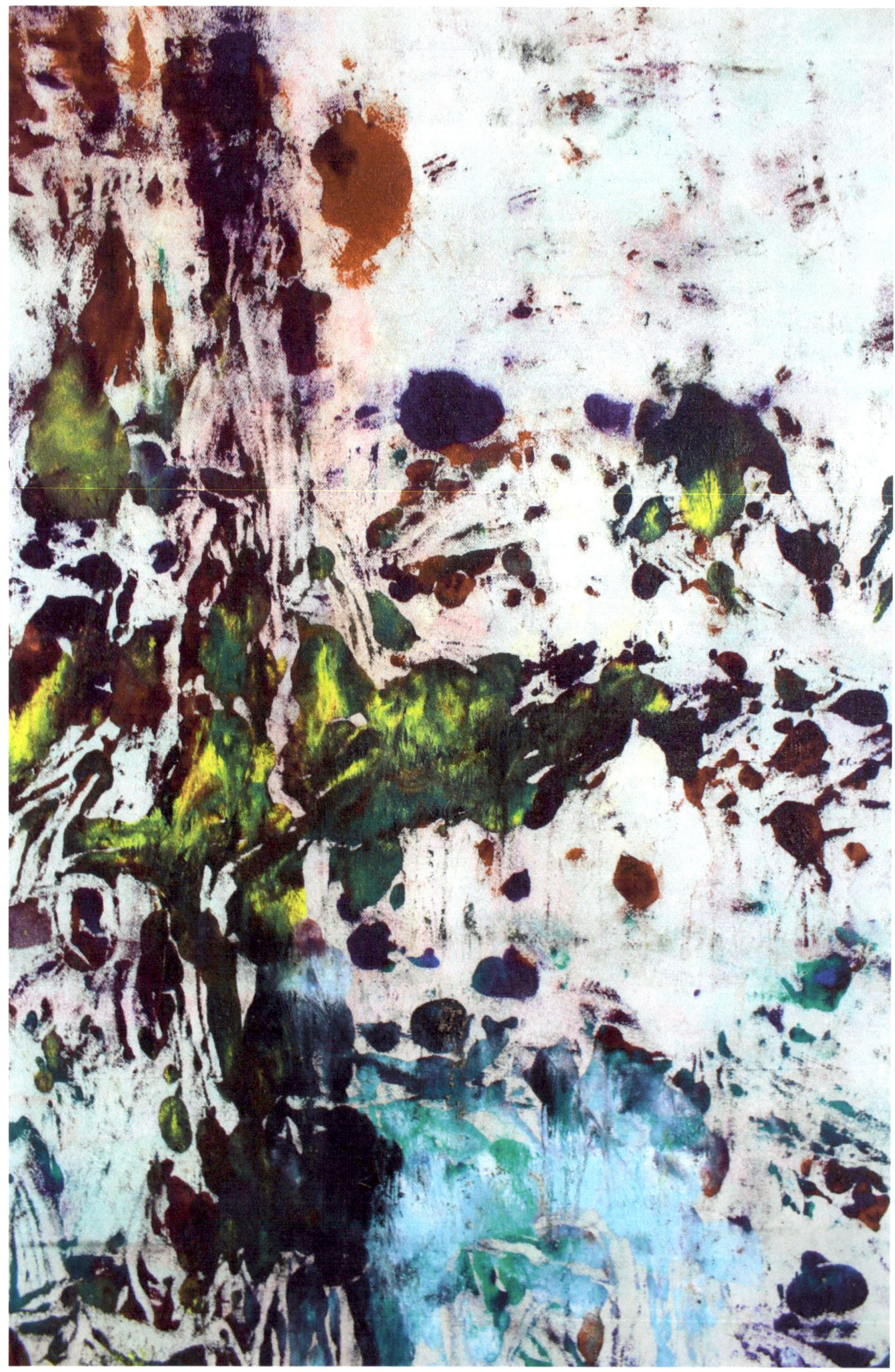

INDEX

Biography   3

Agorà Gallery Forward   5

The Scottish Landscape   7

Photo Gallery   77

Other Works   93

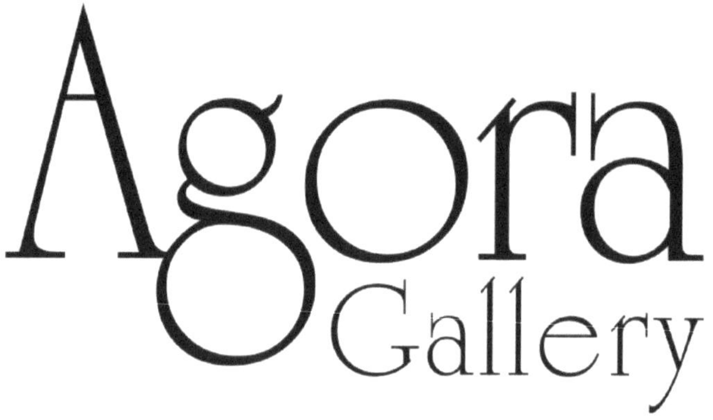

**The artworks were on display at the Agora Gallery
530 W 25th St, Chelsea, New York, USA**

More Artworks by Stephen Najda can be seen:

www.najda.net
Facebook: Najda Art
E-mail enquires: najdaart@gmail.com